New Testament Studies

III

THE ACTS OF THE APOSTLES

BY

ADOLF HARNACK

PROFESSOR OF CHURCH HISTORY IN THE
UNIVERSITY OF BERLIN

TRANSLATED BY

THE REV. J. R. WILKINSON, M.A.

LATE SCHOLAR OF WORCESTER COLLEGE,
OXFORD; AND RECTOR OF WINFORD

Wipf & Stock
PUBLISHERS
Eugene, Oregon

Wipf and Stock Publishers
199 West 8th Avenue, Suite 3
Eugene, Oregon 97401

The Acts of the Apostles
By Harnack, Adolf
ISBN: 1-57910-535-1
Publication date 11/2/2000
Previously published by G. P. Putnam's Sons, 1909

DEDICATED TO

THE SENATE OF THE UNIVERSITY OF GLASGOW

AS AN EXPRESSION OF THE AUTHOR'S GRATITUDE

FOR THE DEGREE OF DOCTOR OF LAWS

CONFERRED UPON HIM

PREFACE

THE two volumes of New Testament studies by Professor Harnack, which have already appeared in this series, may be said without exaggeration to have marked an epoch in New Testament research. The third volume, "The Acts of the Apostles," now presented in English form, is if anything more remarkable than its predecessors. In it Professor Harnack develops the position which he has established in "Luke the Physician," and subjects the Acts of the Apostles to a most searching investigation from almost all possible points of view. A very pleasing feature of this series of studies is the high esteem in which the author holds the researches of distinguished English scholars, such as Sir John Hawkins, Dr. Plummer, and Dr. Hobart. To those who, like the translator, have long felt that from the standpoint of scientific historical criticism it was inconceivable that the author of the Lukan writings could have been a companion of St. Paul, the conclusions of the great German scholar have come with somewhat of a shock. And yet the view—or rather the peculiar psychological solution of the problem of these writings—now propounded by Dr. Harnack, has had at least one champion among English scholars of the so-called critical school. The translator calls to mind a controversy many years ago at a meeting of the "C.C.C."—mystic signs known to the initiated—when the Rev. Dr. Hastings Rashdall, Fellow and Tutor of New College, Oxford, argued almost in the words of Dr. Harnack that the difficult account of Acts ii. could perfectly well have been written by a companion of St. Paul—*i.e.* by one who knew the real nature of the phenomenon of "Speaking with Tongues." The translator then denounced such a position as unscientific; he now assures Dr. Rashdall of his reluctant yet complete conversion, and begs to dedicate to him his own work in rendering these notable researches accessible to the English reader.

CONTENTS

INTRODUCTION

THE magnitude and difficulty of the task which St. Luke set himself in his "Acts of the Apostles," and the ability and skill with which he has mastered this task, cannot be easily overrated. In order to estimate what he has performed, let us transport ourselves into the situation in which he composed his work. It was the time of the Flavian Cæsars, and he—a physician probably already well stricken in years—after many long travels, which had led him as far as Jerusalem in the East and Rome in the West, had now taken up his abode either in Ephesus or in Achaia, or in some other province lying on the shores of the Grecian Sea. The Christian movement had been in progress in these lands for at least thirty to forty years. He himself had taken an active part in its propagation, and had stood in personal relations not only with St. Paul, but also with distinguished members of the Primitive Community. He had received the details of the Gospel history from those who could be described as "from the beginning eye-witnesses and ministers of the Word." An overwhelming flood of impressions stormed in upon the Hellenic mind of the writer—overwhelming where these concentrated themselves into one single impression, overwhelming in their variety and paradox. A sacred volume of inexhaustible content—the portrait of Jesus Christ in a *concordia discors* of testimony, of narrative, and of speculation—the apostles—the churches—that multitude of Spirit-gifted ones experiencing and working Signs and Wonders! Above this surging sea, whose waves are breaking in ever fresh creations in the sphere of thought and action, the heavens are dark with the storm-cloud of the approaching End—and yet at the same time the most strenuous efforts are made after an accommodation with the world as it is, and towards transformation of its life by the new spirit. Lastly, everywhere conflict and controversy: the Jew and the Greek—Paul and the rest of the apostles—knowledge and the absolute contempt of knowledge—the spirit and the letter—tradition and prophecy—speculation opposed to speculation—facts and their commentaries—life and asceticism. In such a situation it was that St. Luke seized his pen and undertook not only to write history, to recount how all that he saw around him had come to pass, but also to unite this history as a second part with the Gospel story.

The first part of his intention was a venture which cannot be easily interpreted from a psychological point of view, unless the writer himself had been in direct and personal touch with the facts which he wished to describe. Those who regard the author simply as an editor of sources only transfer the difficulty of the problem to the shoulders of some early unknown writer, and those who bring him down into a later generation mistake the character of the book, in that they cannot see the wood for the trees. Direct touch with the recorded facts—this alone explains such a history as lies before us in the "Acts of the Apostles." Even so the performance is quite astounding. What religious movement of that epoch, whether of ancient origin or newly born, produced, or even aimed at producing, anything similar? Did the religion of Mithras or of Magna Mater? Had not the author approached the task as—to a certain extent—a biographer of St. Paul, qualified thereto by personal knowledge of the apostle; had he not possessed in this knowledge a guiding principle of his work, how is it even conceivable that he could have mastered, or even thought of mastering, the enormous bulk of unwieldy, chaotic material that lay before him? Even so he was compelled to bring to bear upon his task an unusual measure of that glorious gift—the birthright of the genuine Hellene—the sense for form and arrangement, and the art of right selection.

But the second part of his intention is even more astounding. The author, St. Luke, has actually appended this history of his as a continuation to the "Gospel-book" created by St. Mark and modified by himself.[1] He therewith elevated his subject to the

[1] It follows from this—a thing, indeed, probable in itself—that this kind of narrative of the history of our Lord was not yet formally regarded as "sacred." If I am right, "St. Matthew," *who does not mention himself*, was the first to make the book of the Gospel a *book of the Church*, and accordingly quasi sacred. *From St. Matthew this sacred character was imparted also to St. Mark and St. Luke.* "St. Matthew" by his first words, "Βίβλος γενέσεως Ἰησοῦ Χριστοῦ," has connected his work with the Old Testament,

loftiest heights imaginable, and with it his own work to the same high level. His daring is equally great regarded either from an objective or a subjective point of view. To the sacred history of Jesus was now added a second part of this history, and side by side with the Gospel narrative style, which already possessed a fixed type, there was now established the type of this new history! Here the selection of material was entirely the work of St. Luke, equally so the type of narrative. For the latter the Gospel type could scarcely in any point serve as a model; it was necessarily an entirely fresh creation, and though many have imitated it, their scope has been always more limited,[1] nor have their attempts been either happy or successful.

Thus the new religion, even in its very beginnings, entered into the possession of a *written history*, and this written not by a Jewish Christian or a native of Palestine, but by a Greek. This was a fact of immeasurable significance! It was the Hellene, scarcely yet won to the new religion, who presented Christianity with a history, and so compelled her adherents to follow him in his selection out of the chaotic mass of

and the character of his narrative—he always has the Christian community in view, and his style is liturgical—his anonymity and his solemn conclusion show that he wished to create a book for liturgical use. St. Luke has written under his own name and for private use. Acts i. 1 shows that something has fallen out before St. Luke i. 1—namely, the address. It seems that the beginning of St. Mark has also suffered from correction. This gospel also was not originally a liturgical book.

[1] I mean the series of so-called apocryphal Acts, which begins with the Acta Pauli; though perhaps we should say with the Kerygma Petri.

traditional material, and to regard as their history that which he offered them. In the whole undertaking and in a hundred of its details he might have made shipwreck, and his book might have sunk into oblivion either without effect or condemned by Christendom. But here it remains. Perhaps only *faute de mieux?* Certainly not! Of course it does not satisfy all the requirements of later days,[1] but it abides because that which is excellent is certain to succeed.[2]

History can be narrated in two ways: one can gather together a heap of more or less important and characteristic stories—Memorabilia; or one can concentrate everything round a central point of interest. This central point can be a personality or an

[1] Even in early days those who gave the book the title of Πράξεις τῶν ἀποστόλων wished to see in the book a work wherein information was preserved concerning the acts and the testimony of all the twelve Apostles; for there was need of such a work as a proof of the evangelic truth in opposition to heresy. But the book does not satisfy this requirement, or only partially so. The above title, which is generally received, and was already known to Irenæus, Clement of Alexandria, Tertullian, and the author of the Muratorion Fragment, cannot be original, and yet cannot have been given much later than A.D. 150. The title Πράξεις is only an abbreviation. The name "Commentarius Lucæ," which Tertullian uses once (De Jejun. 10), though not a bad one, is a free invention of Tertullian himself.

[2] In Gentile communities the book, so far as we know, was rejected only by the Marcionites (probably also by some Gnostic sects), and by the problematical Severians (Euseb., "Hist. Eccl.," iv. 29: these are probably not to be reckoned among Gentile Christians, seeing that they rejected St. Paul). In spite of Tertullian (Adv. Marc., v. 2, 3, and De Præscr., 22 *f*) we cannot be quite certain whether the book came into the hands of Marcion; there are good reasons both for and against.

idea, and the idea can be pictured as fixed or as in development. What has St. Luke done? He disdainfully refuses to be satisfied with a collection of stories like the fabricators of Acts of the Apostles who came after him. Neither has he set up a single personality as his central point, though his relations with St. Paul and his veneration for that apostle must well have suggested to him this procedure. On the contrary, he recognised with sure tact that, if he wished to place this new history side by side with the Gospel history as its second part, no single personality ought to stand in the centre of interest; for at once the unique character of the Master Jesus Christ would be threatened and blurred. It followed that he must group his material round an *idea.* If, however, this work was to be regarded as a continuation of the first work, this idea must be derived from the active ministry of Jesus Himself. *The power of the Spirit of Jesus in the Apostles manifested in history*—this theme alone seemed to satisfy all requirements. Everything worthy of memory in the history of the primitive communities could without constraint be ranged under this theme; above all, it would supply an excellent criterion of selection, and at the same time would connect the whole subject-matter most firmly with the first part, with the history of the words and actions of Jesus. A genuine inspiration of genius! which loses nothing of its excellence in that it seems to us now so very natural.

"The power of the Spirit of Jesus *in the Apostles manifested in history*"—here the term "Apostle" is not yet used by St. Luke with an absolutely narrow connotation. The facts themselves, indeed, protested against such a restriction. Of the great majority of the Twelve St. Luke knew nothing, or there was nothing for him to tell about them that passed beyond the limits of a simple uneventful ministry. Hence the term "apostle" must receive a somewhat wider connotation, and this would be allowed by the meaning which was at that time still generally attached to the word. The ministry of Philip, Barnabas, Apollos, but above all of St. Paul, was to be described. And now, under the shadow of the general theme and in subordination thereto, the two great heroes of primitive Christian history, St. Peter and St. Paul, could also come into their full rights. The Acts of the Apostles is *a parte potiori* a description of the ministry of St. Peter and St. Paul. In its first part St. Peter rules almost exclusively, in its second part St. Paul is absolutely supreme. Yet no one can describe this book as the combination of two apostolic biographies. On the contrary, with extraordinary skill, care is taken that the biographical element never passes a certain limit. Biographical curiosity is not fully satisfied, indeed it is compelled to content itself with little or no information on very important points.

St. Peter and St. Paul—this combination which in the memory of the Church occupies the highest place of honour after the Founder Himself—was certainly not created by St. Luke, but by History herself. Yet we may well question whether this combination would have impressed itself so exclusively and so firmly upon the memory of posterity without the Acts of the Apostles. Had the Great Unknown, who at a little later period worked in Asia, and there gathered round him a circle of presbyters—had he found such a biographer as St. Luke, it is probable that the dual monarchy of the two chief apostles in the memory of the Church would have been shaken; and had James, the Lord's brother, won to his side an Hellenic author, in the Jerusalem of the future this James might easily have been regarded as the chief personality of the Apostolic epoch. Attempts were made on behalf of both these personalities, but at too late a date and by unqualified persons. Hence, established and protected by the Acts of the Apostles, the twin apostles St. Peter and St. Paul abide unquestioned on their lofty pedestal, whence they can never be thrown down. Of the change which in later days came over the Church's appreciation of the relative importance of these apostles it is not here the place to speak. Only let it be said that St. Luke does not set either above the other. His narrative of St. Paul is of one personally known to himself, while for what he says of St. Peter he depends upon information from outside—this naturally constitutes an important difference; but apart from this insuperable difference he speaks of both with equal veneration; and questions of rivalry between the two do not lie at all within his horizon. If he allows the orbit of St. Peter to intersect that of St. Paul *once* only—at the climax of his narrative (chap. xv.)—while, as we learn from Acts ix. 27, Gal. i. 18, 1 Cor. i. 12, these orbits often touched one another, this is bound up with a definite conception and treatment of his theme on the part of the author, a circumstance which, in spite of all that has been written on the Acts, has hitherto been left out of consideration.

To demonstrate historically the power of the Spirit of Jesus in the Apostles—this was the general theme of St. Luke. But how indefinite must this theme have ever appeared in the face of the crowd of phenomena which presented themselves to the historian! How was he to master them? where was he to draw the limits of subject-matter, of scene, and of actors? If he was to steer a fixed and sure course over this boundless ocean he must discover some guiding principle. Again his simple solution of the problem shows his genius. The power of the Spirit of Jesus manifested itself most impressively in the *Mission*, in that victorious progress wherein the proclamation of the Gospel was carried from Jerusalem to Rome. That within a few decades the new religion had spread from little Galilee throughout the whole empire, that it had won to itself both Greeks and barbarians, and had been proclaimed even before kings and proconsuls—with this fact nothing else could be compared, and everything worthy of narration could be subordinated to this theme. This fact, therefore—*the expansion of the Gospel*—could not but come to the front as the principle of selection and exclusion, and as the leading idea which was to give form to the whole. At the very beginning of the work it is most distinctly proclaimed: "Ye will receive the power of the Holy Spirit and will be My witnesses in Jerusalem and in all Judæa and Samaria and unto the uttermost parts of the earth"; and it is expressed yet more impressively in the great scene of the second chapter, which, in fact, anticipates the conclusion of the mighty drama, where, in words which sound like a triumphant conqueror's list of nations vanquished in a great campaign, we read: "Parthians and Medes and Elamites, the dwellers in Mesopotamia, Pontus, and Asia"—and the rest. As far as the Roman Imperator rules, and farther still beyond the bounds of his empire, the world now hears the Evangelic message and accepts it!

It is wonderful how firmly, exclusively, and consistently St. Luke throughout the whole book has kept the idea of the Mission and expansion of Christianity in his eye, and has scarcely anywhere allowed himself a digression.[1] Even the long narrative of the particular stages of the trial of St. Paul, and of the perils of the last voyage up to the final arrival in Rome, scarcely forms an exception; for that trial is a grand confession of Christianity before the whole world and its rulers, represented by the Roman governor and King Agrippa; while the voyage and shipwreck tend to intensify the suspense of the reader as he wonders whether after all the Gospel will be proclaimed in the metropolis of the world through the preaching of St. Paul. "And so we arrived at Rome" (καὶ οὕτως εἰς τὴν Ῥώμην ἤλθαμεν, note the article)—with these words the conclusion of the book is introduced, and the conclusion of the conclusion runs: "And Paul preached (there) the kingdom of God, and taught concerning the

[1] Only one single subsidiary aim is to be discerned—the defence of St. Paul against Judaistic calumnies.

Lord Jesus Christ with all boldness, none forbidding him."

But this victorious progress had a dark side which, to the historian St. Luke, is scarcely less important than the bright side: the Jewish nation, among whom Jesus Christ had appeared and from whom the whole movement had taken its origin, had not only rejected their Messiah, but had more and more hardened themselves against the preaching of the Gospel, had everywhere attempted to throw the greatest obstacles in the way of its progress among the Gentiles, and with increasing energy of intrigue had stirred up persecutions against the Christians. Through the malicious machinations of this wretched nation the history which St. Luke has to write becomes a drama, and thus it is that he presents it. Moreover, not only must he describe these machinations, but he must also show that, in spite of all the ceaseless and sincere attempts of the Apostles—of St. Paul also—to bring the Jews to a better mind, they nevertheless became only more and more hostile.

But why? Is it not a sign of the weakness of the Gospel that it could not gain over the Jews, and must therefore pass on to the Greeks and the Barbarians? No thought is more alien to St. Luke than this which so easily suggests itself to us! He turns its point in the opposite direction, in that with St. Paul he sees in the Jews' rejection of the Gospel and their hostile attitude to the Mission the predestined arrangement and the foreordained judgment of God. The divine rejection of the Jews had indeed been already foretold by the Prophets; now it was being fulfilled, in that the Gentiles were being called. Thus the seal is set to the legitimacy of Christianity, the new religion is even thereby shown to be the fulfilment of the Old Testament, and for the future it seizes upon this book also as its own. This negative theme, which runs like a scarlet thread through the whole book, is summarised once again with impressive emphasis in the antepenultimate verse of the Acts: "Be it known therefore unto you that this salvation of God is sent unto the Gentiles; they will also hear."

The Jew is in a sense the villain in this dramatic history, yet not—as in the Gospel of St. John and the Apocalypse—the Jew in the abstract who has almost become an incarnation of the evil principle, but the real Jew without generalisation and exaggeration in his manifold gradations of Pharisee, Sadducee, aristocrat, Jew of Palestine or of the Dispersion. Where St. Luke knows anything more favourable concerning particular sections or persons among the Jews he does not keep silence, and so sacrifice truth to his theology of history. He tells us that very many Jewish priests had entered the new community; he speaks of converted Pharisees; he reports the prudent counsel of Gamaliel; he does not conceal from us that the whole Jewish colony in Berœa accepted the teaching of St. Paul with great goodwill, and that even among the Jews of Rome some were won over by the Apostle. This impartiality of the narrative, in a point where there was such an extraordinary temptation to partiality, is a valuable proof of the careful sense of justice of the historian St. Luke.[1]

[1] Different stages are to be traced in the anti-Semitism (anti-Judaism) of the early Gentile-Christians. St. Luke marks the first stage; for St. Paul was never anti-Judaistic; of course the early Church soon forgot Rom. xi, 25–32, if it ever really gave heed to this passage. St. Luke himself has adopted from St. Paul the theory of the hardening of Israel without Rom. xi. 25 *ff*; yet he regards the religion and piety of the Old Testament with the deepest reverence; he still joys over every Jew who is converted, and does not in the least place the individual under the ban of his general theory. "St. John" marks the next stage. Here the Jews are already almost always mentioned only in terms which imply the Divine Rejection, and are treated as *massa proditionis et perditionis;* yet the author, looking back to the pre-Christian epoch, suffers them to stand in their privileged position (iv. 22: ἡ σωτηρία ἐκ τῶν Ἰουδαίων ἐστίν, i. 47: ἴδε ἀληθῶς Ἰσραηλείτης, ἐν ᾧ δόλος οὐκ ἔστιν, x. 8 is to be confined to false Messiahs). The third stage is marked by the Apologists, who, agreeing with St. Luke and St. John in the theory of Israel's hardening, regard the ordinances revealed to the Jews in the Old Testament as a means of discipline and punishment; who, by forced interpretation, deprive the Jews of all the promises referring to their nation, and separate the men of God of the Old Testament from connection with the Jewish people. The fourth stage is characterised by the so-called Epistle of Barnabas, the author of which rejects, together with the Jewish nation, the whole cultus and all the legal ordinances of the Old Testament as a diabolical misrepresentation of the truth, and accordingly admits the Old Testament, which he claims exclusively for Christianity, only under an allegorical interpretation. The fifth and last stage is given in Marcion and the Gnostics. Here, together with the Jewish nation and Judaism, the whole Old Testament is thrown overboard, either as a book of the devil or of the Demiurge; either as a complicated work composed of utterly different elements, or as a book full of absurd myths and lying invention. *All these standpoints have their roots in Paulinism, and their champions sought to establish them by appealing to the teaching of St. Paul* This fact is perhaps the strongest proof that St. Paul was a writer essentially incomprehensible to his age, however well he must have been understood

Moreover, it is not only the regard paid to the conduct of the Jews that brings the play of action and reaction into the narrative of the Acts; this is also brought about in the first part of the Acts by the open acknowledgment of the fact that at the beginning not only was there no mission to the Gentiles in existence, but that at first no one had even thought of such a mission, and that it was only through a slow process of development that this mission was prepared for and established. Practically all that lies written in the Acts between the sixth and the fifteenth chapters, thus more than a third part of the book, is dedicated to the demonstration of the historical problem, how it came about that there was a mission to the Gentiles at all.

The longer I study the work of St. Luke the more am I astonished that this fact has not forced his critics to treat him with more respect than they show him. but not a few of them treat their own conceits in regard to the book with more respect than the grand lines of the work, which they either take as a matter of course, or criticise from the standpoint of their own superior knowledge. Yet it was by no means a matter of course that the

as the great pioneer missionary. As a theological thinker he came out of another generation of long ago, and passed over into another generation far in the future. He was and he remained a Jew, and yet he anticipated, with his doctrine of freedom bound by Faith alone, the development of a whole epoch. The great region lying between these extreme points, with its gradual ascent, did not exist for him. His contemporaries, however, only knew this region. Like all natures of true genius, he lived in the past and in the future.

author should have raised the question: "How is it that within the Christian movement, originally Jewish, there arose a mission to the Gentiles?"—nor that he should have at once treated it as a problem of the first importance and have exerted himself to give it an historical solution. Who else in the early Church except St. Luke, whether of his contemporaries or of a later generation, even proposed this problem? And when it was proposed, who has treated it otherwise than dogmatically with the worthless and absolutely fallacious explanation that the mission to the Gentiles was already foretold in the Old Testament, and had, moreover, been expressly enjoined by our Lord? What other idea than this is given by the Apostolic Fathers and the Apologists? Or to say nothing of these—what else do we learn from St. Matthew and St. Mark (chap. xvi.)? Thus, the very fact that St. Luke has raised this question, and has made its consideration a chief point of his historical work, shows an amount of historical insight which claims the highest appreciation. It is, moreover, a proof that St. Luke himself had in some way taken part in this great historical development, or at least stood in some pretty close relationship to it, for what in the wide world could make a Greek of about the end of the first century feel that he ought to explain how the Gospel came to be preached to the Gentiles; how could he have even proposed to himself such a question whose answer seemed given in the short and simple language of accomplished fact—a question which was indeed no longer a problem for consideration, but a dogmatic postulate—unless he had been in personal touch with the development of days gone by?

But in far higher measure than for the statement of this problem, St. Luke deserves recognition for the manner in which he has answered it. It has, of course, always been thought necessary to criticise with especial rigour this aspect of St. Luke's narrative; here, however, the critics have both overlooked points in his narrative which are undoubtedly correct, and also have set themselves to assail historical positions which upon closer investigation they necessarily would have found to be unassailable. We have in the first place to note what answers he has *not* given. He has ascribed the beginnings of the mission to the Gentiles neither to St. Paul—as it would have been so natural for him to do—nor to the Twelve, nor to St. Peter, indeed he has expressly described the course of events in such a way as to show that St. Peter after receiving an isolated Divine command to baptize a Gentile, did not for years draw therefrom any further practical conclusion. Therefore the representation which is given in the Acts of the Apostles is not one that has been manufactured in favour of the Apostles. Again, what St. Luke tells us of the Christian Hellenists in Jerusalem and their conflict with the Christian Hebrews; of the Hellenist Stephen who prophesied the destruction of the Temple and the change of the ordinances given by Moses; of the Evangelist Philip who first preached the Gospel among the Samaritans and baptized the eunuch of the Queen of Ethiopia; of the unnamed men of Cyprus and Cyrene who first preached the Gospel to Greeks and formed them into a Christian community; of the college of Elders at the head of the Church in Jerusalem who made no protest when Christians from Jerusalem went to distant Antioch and demanded that the Gentile Christians in that city should be circumcised; lastly, of that same college of Elders who found themselves compelled to recognise the Gentile mission in the face of the grand *fait accompli* which St. Paul and St. Barnabas had brought about in South-eastern Asia Minor[1]—all these records bear the stamp of historical truth. And if towards the close of his narrative he remarks by the way that the great majority of Christians in Jerusalem were still zealous of the Law, and needed to be protected from the danger of yielding credence to calumnious charges against St. Paul—how can he be accused of concealing the true course of events? Though he may indeed have erred elsewhere in this or in that particular point, he cannot be charged with a definite bias or with a want of knowledge obscuring his whole presentation of the history. If he is silent upon many points on which we to-day would gladly have information, this surely cannot be justly reckoned to his discredit!

And the less so seeing that he has confined himself strictly to the theme which he had marked out for himself. The seeming gaps in his narrative become no gaps for us so soon as we realise

[1] Chapters xiii. and xiv. are simply written to prepare for chapter xv., and what they relate must be interpreted in the light of that chapter.

the task he set himself. What this was is clear from what we have already said; it was to show how *the power of the Spirit of Jesus in the Apostles founded the Primitive Community, called into being the mission to the Gentiles, conducted the Gospel from Jerusalem to Rome, and set the receptive Gentile world in the place of the Jewish nation, which hardened its heart more and more against the appeal of Christianity.* From these main lines upon which the work was planned, and which were abstracted in the happiest way from the actual situation of events, St. Luke scarcely ever deviates. If one keeps this fact well in view, one will no longer wonder that he tells us so little about the Churches, and that he scarcely touches upon the inner life of individuals—even of St. Paul—and of the Christian community.[1] When he conducts the missionaries to a new scene of action he only asks himself: how it was that they came there?—what reception they found among the Jews? what among the Gentiles?—and, if any material was to hand on this point, how they were received by the Roman authorities of the place?—about how long they stayed there?—and what was the manner of their departure? If in his narrative he gives anything more than bald answers to these questions, it must be because of specially important personages and events in which the power of the Spirit manifested itself in extraordinary ways. There is also no justification for charging him with a distinctly *politico*-apologetic bias. The dedication

[1] We should, however, here remember the limitations of ancient historical literature.

of the work shows that it was addressed to a man who was an instructed Christian, and there are no indications that St. Luke had heathen readers in his mind as he wrote. We need not assume that he excluded these, but they were not distinctly in his view. If in spite of this he has laid so much stress upon showing that the Gospel was proclaimed before magistrates, proconsuls, and kings, and that these adopted towards it on the whole a not unfriendly attitude, this fact does not necessarily imply some political tendency of a special character on the part of the author. With every new religious movement the attitude of the public very quickly becomes a question of the deepest interest, and the public is in the first line represented by the authorities. In this case, moreover, the interest must have been deepened by the contrast between the behaviour of the *Roman* authorities and those of the *Jews*. What St. Luke tells us in this connection simply answered to the facts; and if, beginning with Pilate, he regards hostile behaviour on the part of the Roman authorities as far more pardonable than similar behaviour on the part of the Jewish authorities, surely no Christian could judge otherwise. Besides he is as far from suppressing instances of unfriendliness and hostility on the part of the Roman and civic police authorities as he is, on the other hand, from keeping silence concerning friendly behaviour on the part of the Jews (*vide supra*).

Whilst the first half of the first part of the Acts (chaps. i.–v.) captivates the reader with its record of the mighty deeds and the great sermons by which the foundation of the Primitive Community was firmly laid, the second half of the first part (chaps. vi.–xv.), with its thronging abundance of facts of the most varied character yet all pointing towards and preparing for the triumphant appearance of the mission to the Gentiles, holds him in a dramatic suspense. This suspense would be well-nigh intolerable if the author had not understood how to temper it by his skill in narrative and by a style which has about it something of the epic—full of life, and yet not unrestful. Though Stephen is martyred, though St. Paul after his first appearance again vanishes from the scene of action, though St. Peter draws no further practical conclusion from the Divine vision, though unbidden guests from Jerusalem seek to trouble the Gentile Church in Antioch — yet they find one another at last, Jerusalem and Antioch, the Gospel and the Gentile world.

The second part of the book lacks a special theme of such vivacious character as that of the first. There now remained only to describe the extension of the gospel to Rome.[1] What means has St. Luke here employed to ensure the continued interest of his readers? In the first place, the "we"-narrative now makes its appearance, and gives to several long passages vivacity and a distinct charm. In the second place, throughout the first half of this part the interest of the reader is kept alive by the rapid progress of the narrative, by the variety of important

[1] The line of division quite plainly comes after xvi. 5; but xv. 36–xvi. 5 forms the transition from the first to the second part. The first part closes with xv. 35.

events, by the change of scene (Philippi, Thessalonica, Berœa, Athens, Corinth, Ephesus), finally by the culmination in the long abode in Ephesus and in the great and significant farewell discourse pronounced before the Ephesian elders.[1] At the close of this third quarter of the work Rome now appears on the horizon and remains the goal of the last quarter of the narrative. Just as the central point of interest in the second quarter of the book is this—whether the Gospel and the Gentile world will ever meet, so now in the fourth quarter the sole subject of enthralling interest is this—whether St. Paul will ever succeed in carrying the Gospel to Rome. Hindrance follows hindrance—yet each affords St. Paul an opportunity for giving noble testimony—finally sea and storm-wind seem to have conspired together against his undertaking; and yet he succeeds—his desire, his appropriate destiny is fulfilled; *he brings the Gospel to Rome.* But in this last section St. Luke perhaps is influenced by yet another interest allied to that of the second quarter (the question of the origin and legitimacy of the mission to the Gentiles). St Paul and his work must be set forth in their pure nobility and grandeur, *i.e.* his mission to the Gentiles must be shown to have been legitimate (there are three narratives of his call!) The Gospel was brought to the Gentile world by no unworthy minister, but by a "*vas electionis.*" He was no destroyer of the Jewish religion, but the most powerful and strenuous affirmer

[1] In order to avoid repetition and not to weaken the impression of continued progress, the narrative is so skilfully managed that the reader scarcely notices St. Paul's second visits to these places.

of its hopes; he was no revolutionary, "neither in respect to the Jewish Law nor to the Temple nor to Cæsar." Here, however, the emphasis—this is worthy of note!—is laid upon his relationship to the Jewish religion (*not* to Cæsar), and this is a further proof that St. Luke still stood in very close personal touch with the primitive times; for what Hellene has ever treated the Jewish religion and the Old Testament piety, existing side by side with Christianity, with such tender, indeed to us almost unintelligible, respect as the author shows here and elsewhere in his work! It is not till we reach Irenæus that the sympathy of the Gentile Church with Old Testament piety becomes again awakened; and this was an artificial awakening, the exciting cause of which was the conflict with Gnosticism.

There is another very important question which presents itself in connection with the subject-matter of the work—Why is it that St. Luke in working out his theme, the extension of the Gospel to Rome, has confined himself so exclusively to the ministry of St. Paul? He must surely have known of several provinces, wherein in his times Christians were found, that had not been converted by St. Paul (he himself notes by the way that Apollos was won over to Christianity in Alexandria). He must also have known that the Gospel was not first brought to Rome by St. Paul. In my opinion, the question can only be answered by assuming that St. Luke's conception of the term "Apostle," though not absolutely narrow, was yet already very definite, and that in his narrative of the propagation of the Gospel he is satisfied with describing only *its progress across the world* from Jerusalem to Rome. The latter procedure was certainly wise; for his narrative would have exceeded all bounds if he had aimed at even approximate fulness in geographical statistics. If the former assumption is true, it necessarily resulted in the glorification of St. Paul; for the Twelve never took part in the mission to the Gentiles, and St. Luke scarcely regards such persons as Stephen, Philip, Silas, Priscilla and her husband, and Apollos as standing to a certain degree on a level with the Twelve. Accordingly, he was left with Paul and Barnabas. Men like Mark and Timothy might have felt hurt, yet note how St. Luke refers to his own missionary activity in only the most modest terms. The title Apostle had already received an exclusive connotation, and it was the apostle alone who really legitimised the mission. If even for people like St. Luke, holding "spiritual" gifts in such high regard and really so spiritually free, the office of apostle had so quickly attained to an exclusive authority, what a multitude of unauthorised missionaries preaching "Jesus" must even at that time have been carrying on their work in the provinces of the Empire! Moreover, though St. Peter during the time of St. Paul's ministry not only visited Antioch, but may also not improbably have paid a passing visit to Corinth, the silence of the Acts concerning him is sufficiently explained by the purpose of the book, which did not admit the narration of the experiences of any church after its foundation.

Of the ancient historian's liberty to insert speeches at appropriate places in his work, whether reports of speeches actually made or free compositions, St. Luke has made an extensive and a happy use. Just as in the Gospel we find a succession of actions and sayings of our Lord (Acts i. 1, *περὶ πάντων ὧν ἤρξατο Ἰησοῦς ποιεῖν τε καὶ διδάσκειν*), so also in the second part of his work he must report both actions and discourses. The discourses predominate in the first and in the last quarters of the Acts; while in the second and third quarters, though occupying less space, they are only the more weighty in substance. The highest level, according to our taste and perhaps also according to the taste of the first readers, is reached in the speeches of chapters xv., xvii., and xx.; but the speeches at the beginning of the work are really fundamental in their Christology, and those at the close assure the readers that their great missionary St. Paul was the divinely appointed instrument of the mission, and the great witness for Christ before governors and kings.

During the last decade ever deeper insight has been gained into the language in which St. Luke has composed his work, and in consequence hasty generalisations of old standing have been corrected. In this connection Blass deserves specially high credit. A very large portion of the supposed Semitic idioms have vanished—the "Κοινή" already included these Semitisms—nor as a rule should they be so regarded, but rather as natural productions of the Κοινή that more or less accidentally coincide with Semitic forms. Some, of course, are still left, especially in well-marked divisions of the work, and it remains to be investigated—just as in the case of the Gospel—whether these divisions are not translated from Aramaic sources. In general St. Luke's style very nearly approaches that of the Septuagint, more particularly that of the books of the Maccabees (but this itself is nothing but the style of the spoken language of educated men). Non-classical words and words of the vulgar idiom are comparatively rare. The syntax and certain stereotyped syntactical formulæ are "vulgar" and non-classical; but it is probable that these also had already gained a recognised place in the more refined literary version of the language of the people. It is now also recognised that St. Luke was a master of language who, with careful purpose, has accommodated his style in different portions of his work to the scene of action and the dignity of his subject-matter. Just as in the Gospel he has so treated the stories of the Infancy that one might imagine that one was reading a piece of history from the Septuagint, so also in the Jerusalem sections of the Acts, especially at the beginning, he retains this style; and so long as the scene of action remains in Palestine he holds fast, in vocabulary, syntax, and style, to the type of narrative which he has followed in the Gospel. Very gradually he passes over to a freer and at the same time more classical type of narrative. The style becomes, so to say, more profane, and even thereby more cosmopolitan, yet without detracting from the dignity of the narrative. In the last quarter of the book, although the scene again lies for the most part in Palestine, the later style is still preserved, for the new movement is no longer simply Palestinian, but now plays out its part on the stage of the world. The author intended that this fact should here find expression even in his style. It is, however, most remarkable that St. Luke, in spite of all the variety which he has introduced into the form of his narrative, has understood how to preserve the stylistic unity of his work. In reading one receives no impression of patchiness or of want of organic connection. The style also is free from all suspicion of pose, and there is a complete absence of vain and empty rhetoric. Scarcely ever does the writer use a single superfluous word. He is ever concerned only with the root of the matter in hand, he knows how to tell a very great deal in a few words, and he never tries to bribe his readers with tricks of oratory. In respect of its style this work can be compared with the best literary productions of the Hellenico-Roman period. Read the descriptions of the Pentecostal scene, of the conversion of St. Paul, of that apostle's mission in Athens, of the shipwreck, and many another passage!

And now where are to be found the weak points of this author? We cannot say that he is on the whole either credulous or uncritical. Credulous and uncritical writers of those days produced works of an entirely different character from his! Again, for the larger half of the work we possess in the epistles of St. Paul a test of the accuracy of the historian than which we can scarcely imagine a more stringent. That these epistles were creations of the moment, the offspring of a personality of the most marked subjectivity, only increases the stringency of the test. And yet it is only the over-scrupulous and the dividers of hairs who cannot recognise that in dozens of important and unimportant passages the Acts of the Apostles has stood the test imposed upon it by the Pauline epistles. Leaving out of account a few minute details, the descriptions of the Council of Jerusalem and of St. Paul's apology in the last speeches, in fact the whole account of his attitude towards the Jews at his last visit to Jerusalem, alone remain questionable. In reference to the latter point, it seems to me that what St. Luke records may be very easily harmonised with the character and theology of St. Paul as set forth in the epistles, if one only does not confine oneself narrowly and rigidly to the Epistle to the Galatians, as of course every one still does. And in reference to the Council of Jerusalem, it remains to be proved whether such serious mistakes occur in the Acts as to render its authorship by St. Luke inconceivable. His real weaknesses as an historian seem to me to lie elsewhere—in the first place, in his credulity in reference to cases of miraculous healing and of "spiritual" gifts; secondly, in a tendency to carelessness and inaccuracy, often of a very far-reaching influence in his narrative, which may be partly due to his endeavour after brevity; lastly, in a tendency to work up important situations. The last failing, measured by the standards of ancient historians, can scarcely be regarded as a fault in method, and in reference to the first, we must take into consideration that, as is the case in every enthusiastic religious movement, "wonders and signs" really occurred, and especially that class of phenomena with which what is to-day called "Christian Science" is concerned. But only he that is acquainted with the religious charlatanism of that age and the extravagancies of its productions can know from what a mass of esoteric rubbish, of fraudulent magic, and pious absurdity the author has kept himself free. All these things we know found their way even into Christianity at that time or soon afterwards. From these St. Luke, however, kept himself free.

We must also in this connection remember the fact that St. Paul (Col. iv. 14) calls St. Luke expressly, and in a context where the epithet has doubled weight, "the physician, the beloved." He had therefore tried him and approved him as a *physician* and a *friend*, and from his experience of St. Luke he is impelled to give him this public testimony. If one now compares how modestly and yet with what firm assurance St. Luke cursorily mentions his successful cures (Acts xxviii. 9–10 . . . ἐθεραπεύοντο, οἳ καὶ πολλαῖς τιμαῖς ἐτίμησαν ἡμᾶς—Ramsay has justly laid stress upon the fact that in verse 8 the word used of St. Paul is ἰάσατο), one by no means receives the impression of some wild enthusiast who cured diseases, but of a man who continued to practise his profession of physician with success, and who in it had earned the permanent esteem of a man of such high temper as St. Paul. That he took account also of cures in answer to prayer, that his attitude towards them was uncritical, that in fact he has no clear knowledge of the boundary-line separating science from magic—what special reason is there here for surprise! And lastly, as to the instances of carelessness and inaccuracy in his narrative, we must indeed keep these closely in view, for he has suffered from them more than anything else in that they have laid him open to the exaggerated calumnies of those who would blacken his literary character. Against these vulnerable points the critics hurl themselves in order to tear down and to scatter in pieces. And yet these many instances of inaccuracy, which are easily discerned as such just because they are a constant quantity, are as a rule harmless and unfitted to serve as a base for far-reaching critical operations.

The account which we have here given of the character of the Acts of the Apostles and of its author St. Luke does not yet enjoy universal acceptance; rather it is entirely, or almost entirely, rejected by numerous critics. With them the book passes as a comparatively late patchwork compilation, in which the part taken by the editor is insignificant, yet in all cases detrimental; the "we"-sections are not the property of the author, but an extract from a source, or even a literary fiction; historical errors are as numerous as gaps and ill-disguised joinings; the portrait of St. Paul is drawn with bias, or in ignorance; the description given in the first chapters is scarcely anywhere other than pure fancy—Peter is Pauline, Paul is Petrine; but who can number the objections that have been raised against this book! If they were only objections that one could take hold of! But after no small number of these has been finally refuted, one has to deal not so much with definite objections, as with an attitude of general mistrust in the book, with airy conceits and lofty contempt; most of all, however, with the fruits of that vicious method wherein great masses of theory are hung upon the spider's thread of a single observation, wherein a writer of the New Testament is allowed no weakness, no possibility of ignorance, wherein instances of such failing are used as powder to blow the whole book into the air. In the first volume of this series, entitled "Luke the Physician" (Crown Theological Library, 1907), I have therefore tried in the first place to prove the identity of the author of the "we"-sections with St. Luke, and at the same time to refute some of these objections and critical vagaries—not by means of the more or less subjective apologetic of the harmonist, but by assiduous attention to, and exhibition of, facts and observations that confirm one another. In the following pages I continue these investigations in order to arrive at a more assured judgment as to how far the book is homogeneous, as to its sources and its degree of trustworthiness, and by this means to prove afresh the identity of the author of the "we"-sections with the author of the whole work. In an age wherein critical hypotheses, once upon a time not unfruitful, have hardened themselves into dogmas, and when if an attempt is made to defend a book against prejudice, misunderstanding, and misrepresentation, scornful remarks are made about "special pleading," it is not superfluous to declare that the method which is here employed is influenced by no prepossession of any kind. It is of course disgraceful that the circumstances of criticism at the present day make such a declaration necessary

CHAPTER I

CHRONOLOGICAL DATA[1]

In the prologue to his twofold historical work St. Luke has announced that he wishes to write down everything "καθεξῆς." This word, as well as the synonym "ἑξῆς," occurs in the New Testament only in the Lukan writings (St. Luke i. 3; viii. 1; Acts iii. 24; xi. 4; xviii. 23; ἑξῆς: St. Luke vii. 11; ix. 37; **Acts xxi. 1**; xxv. 17; **xxvii. 18**).[2] The word does not necessarily denote a chronological arrangement, though as a rule it means this, and its use in the other places suggests that this signification is to be understood here. We have not in all cases the means of judging how far St. Luke has succeeded in establishing a correct chronological arrangement. In his gospel it is obvious that he does not come up to an even moderate chronological standard; but in the Acts every one allows that he had the opportunity of doing, and has done, better things. His procedure in regard to chronology in the Acts, so far as I know, has not yet been subjected to a

[1] This chapter was read at a meeting of the Prussian Academy, and was published in their reports (*Sitzungsberichten*, 25th April 1907). It appears here in a somewhat different and more developed form.

[2] Throughout this book the numbers in bolder type denote passages in the "we"-sections.

thorough and connected investigation. And yet more accurate knowledge on this point is of interest in two respects, both in relation to the question of the trustworthiness of the work (or of the literary conscientiousness of the author) and in relation to the question of its unity.

In the first place, the book is disappointing in so far as it gives evidence of no trace of a connected chronological framework. The construction of such a framework, for at least the principal part of the narrative, could not have presented special difficulties to a man with the author's culture and access to sources of information, even if he were not the companion of the Apostle.[1] He must, therefore, have regarded it as of no importance, and have used καθεξῆς not in this sense. In this attitude he, moreover, shows himself an adept in the historical writing of those days which, especially if it aimed at edification or amusement, set up no chronological framework and was sparing in the use of definite dates. So also St. Luke is content to refer to contemporary history in only a few passages where such reference seemed to him fitting—if these few passages may be so understood—elsewhere he only gives relative dates. Even the passages where the succession of years is mentioned are few in number; on the other hand, the author shows interest in times of festivals, in days, and in hours—again in accordance with the custom of writers of his day. These references are intended to give life to the narrative, *i.e. to the narra-*

[1] And yet all chronological systems of those days were wanting in connection, in clearness, and exactitude.

tive of particular events. He does not, as a rule, place the reader in a position to judge whether he represents events in their correct order; his desire is rather that the reader should simply trust him in this matter. But for this very reason, because he has not thought of consistently dating events by the year in which they occurred, nor of a chronological framework for his work, the passages wherein he produces chronological material have special value; for they do not belong to a system, but are scattered throughout the book apart from any tendency whatever. Let us consider in order the chronological expedients of which the writer has availed himself, distinguishing the while his use of them in connection with the history of Christianity in Palestine, from his use of them in connection with the history of Christianity in the Diaspora.

I. *Chronological References to Contemporary History.*

As concerns the history in Palestine, apart from a few references to the past,[1] and to person-

[1] Our Lord executed under Pilate and Herod Antipas (iv. 27, &c.); in the days of "the enrolment" (v. 37); Theudas (v. 36); Judas the Galilæan (v. 37); the "Egyptian" (xxi. 38). Here let it be noted by the way that St. Luke gives us certain information, nowhere else recorded, concerning the relationship of Herod Antipas and his court to Christ and the new religion. He expressly refers to this Herod when giving the date of the public appearance of our Lord (St. Luke iii. 1); he records (viii. 3) that among the women who followed our Lord was to be found one Joanna, the wife of a steward of Herod (*cf.* xxiv. 10), and (Acts xiii. 1) that among the spiritual leaders of the Primitive Community of Antioch was a "syntrophos" (confidential friend) of Herod,

ages[1] of note whose date was known or could easily be ascertained, the only information that the author gives us is that the general famine foretold by Agabus, the prophet from Jerusalem, actually came to pass "under Claudius" (xi. 28), and that at the same time[2] (xii. 1) a persecution of the Christians was set on foot by King Herod Agrippa I. (the name of Herod tempts the author to a digression concerning the circumstances under which Herod died soon afterwards: the quarrel with the people of Tyre and Sidon; Blastus the chamberlain; the presumptuous pride of the king; *mors persecutoris!* xii. 20–23). The former chronological note is due simply to the author's desire to bear witness to the fulfilment of the prophet's prediction; the latter notice arises in the natural course of events, seeing that Herod himself (in order to please the Jews) had thrown himself in the path of

Manaen by name. He hands down to us an utterance of our Lord concerning Herod (St. Luke xiii. 32), otherwise unknown, and he relates that our Lord was sent by Pilate to Herod for judgment (xxiii. 7 *ff.*).

[1] Gamaliel (v. 34; xxii. 3); the chief priests Annas and Caiaphas, and John (Jonathan) and Alexander (iv. 6); the high-priest Ananias (xxiii. 2; xxiv. 1 *f.*); the procurator Felix (xxiii. 6, &c.); Drusilla the wife of Felix (xxiv. 24); the procurator Festus (xxiv. 27, &c.); the king Agrippa II. and Bernice (xxv. 13, &c.). In mentioning the Ethiopian queen Candace, St. Luke does not give us an indirect chronological reference, seeing that at that time and afterwards all the Ethiopian queens were called by that name.

[2] *κατ' ἐκεῖνον τὸν καιρόν.* Weiss describes the expression as chronologically incorrect, because he regards it as referring to the time of the first origin of a Gentile Christian community, a time which was far in the past. But it really refers to the time of the Famine, or rather to the time of the journey of St. Paul and St. Barnabas to Jerusalem, and is therefore not incorrect.

the youthful Church. Neither in the one case nor in the other can we therefore trace any real chronological interest on the part of the author.

As concerns the history in the Diaspora, here again Claudius is the only emperor mentioned by name, and his name forms the sole directly chronological notice. When St. Paul came to Corinth he found there one Aquila with Priscilla his wife, who had lately come from Italy; they had been compelled to leave their place of abode διὰ τὸ διατεταχέναι Κλαύδιον χωρίζεσθαι πάντας τοὺς Ἰουδαίους ἀπὸ τῆς Ῥώμης (xviii. 2).[1] Here again this information is not given for the sake of chronology, but quite casually. That St. Luke knows of the edict of Claudius, and records it, shows that he interested himself in the fortunes and doings of the Jews in the Diaspora. Besides this piece of information mention is made of a few notable persons, such as the pro-consul Sergius Paulus in Cyprus (xiii. 7), and the pro-consul Gallio in Corinth (xviii. 12 *f.*). Here again the names are mentioned in the natural course of the narrative; there is nothing that is intentionally chronological.[2]

[1] In both cases (here and xi. 28) St. Luke has omitted all titles, and gives only the name of the emperor. Even in this point the consistency of his style is remarkable. Orosius gives the date of the edict of Claudius. We do not know where he got his information; there is, however, no reason for doubting its accuracy.

[2] For further references to general history and matters connected with heathen cultus, *cf.* the Chiliarch Claudius Lysias (xxiii. 26), the centurion Julius (**xxvii. 1**); the σπεῖρα Ἰταλική (x. 1), and the σπεῖρα Σεβαστή (**xxvii. 1**)—note the coincidence; the Epicureans and Stoics (xvii. 18; we are surprised that no mention is made of the Academicians; did the author intend to represent them as not opposed to St. Paul?); the Areopagus (xvii. 19); Dionysius the

It cannot therefore be shown that St. Luke was influenced by a chronological interest in any of the few passages wherein he produces what is practically chronological material from contemporary history. *Such a passage as St. Luke iii. 1, wherein the chronological situation is scientifically determined, is to be found nowhere in the Acts of the Apostles.* Moreover, there is *no difference* here between the treatment of the history of Christianity in the Diaspora and in Palestine.

II. *Exact statements of years, months, and days.*

Dates of years and months occur only in the following passages:[1]—

xi. 26. St. Barnabas and St. Paul abide a full year (ἐνιαυτὸν ὅλον) in Antioch (fostering the youthful Church).

xvii. 2. On three Sabbath days (ἐπὶ σάββατα τρία) St. Paul preached in the synagogue at Thessalonica, and was therefore nearly a month in that city.

xviii. 11. St. Paul on his first visit to Corinth remained there a year and six months (ἐνιαυτὸν καὶ μῆνας ἕξ).

Areopagite (xvii. 34); the στρατηγοί in Philippi (xvi. 20); the politarchs in Thessalonica (xvii. 6); the Asiarchs (xix. 31); the school of Tyrannus (xix. 9); the γραμματεύς (xix. 35); the ἀγοραῖοι καὶ ἀνθύπατοι (xix. 38); and the ἔννομος ἐκκλησία in Ephesus (xix. 39); Zeus and Hermes (xiv. 12); the great Artemis (xix. 27); the πόλις νεωκόρος (xix. 35); Dike (xxviii. 4); the Dioscuri (xxviii. 11); the Unknown God in Athens (xvii. 23). Each trait is correct and true to its situation.

[1] Passages wherein the years of duration of disease are given are left out of consideration.—*Vide* iv. 22 and ix. 33.

xix. 8. St. Paul on his visit to Ephesus taught for three months (ἐπὶ μῆνας τρεῖς) in the synagogue there, and then

xix. 10. he taught for two years (ἐπὶ ἔτη δύο) in the school of Tyrannus in the same city. These two periods together are described in

xx. 31. as making up a period of three years (τριετίαν).

xx. 3. St. Paul made a second stay of three months (ποιήσας μῆνας τρεῖς) in Greece (Corinth).

[xxiv. 10. Felix at the time that St. Paul first appeared before him had been procurator in Judæa for many years (ἐκ πολλῶν ἐτῶν).]

[xxiv. 17. St. Paul, after the lapse of several years (δι' ἐτῶν πλειόνων), had again returned to Jerusalem, bringing alms.]

xxiv. 27. After two years (διετίας πληρωθείσης)—reckoned from St. Paul's first hearing—Felix was replaced by Festus.[1]

[1] Wellhausen (*Nachr. d. K. Gesellsch. d. Wissensch. z. Göttingen*, 12. Jan. 1907, s. 8 *f.*) makes the following remarks on this passage:—

"Διετία is generally referred to the stay of *St. Paul* in Jerusalem (read: Cæsarea), and as a necessary consequence it is considered characteristic of the narrative of St. Luke that out of a period of the apostolic ministry of St. Paul, lasting more than two years, he should only have been able to tell us of the progress of the trial of the Apostle. The hypothesis of a cessation of two years in the consecutive and consistent course of the trial, which naturally and necessarily forms the proper subject of the narrative, is however rather characteristic of the exegetes, who one and all hang on like bulldogs to only a single exegetical possibility. It is just as possible that the words quoted refer to *the departure of Felix from office* at the end of two years. This interpretation is indeed the first that suggests itself, and has the advantage of disposing of the absurd hiatus in the trial of St. Paul. The exegetes have

xxviii. 11. After three months (μετὰ τρεῖς μῆνας) St. Paul left the island of Malta.

xxviii. 30. St. Paul abode in Rome two full years (διετίαν ὅλην) in his own hired lodging.

We have in addition the following dates by days:—

i. 3. Our Lord manifested Himself for forty days (δι' ἡμερῶν τεσσαράκοντα) after His Resurrection.

[ix. 9. Saul was blind for three days (ἡμέρας τρεῖς) after Christ had appeared to him.]

x. 30. Cornelius had the vision three days (ἀπὸ τετάρτης ἡμέρας) before St. Peter's visit to him.

xx. 6. Within five days (ἄχρι ἡμερῶν πέντε) we came from Philippi to Troas.

xx. 6. Seven days (ἡμέρας ἑπτά) we abode in Troas.

probably allowed themselves to be led away by the πολλὰ ἔτη of xxiv. 10. As if St. Luke in his discourses cared for historical exactitude and not rather for anything that suited his purpose! He constantly contradicts himself even when his speakers give a rhetorical summary of events described in the narrative (? ?). In xxiv. 10, however, there is no need to suppose that he thought of xxiv. 27. It is not my business to investigate whether Felix was really superseded so early as the end of 54 or the beginning of A.D. 55."

So far as I know, Wellhausen has had no predecessor in his interpretation which in my opinion will not stand investigation; for—(1) St. Paul, not Felix, is here the principal figure. It would be singular, and it is not suggested by the context or by the general procedure of St. Luke, that the author should have thought it necessary to state the time during which a procurator held office. (2) The preceding words, διὸ καὶ ὁ Φῆλιξ πυκνότερον τὸν Παῦλον μεταπεμπόμενος ὡμίλει αὐτῷ form an excellent introduction to the statement that this lasted for a somewhat long time, while they are out of any connection with the supposed statement concerning the length of Felix's term of office. (3)

xxi. 4. Seven days (ἡμέρας ἑπτά) we abode in Tyre.

xxi. 7. One day (ἡμέραν μίαν) we abode in Ptolemais.

xxiv. 1. After five days (μετὰ πέντε ἡμέρας), reckoned from the conveyance of St. Paul to Cæsarea, the high-priest Ananias came thither.

xxiv. 11. There are not more than twelve days (οὐ πλείους εἰσίν μοι ἡμέραι δώδεκα), says St. Paul, since I came to Jerusalem.

xxv. 1. Three days after his entry into office (μετὰ τρεῖς ἡμέρας) Festus came to Jerusalem.

xxv. 6. After not more than eight to ten days (ἡμέρας οὐ πλείους ὀκτὼ ἢ δέκα) Festus returned back to Cæsarea.

xxvii. 27. The fourteenth night (τεσσαρεσκαιδεκάτη νύξ) in the raging storm (**xxvii. 33**).

Felix was in office longer than two years—there can be no doubt upon this point—and St. Luke himself says as much a few verses previously. It is somewhat out of place to charge him unnecessarily with such an extraordinary instance of discrepancy. Moreover, (4) διετία cannot be regarded as the general technical expression for the term of office of a procurator (so that διετίας πληρωθείσης would simply mean "after the end of his term of office"); for the term of office was not at that period fixed (*vide* Hirschfeld, *Die kaiserl. Verwaltungsbeamten*, 2 *Aufl.*, 1905, s. 445 *ff.*), and διετία is found a few chapters later (xxviii. 30) in its ordinary sense. (5) There is no justification for speaking of an absurd hiatus in the trial of St. Paul as being implied by the traditional interpretation, for when St. Luke gives a date in years he never tells us what details occurred within this period, but leaves it to the reader to derive this information from the context, that is, from his general statement concerning the situation of the Apostle. Therefore the statement in xxiv. 27, when referred to St. Paul, is in conformity with the other statements giving the years of the Apostle's stay in great cities (*vide supra*).

xxviii. 7. For three days (τρεῖς ἡμέρας) Publius entertained St. Paul at Malta.

xxviii. 12. For three days (τρεῖς ἡμέρας) we abode at Syracuse.

xxviii. 13. After one day (μετὰ μίαν ἡμέραν) we sailed from Rhegium.

xxviii. 13. In two days (δευτεραῖοι) we came to Puteoli.

xxviii. 14. For seven days (ἡμέρας ἑπτά) we abode with the brethren in Puteoli.

xxviii. 17. Three days after his arrival in Rome (μετὰ ἡμέρας τρεῖς) St. Paul invited the leaders of the Jews in that city to an interview.

We add lastly the passages in which the next day is mentioned:—

Passages	
x. 9 x. 23 x. 24 xiv. 20 **xx. 7** **xxi. 8** xxii. 30 xxiii. 32 xxv. 6 xxv. 23	ἡ ἐπαύριον (ἡμέρα)
iv. 3 iv. 5 [xxiii. 15] xxiii. 20 xxv. 22	ἡ αὔριον (ἡμέρα) *vel* αὔριον
[vii. 26] **xvi. 11** **xx. 15** **xxi. 18** xxiii. 11	ἡ ἐπιούσῃ (also with ἡμέρα or νύξ)

xx. 15 . . . . **xxvii. 3**	ἡ ἑτέρα (ἡμέρα)
xx. 15 . . . . xxi. 26 . . . . [xiii. 44. Reading uncertain] . .	ἡ ἐχομένῃ (xxi. 26 with ἡμέρα, xiii. 44 with σάββατον)
xxi. 1 . . . . xxv. 17 . . . . **xxvii. 18**	ἡ ἑξῆς ἡμέρα (in **xxvii. 18** followed by ἡ τρίτῃ)

From these lists we derive the following conclusions:—

1. Exact statements of longer periods of time occurring in this book refer *exclusively* to the duration of the stay or the ministry of *St. Paul* in some important place: St. Paul was a *full* year in Antioch, nearly a month in Thessalonica, eighteen months in Corinth, two years and three months (thus a τριετία) in Ephesus, three months in Greece (on his second visit), two years (διετία) in Cæsarea in prison, [three months in Malta], and two *full* years (διετίαν ὅλην) in Rome.[1] The duration of the ministry of the Apostle in these places was so important to St. Luke that he has expressly mentioned it. For questions connected with the inner development of the Christian communities, *so far as these had nothing to do with the Jews and heathen*, he in his book evidently betrays no interest; but the length of time during which these communities had the good fortune to see the Apostle in their midst is a matter in which he had, and he

[1] The two instances which I have included above among the years and months, but in brackets, do not come into account; for in xxiv. 10, 17 only passing mention is made of "several years" without any closer determination of the periods.

shows, the most lively interest. For ascertaining the absolute chronology of the Acts these exact statements, together with the references to contemporary history, afford almost the only material we can use.

With these ten notices concerning a lengthy ministry of St. Paul in definite localities are connected the five notices of similar character wherein it is a question only of a period of days: seven days we abode in Troas, seven days in Tyre, a day in Ptolemais; ten days was the length of St. Paul's last visit to Jerusalem; seven days we abode in Puteoli (brethren were found in all these places).

2. But of these five notices, four—and of the ten, one—belong to another connection, namely, to the diary of the "we"-account. Here in twenty-one instances dates are given in days (including one instance of like character—the stay in Malta—where the duration is given in months—*vide supra*), and within this "we"-account the times spent in the different stages of the journey are to the author seemingly of equal importance with the times spent in visits at various places.[1] From **chap. xx. 6** until the arrival in Jerusalem it is possible to make a connected calculation of the time spent. According to **xx. 6** the start was made from Philippi after the days of unleavened bread, and St. Paul wished to be in Jerusalem for the feast of Pentecost. He had therefore about 44 days for his journey. The

[1] The passage, **chap. xxvii. 12**, should also be added to the chronological passage of the "we"-account. We are here told that it was at the beginning of winter that the ship touched at Crete on the voyage to Rome.

journey from Philippi to Troas occupied 5 days, 7 days were spent in Troas, *x* days in the voyage to Mitylene, 1 day at Chios, 1 day to Samos, 1 day to Miletus, *x* days in Miletus, 1 day to Cos, 1 day to Rhodes, *x* days to Patara, *x* days from Patara to Tyre, 7 days in Tyre, 1 day to Ptolemais, 1 day in Ptolemais, 1 day to Cæsarea, "several" days in Cæsarea, *x* days in the journey from Cæsarea to Jerusalem. Thus a period of 27 days is given, while about 17 days are left for the six indefinite periods. The voyage from Troas to Mitylene would probably last one day; in Miletus also St. Paul probably halted for only one day, otherwise he could have gone himself to Ephesus; from Rhodes to Patara would take one day; from Patara to Tyre the voyage would last at least five days (Chrysostom), from Cæsarea to Jerusalem would be a journey of two days. Thus six to seven days are left for the stay in Cæsarea. We are not, of course, expressly told that St. Paul really reached Jerusalem in time for the feast; but we may assume this as probable (Weiss contests this point; but in this case would it have been thought worth while to mention St. Paul's plan in the narrative?). In Jerusalem St. Paul stayed scarcely a week, then he was conveyed to Cæsarea. It is, moreover, worthy of note that St. Luke did not himself count up the days, otherwise he would not have left so many items of the sum indefinite.

3. In addition to these two great groups of chronological statements there still remains two smaller groups, namely, the four dates by days in the story of Cornelius (chap. x.)—these are insignificant and

belong to the type of narrative[1]—and the fourteen (13) important dates by days referring to the (làst) stay in Jerusalem and in Cæsarea (xxi. 26—xxvi. 32).

4. The following isolated chronological statements are found in the book: (1) that our Lord allowed Himself to be seen for forty days after His Resurrection (i. 3); (2) that St. Peter and St. John remained in prison until the next morning (iv. 3, 5); (3) that St. Paul was blind for three days after his vision (ix. 9); (4) the notice of the *next* Sabbath and the *next* day in xiii. 44 and xiv. 20; (5) the information that St. Paul invited the leaders of the Jews in Rome to an interview three days after his arrival (xxviii. 17). Of these (2), (3), and (4) are unimportant; (5) is closely connected with the dates by days in the "we"-account, which directly precedes it; (1), which is found nowhere else in the contemporary literature—its occurrence in later literature is dependent upon this passage—can only be derived from Messianic legend, and is certainly manufactured, but not by St. Luke himself.[2]

[1] When one carefully compares the style of this narrative with the narratives of occurrences in Philippi, Corinth, Ephesus, and other places, one cannot but notice that St. Luke is in the latter cases writing as an eye-witness or at very good second-hand; whereas in the former case he follows a tradition that had been already worked up and had already lost many concrete traits, though some here and there had still been preserved.

[2] The manner in which St. Paul speaks in 1 Cor. xv. of the visions of the Risen Christ, including among them that to himself, makes it quite improbable that he knew of or, if he did, believed in this period of forty days; his record is, moreover, quite opposed to St. Luke's statement: "*ἐν πολλοῖς τεκμηρίοις ὀπτανόμενος αὐτοῖς καὶ λέγων τὰ περὶ τῆς βασιλείας τοῦ θεοῦ.*" "Forty days" is a significant sacred number (*cf.* the "forty days" of temptation in the wilderness). One only wonders that the period was not extended to

As we now survey all these chronological statements, grouped as we have placed them, they impress us most favourably, and show that from the standpoint of the chronologist this historical work can scarcely be put on a level with the apocryphal Acts and other such books of fables.[1] *Where St. Luke was not himself present, and therefore could not give dates in days, he contents himself with ascertaining and recording the length of St. Paul's stay in the centres of his activity by years and months. Otherwise he refrains almost entirely from giving direct chronological information.* The only exception is formed by the dates by days in the description of the last stay in Jerusalem and in Cæsarea; but (1) it is possible that St. Luke himself was here an eye-witness; (2) these items of information give no cause for objection. If St. Luke himself was not present—which is to me probable [2]—then for this period he must have had excellent records at his disposal.[3] As for the information con-

Pentecost (*vide infra*), so that an hiatus might have been avoided. We may assume that underlying the tradition of the forty days there is this amount of truth, namely, that within this period (or just at its close) the return of the disciples from Galilee to Jerusalem really took place. The visions at Jerusalem, which occurred after this but before Pentecost, were transferred by later legend into the Easter octave.

[1] Therefore also the "we" of the Acts of the Apostles has nothing whatever to do with the artificial stylistic "we" in the later Acts of Apostles and martyrs. In particular instances the former "we" may have served as a model for this class of novels with a religious purpose.

[2] Except that St. Luke came again to Cæsarea during the time of Festus.

[3] This naturally does not cover the trustworthiness of the discourses, which are especially numerous in this section of the work, and of several other details.

cerning the duration of the longer visits to the chief centres—presupposing careful investigation on the part of St. Luke—we can only here and there, and that inadequately, control its accuracy from the Epistles of St. Paul.[1] So far, however, as the test can be applied, all the chronological statements pass muster.[2] All of them, or almost all of them, refer to the times of the author's partnership with St. Paul in the mission and to the periods lying between. In the former he reckons by days, in the latter by years and months; elsewhere—*i.e.* in the whole first half of the book—he almost entirely refrains from giving dates. What condition of things could we wish for that would inspire us with greater confidence in the writer?[3]

[1] Still less are we able to exercise control over the dates given in the "we"-account; however, their whole character is such as to render control unnecessary.

[2] Some would conclude from the Epistles to the Thessalonians that St. Paul must have stayed in the capital of Macedonia for a longer time than is recorded in the Acts of the Apostles. But even here there is no compelling reason for questioning the statement of the Acts.

[3] For completeness' sake let us cast another glance over the reference to days and hours. The information that the events recorded happened in the *night* was self-evident in the case of visions in dreams, **xvi. 9**, xviii. 9, xxiii. 11, and **xxvii. 23** (*διὰ τῆς νυκτός, ἐν νυκτί, τῇ ἐπιούσῃ νυκτί* and *ταυτῇ τῇ νυκτί*); in the case of the miraculous occurrences in prison, v. 17, xii. 6, and xvi. 25, 33 (*διὰ τῆς νυκτός, τῇ νυκτὶ ἐκείνῃ, κατὰ τὸ μεσονύκτιον*, and *ἐν ἐκείνῃ τῇ ὥρᾳ τῆς νυκτός*); and in the case of the secret arrangements in Damascus, ix. 25 (*νυκτός*), xvii. 10 in Thessalonica (*διὰ νυκτός*), and xxiii. 23, 31 in Jerusalem (*ἀπὸ τριτῆς ὥρας τῆς νυκτός* and *διὰ νυκτός*). Elsewhere it is only in the "we"-account (the story of the shipwreck) that mention is made of the fourteenth night and midnight (**xxvii. 27**, *κατὰ μέσον τῆς νυκτός*), and that we are told concerning

But now for the other side of the picture! From this condition of things—*no manufactured dates!*—it follows that the history of the Primitive Community of Jerusalem and of the earliest period of the mission in Palestine is practically destitute of chronology. *Only two points stand out in this desolate chronological plain, and are therefore worthy of special notice and consideration. These are the date of St. Paul's first and fundamentally important visit to Antioch,*[1]

St. Paul's sermon in Troas that it lasted μέχρι μεσονυκτίου (**xx. 7**), indeed even ἄχρι αὐγῆς (**xx. 11**). In xxviii. 23 we are informed that the meeting in Rome in which St. Paul delivered his apology before the Jews lasted ἀπὸ πρωΐ ἕως ἑσπέρας; in xxii. 6 and xxvi. 13 it is recorded that St. Paul saw the vision of Christ περὶ μεσημβρίαν and ἡμέρας μέσης respectively (this detail does not occur in ix. 3); and in iv. 3 we hear that the imprisonment of the Apostles took place in the *evening;* lastly, in v. 21, that the Apostles when set free entered into the Temple ὑπὸ τὸν ὄρθρον—both statements almost necessarily follow from the context. As for the *hours*, ὥρα is used pleonastically, or at least not in a strictly technical sense, in x. 30 (μέχρι ταύτης τῆς ὥρας), xvi. 18 (αὐτῇ τῇ ὥρᾳ), xvi. 33 (ἐν ἐκείνῃ τῇ ὥρᾳ), and xxii. 13 (αὐτῇ τῇ ὥρᾳ). Signifying hour of prayer, ὥρα occurs in iii. 1 (ἐπὶ τ. ὥραν τ. προσευχῆς τ. ἐννάτην), x. 3, 30 (ὡσεὶ ὥραν ἐννάτην τ. ἡμέρας and ἐνάτην respectively), and x. 9 (περὶ ὥραν ἕκτην). Otherwise only in four places, namely, ii. 15 (the Pentecostal miracle happened at the third hour of the day; this is expressly recorded in order to refute the calumnious charge that the Apostles were intoxicated), v. 7 (Sapphira's act of deceit and her sudden death followed three hours after that of her husband), xix. 34 (the Ephesians cried out, ἐπὶ ὥρας δύο), and xxiii. 23 (this passage is given above). These accounts certainly are not all of them quite trustworthy; yet there is in them no trace of systematic tendency, nor, where they have something of the conventional about them, do they go beyond the literary expedients of which the best historical writers of antiquity availed themselves.

[1] The fact that this notice is unique in the first half of the book suggests that the account of the mission in Antioch, in regard to its source, either belongs to the accounts of the second half or is not inferior to them in value.

and the reference to the famine under Claudius together with the reference to Herod Agrippa.[1] We have, therefore, no certainty whether the author has been able to give us the events of the first period in their correct order,[2] and it is most difficult to discover the actual date of each occurrence. In regard to the chronological order one for instance may, indeed must, question whether the election of an apostle (if it took place at all and in the manner recorded in the Acts) fell within the first forty days; whether the different accounts of the imprisonment of apostles are to be distinguished from one another; when it was that the conversion of St. Paul took place; when the conversion of the Samaritans (we are told that whole villages were to a great extent Christianised, viii. 25); when the mission of St. Philip to the coastland; when it was that Cornelius was converted; when it was that the first Gentile Christian community was founded in Antioch; and above all, whether the

[1] This notice affords us the best datum for the absolute chronology of the first half of the Apostolic epoch. The persecution of the Apostles by Herod Agrippa (king of Judea A.D. 41–44), which was shortly followed by the death of the king, took place not long before the year A.D. 44, the year of Herod's death. At that time the Apostles left Jerusalem. Now a very ancient tradition (see my Chronologie, I. s. 243 *f.*) reports that the Apostles remained twelve years in Jerusalem in accordance with a command given by our Lord. The command was undoubtedly invented in order to justify the departure of the Apostles in the twelfth year. It brings us to the year A.D. 42, a calculation which is confirmed by Acts xii. 1 *ff.* 17: "Peter departed to another place"; while in viii. 1 stress is laid upon the fact that the Apostles remained in Jerusalem during the first persecution.

[2] In v. 36 (Theudas) there probably lies a gross chronological error.

journey of St. Paul to Jerusalem (xi. 30, xii. 25) is rightly distinguished from the journey of chap. xv. But even if in these cases there is more that is questionable or erroneous than the average critic is accustomed to assume,[1] the author would not therefore be deserving of severe blame; for he has not pretended to more knowledge than he possesses, but has clearly told us where alone in his narrative dates stood at his disposal. Before, however, we can give a final verdict on his chronological procedure, it is also necessary both to examine the instances where he refers to *Festivals*, and to investigate his chronological statements of an indefinite character.

III. *References to Festivals.*

From the chronological point of view it is the greatest paradox in the Acts of the Apostles that in this book, written by a Greek for another Greek of high position,[2] it not infrequently occurs that Jewish feasts are referred to, and are presupposed as well known. These references do not come from the sources of the work, or at least only in part, for they are just as numerous in the second half as in the first half of the Acts, and are not absent even from the "we-sections." We are therefore led to conclude

[1] In my opinion this is not the case.

[2] That this Greek noble bore the name of Theophilus from his birth is possible, but not probable. Either St. Luke in the address has given to him a lofty spiritual title side by side with his high worldly title "κράτιστος," or he himself as a Christian had taken the name "Theophilus," just as a few decades later the Christian Ignatius took the name "Theophorus."

that St. Luke had already, before his conversion to Christianity, come into close touch with the Judaism of the Diaspora,[1] and that he could presuppose a like acquaintance in the person to whom he addressed his work and in the majority of his readers. This tends to confirm a statement once made by Renan that in the Apostolic epoch there could have been only a few Gentile Christians who, before they became Christians, had not come into touch with Judaism.

The passages which here come under consideration are the following:[2]—

i. 12. Distance is given in terms of a "Sabbath day's journey"; the knowledge of the length of this standard is therefore presupposed.

xx. 7. The Christian sacred day is called *ἡ μία τῶν σαββάτων* (is thus named by reference to the Jewish sacred day).

ii. 1 and **xx. 16.** *ἡ ἡμέρα τῆς πεντακοστῆς*—it is presupposed that it is known at what time the feast of Pentecost fell.[3]

[1] His by no means contemptible knowledge of the Old Testament lends additional probability to this conclusion.

[2] We must naturally exclude those passages where it is recorded that St. Paul came into the synagogue on the Sabbath day and taught there. Every reader would certainly be acquainted with the "Sabbath," and the record concerning St. Paul's preaching on the Sabbath day in the synagogue (at the beginning of his ministry in every city) is to be accepted as trustworthy, though some critics of the Acts think otherwise, seeing especially that the "we"-account gives the same tradition (**xvi. 13**).

[3] The wording of ii. 1 is, moreover, of such a character that there is room for doubt whether the author intended to say that the pouring forth of the Spirit occurred on the day of Pentecost itself. It is more natural to suppose that it occurred shortly before this day. The matter is perhaps purposely left indefinite.

xii. 3 and **xx. 6.** *ἦσαν ἡμέραι τῶν ἀζύμων* and *ἐξεπλεύσαμεν μετὰ τὰς ἡμέρας τῶν ἀζύμων*—it is not said, and is therefore assumed to be generally known, when these days fall.

xii. 4. Herod intended to deliver St. Peter to the people *μετὰ τὸ πάσχα*—the time of the Passover is thus known.

xxvii. 9. *ὄντος ἤδη ἐπισφαλοῦς τοῦ πλοὸς διὰ τὸ καὶ τὴν νηστείαν ἤδη παρεληλυθέναι*—the fast of the great Day of Atonement is meant; the author's recourse to the Jewish Festival-calendar is here especially remarkable; even a Gentile in becoming a Christian at first accepted, along with Christianity, a slice of Judaism.

xxi. 23, 27. *αἱ ἑπτὰ ἡμέραι (τοῦ ἁγνισμοῦ)*—the readers know that a Jewish vow of this kind lasted seven days.[1]

In regard to the trustworthiness of these dates given in terms of the Jewish Festival-calendar and in the most different contexts, that of ii. 1 alone can give cause for doubt.

Besides the consideration of these passages it is necessary to point out the extensive use that is made in this book of the word "*ἡμέραι*" in all kinds of chronological notices. This use is, so far as I know, contrary to Greek idiom. In St. Luke's gospel *ἡμέρα* and *ἡμέραι* are found eighty-four times, in the Acts ninety-four times (in St. Matthew forty-six times, in St. Mark twenty-eight times, in St. John

[1] Perhaps mention might also be made here of v. 37 (*ἐν τ. ἡμέραις τ. ἀπογραφῆς*); yet a reference to St. Luke ii. 1 *f.* is probably intended here. Note also the Hebraic *νύκτα καὶ ἡμέραν*, xx. 31, xxvi. 7 (but *ἡμέρας τε καὶ νυκτός* stands in ix. 24).

thirty-one times). The numerous constructions in which the word stands are in many cases Hebraic, or rather imitated from the Greek of the Septuagint. By this means, and moreover by other similar expedients which must have been quite customary with him, St. Luke has probably purposely given his style a Biblical character. We shall at once make acquaintance with a portion of these passages as we now turn to consider his indefinite chronological notices.[1]

IV. *Indefinite Dates.*

i. 5. Ye shall be baptized with the Holy Ghost *οὐ μετὰ πολλὰς ἡμέρας*—*i.e.* in a few weeks' time.

i. 15. *ἐν ταῖς ἡμέραις ταύταις*—in the days between the Ascension and Pentecost, St. Peter stood up and proposed the completion of the number of the Apostles.

v. 36. *πρὸ τούτων τῶν ἡμερῶν* (quite indefinite in regard to the length of the time—meaning "before this our time")—Theudas rose up.

vi. 1. *ἐν ταῖς ἡμέραις ταύταις* (=at that time; it is more closely defined by *πληθυνόντων τῶν μαθητῶν*) arose a dispute between the Hebrews and the Hellenists in the Primitive Community.[2]

[1] Compare, moreover, the word "ἡμέρα" in a concordance.

[2] *Cf.* in St. Stephen's speech, vii. 41: *ἐν ταῖς ἡμέραις ἐκείναις ἐμοσχοποίησαν*. Note also that St. Peter in his speech (xv. 7) describes the conversion of Cornelius as having taken place *ἀφ' ἡμερῶν ἀρχαίων*, and that Mnason *in the we-account* (**xxi. 16**) is called an *ἀρχαῖος μαθητής*.

viii. 11. ἱκανῷ χρόνῳ (*i.e.* probably for many years) had Simon Magus practised his sorceries in Samaria.

ix. 19. St. Paul, after his conversion, continued with the brethren of Damascus ἡμέρας τινάς, and began at once his active ministry.[1]

ix. 23. ὡς ἐπληροῦντο ἡμέραι ἱκαναί (it may have been years)—the Jews of Damascus prepared a plot against St. Paul.

ix. 37. ἐν ταῖς ἡμέραις ἐκείναις (*i.e.* when St. Peter was staying in Lydda)—it happened that the disciple Tabitha died in Joppa.

ix. 43. St. Peter abode in Joppa with a tanner named Simon, ἡμέρας ἱκανάς (as in viii. 11 and ix. 23 it may have been for years).

x. 48. St. Peter accepted an invitation to stay in Cæsarea, ἡμέρας τινάς (*i.e.* a few days, *vide* ix. 19).

xi. 27. ἐν ταύταις ταῖς ἡμέραις, namely, at the time of the foundation of the Church of Antioch, or more exactly, at the time when St. Barnabas and St. Paul were working there.[2]

xii. 1. κατ' ἐκεῖνον δὲ τὸν καιρόν—namely, at the time when what had been narrated in chap. xi. took place—Herod turned against the Church.[3]

[1] As it is said in ix. 23 that his stay in Damascus lasted ἡμέρας ἱκανάς, the above passage must be paraphrased as follows: "After a few days, which he spent in the company of the disciples in Damascus, he began at once to preach as a missionary."

[2] Ἐν ταύταις ταῖς ἡμέραις cannot possibly refer to verse 26[b], but only to 26[a].

[3] The passage introduced by these words is not an interpolation without chronological reference, as Weiss thinks; for the expression κατ' ἐκεῖνον τὸν καιρόν need not refer to the time of the foundation of the Antiochean Church in the strictest sense of the word, but refers to the whole early history of that community so far as it had been narrated.

xiii. 31. Our Lord showed Himself after His Resurrection—*ἐπὶ ἡμέρας πλείους*, *i.e.* forty days.

xiv. 3. *ἱκανὸν χρόνον*—St. Barnabas and St. Paul worked in Iconium (see above on viii. 11, ix. 23, and ix. 43).

xiv. 28. *χρόνον οὐκ ὀλίγον*—they then abode in Antioch (no doubt a shorter time than *ἱκανὸν χρόνον* is intended).

xv. 33. *ποιήσαντες χρόνον* (quite indefinite)—Judas and Silas in Antioch.

xv. 35. *Παῦλος κ. Βαρνάβας διέτριβον ἐν Ἀντιοχείᾳ* (without any mention of time as in xii. 19).

xv. 36. *μετὰ δέ τινας ἡμέρας*—*i.e.* (*vide* ix. 19, x. 48) after a few days St. Paul proposed to St. Barnabas that they should join in a fresh missionary journey (preceded by the narrative of the Council of Jerusalem and the notice of the stay of St. Paul and St. Barnabas in Antioch: this stay must, therefore, have been quite a short one).

xvi. 12. We abode in Philippi *ἡμέρας τινάς* thus only a few days.[1]

xvi. 18. The possessed woman cried after us *ἐπὶ πολλὰς ἡμέρας*.

xviii. 1. *μετὰ ταῦτα*, *i.e.* after his stay in Athens St. Paul came to Corinth.

xviii. 2. *προσφάτως* Aquila had come from Rome to Corinth.

xviii. 18. After the trial St. Paul remained yet *ἡμέρας ἱκανάς* in Corinth, thus a long time (*vide* ix. 23, 43; viii. 11; xiv. 3).

[1] Weiss tries to show that this does not refer to the whole time of their stay in Philippi; but I do not think he proves his point.

xviii. 23. St. Paul stayed (the third time) χρόνον τινὰ ποιήσας (*vide* xv. 33) in Antioch.

xix. 22. St. Paul abode yet some time (χρόνον) in Asia[1] (*vide* xv. 33; xviii. 23).

xix. 23. κατὰ τὸν καιρὸν ἐκεῖνον, namely in the last days of St. Paul's stay in Ephesus, when his departure had been already settled, a riot broke out.

xxi. 10. We abode in Cæsarea ἡμέρας πλείους.

xxi. 15. μετὰ δὲ τὰς ἡμέρας ταύτας (*i.e.* after the stay in Cæsarea) we started for Jerusalem.

xxi. 38. St. Paul is asked whether he was not the Egyptian who πρὸ τούτων τῶν ἡμερῶν (*vide* v. 36), rose up as a deceiver of the people.

xxiv. 24. μετὰ δὲ ἡμέρας τινὰς (thus after a few days, *vide* ix. 19; x. 48; xv. 36; xvi. 12), Felix ordered St. Paul to be called that he might hear him concerning Christ.

xxv. 13. ἡμερῶν δὲ διαγενομένων τινῶν (*cf.* xxiv. 24), came Agrippa and Bernice to Cæsarea.

xxv. 14. They remained there ἡμέρας πλείους.

xxvii. 7. ἐν ἱκαναῖς δε ἡμέραις βραδυπλοοῦντες, we arrived with difficulty at Crete (probably several weeks, *vide* ix. 23, 43; xviii. 18).

xxvii. 9. ἱκανοῦ δὲ χρόνου διαγενομένου, we loosed from Crete (*vide* **xxvii. 7,** viii. 11, xiv. 3).

xxvii. 14. μετ' οὐ πολύ, the tempest arose.

xxvii. 20. Neither the sun nor the stars appeared, ἐπὶ πλείονας ἡμέρας.

[**xxviii. 6.** ἐπὶ πολύ, they expected that St. Paul

[1] This is preceded in xix. 21 by the quite indefinite ὡς δὲ ἐπληρώθη ταῦτα (the successful progress of the mission in Ephesus).

would fall down dead after being bitten by the snake.[1]]

In the first place, it is an important point in favour of the identity of the author of the we-account with the author of the whole work, that indefinite chronological notices are of no rarer occurrence in the we-account than in the rest of the work, nor are they different in form. This circumstance will be considered in Appendix I. Next we must distinguish those passages, where the fact that the time is not defined is by no means remarkable, from those where it seems at first sight strange. Of the former we may at once simply dismiss the passages i. 5; v. 36; viii. 11; ix. 37; xiii. 31; **xvi. 18;** xviii. 2; xxi. 38; **xxvii. 7, 9, 14, 20; xxviii. 6;** in some of these instances the author could have given us more accurate information had he wished it, in others the context required or allowed only a general reference to time. But from the remaining passages we may not as a rule argue ignorance on the part of the author. Thus the duration of the stay at Philippi and in Cæsarea (**xvi. 12; xxi. 10, 15**) is only given indefinitely, although the author, if he had wished it—we are here in the we-account—could

[1] *τότε* is found 21 times in the Acts (including 4 occurrences in the "we"-sections). It has, however, *in no case* chronological significance in the strict sense of the word. In xvii. 14, it is combined with *εὐθέως*, in **xxvii. 21**, it follows a genitive absolute, in **xxviii. 1** a participle (*διασωθέντες τότε ἐπέγνωμεν*).—Εὐθέως, *εὐθύς* (the latter only in x. 16) is not very frequent in the Acts; it occurs 10 times (including *καὶ εὐθέως* 5 times). It is a favourite word in stories of miracles and visions (ix. 18, 34; x. 16; xii. 10; **xvi. 10**); elsewhere only in ix. 20; xvii. 10, 14; xxi. 30; xxii. 29.

have afforded us more accurate dates. Why he has not done so we are unable to say. It should, however, be noticed that in reference to the stay in Philippi he uses the expression ἡμέρας τινάς, in reference to the stay in Cæsarea the words ἡμέρας πλείους, and again in the we-account (**xxvii. 7, 9**) he speaks of ἱκαναὶ ἡμέραι (ἱκανὸν χρόνον).[1] If we find the same distinctions in statements of time also made outside the we-account, we may assume with a certain degree of probability that they are not chosen arbitrarily, but—as is certain in the case of the we-account—rest upon more accurate information than is clearly expressed. Accordingly when we are told (ix. 43) that St. Peter remained in Joppa ἡμέρας ἱκανάς, but in Cæsarea (x. 48) ἡμέρας τινάς (in the former place he had his abode for the time being, at the latter he was only on a visit), again (ix. 19) that St. Paul had already begun his missionary preaching in the synagogues ἡμέρας τινάς after his conversion, while the whole period of his activity in Damascus lasted ἡμέραι ἱκαναί (ix. 23), again that St. Paul was in Iconium (xiv. 3) ἱκανόν χρόνον, in Antioch for the second time (xiv. 28) χρόνον οὐκ ὀλίγον, in Antioch for the third and fourth times

[1] Ἱκανός in chronological statements occurs in the New Testament only in the Lukan writings, namely, twice in the gospel (viii. 27; xx. 9) and seven times in the Acts (including two occurrences in the we-sections). Combined with χρόνοι it appears in St. Luke viii. 27; xx. 9; with χρόνος in Acts viii. 11; xiv. 3; **xxvii. 9**; with ἡμέραι in Acts ix. 23, 43; xviii. 18; **xxvii. 7**. The approximate length of the time indicated by ἱκανός is always to be understood from the context. It may be years (viii. 11; ix. 23; ix. 43 [?]; xiv. 3 [?]), but also only weeks (**xxvii. 7, 9**).

(xv. 36 and xviii. 23) ἡμέρας τινάς and χρόνον τινά respectively, and that he remained in Corinth (xviii. 18) yet ἡμέρας ἱκανάς after the trial, moreover, that Felix summoned St. Paul before him (xxiv. 24) μετὰ ἡμέρας τινάς, finally that Agrippa and Bernice came to Cæsarea (xxv. 13) ἡμερῶν διαγενομένων τινῶν after the first appearance of St. Paul before Festus and abode there (xxv. 14) πλείους ἡμέρας—in face of all these instances we can scarcely regard the epithets used with ἡμέρας as meaningless, or as quite arbitrarily chosen—especially seeing that in several cases we can prove that they have been most suitably chosen — rather we are led to suppose that St. Luke[1] in these cases was in possession of good information, even though it were not exact but only

[1] It follows from Gal. i. 17 *f.* that the stay of St. Paul in Damascus, including a journey into Arabia which came just at the beginning, lasted three years. St. Luke says nothing of the journey into Arabia; probably it was of no importance or he had no knowledge of it. St. Paul only mentions it in order to explain that he, although he had taken a journey, had nevertheless not journeyed to Jerusalem. That St. Paul soon (after ἡμέρας τινάς) began his missionary work "in the synagogues," is not excluded by the Galatians, for "in the synagogues" may well include those without Damascus, and Arabia extended to the very gates of that city; moreover, the ἡμέραι ἱκαναί of the Acts would correspond with the three years of the Epistle.—That St. Paul on his last visit to Antioch could only have remained a short time can also be shown to be probable from the epistles. It can also be shown that the approximate chronological statements of the section dealing with St. Paul, Felix, and Festus are correct, especially as many definite dates are found side by side with them. It is strange that in xv. 36 we read only of "some days" which St. Paul and St. Barnabas spent at that time in Antioch, while it was during this time—some scholars place it earlier—that the visit of St. Peter to this city (Gal. ii. 11 *ff.*) seems to have occurred.

approximate.[1] This supposition also may be extended to the instances xviii. 1 and xix. 21–23; for the description of the visit to Athens, taken in connection with the context, makes it clear that St. Paul made only a quite short stay in this city, a fact which is confirmed by the Epistles to the Thessalonians; and likewise there was no need that *exact* dates should be given in order to explain that the events narrated in xix. 21 *ff.* happened at the end of the long ministry in Ephesus.

Accordingly, there remain only four passages in which the indefinite chronological statement possibly or probably disguises inadequate knowledge, namely, i. 15, vi. 1, xii. 1, xv. 33 (the date of the completion of the College of Apostles and of the uprising of the Hellenists; the chronological relationship of the Herodian persecution to the history of the planting of Christianity in Antioch; the length of the stay of Judas and Silas in Antioch). This is a small number, and we may accordingly maintain that the Acts of the Apostles even in regard to its indefinite, and still more in regard to its definite, chronological statements is, on the whole, a very respectable historical work (in spite of its want of a *chronological scheme*). In this respect it can very well hold its own when

[1] Naturally in a number of these instances he may also have possessed quite exact information, but did not consider it necessary to impart it. Thus in xiii. 31 he says that our Lord after His Resurrection showed Himself ἐπὶ ἡμέρας πλείους; in an earlier passage, however, he has given the more exact statement: δι' ἡμερῶν τεσσαράκοντα (i. 3). Also in i. 5 we read that the disciples received the baptism of the Spirit, οὐ μετὰ πολλὰς ταύτας ἡμέρας, and in ii. 1 the exact date is given.

compared with the historical works of that period. That in point of chronology it leaves much to be desired is a fact so obvious as to require no express statement; but if, for example, the narrative of the so-called first missionary journey of St. Paul when compared with that of the second and third journeys leaves much to be desired in respect of chronological data (though here also the chief stations are carefully given), this circumstance is only a proof that the author, though he generally shows such interest in the times of duration of journeys and visits, did not wish to say more than he could vouch for, and has therefore kept silence on these points in this part of his work. Our recognition of the trustworthiness of the book is thus enhanced by a close investigation of the procedure of the author in chronological questions. In the case of a few incidents the narrative is of a conventional type; but as a whole it is, both in accordance with the purpose of the writer and in reality, a genuinely historical work.

APPENDIX I

The Consistency of the Form in which Chronological Statements are given in the Acts

In order to establish the consistency of the chronological expressions in the Acts, we shall do best to start with the data given in the we-sections and to compare with them those in the rest of the book.

xvi. 11, xx. 15, xxi. 18. τῇ ἐπιούσῃ [ἡμέρᾳ] (twice elsewhere in the book).

xx. 7, xxi. 8. τῇ ἐπαύριον [ἡμέρᾳ] (eight times elsewhere in the book).

xx. 25. τῇ ἐχομένῃ [ἡμέρᾳ] (*vide* xxi. 26).

xxi. 6, xxvii. 18. τῇ ἑξῆς [ἡμέρᾳ] (*vide* xxv. 17).

xvi. 12. ἡμέρας τινάς (five times elsewhere in the book).

xxvii. 7. ἡμέρας ἱκανάς (three times elsewhere in the book).

xxvii. 20. ἐπὶ πλείονας ἡμέρας (xiii. 31 : ἐπὶ ἡμέρας πλείους).

xxi. 10. ἡμέρας πλείους (elsewhere xxv. 4 ; xxiv. 11: οὐ πλείους ἡμέραι ιβ', xxv. 6 : ἡμέρας οὐ πλείους η', *cf.* **xxvii. 14** : μετ' οὐ πολύ, xviii. 20 : ἐπὶ πλείονα χρόνον).

xvi. 18. ἐπὶ πολλὰς ἡμέρας (i. 5 : οὐ μετὰ πολλὰς ταύτας ἡμέρας).

xxi. 10 ; xxviii. 12, 14. ἐπιμεῖναι ἡμέρας (*vide* x. 48).

xvi. 12; xx. 6. *διατρίβειν ἡμέρας* (*vide* xxv. 14).

xxvii. 29, 33, 39. *ἡμέραν γίνεσθαι* (three times elsewhere in the book).

xxvii. 9. *χρόνου διαγενομένου* (*vide* xxv. 13: *ἡμερῶν διαγενομένων*).

xxvii. 9. *ἱκανὸς χρόνος* (*vide* viii. 11: *ἱκανῷ χρόνῳ*, xiv. 3: *ἱκανὸν χρόνον*).

xxi. 15. *αἱ ἡμέραι αὗται* [*ἐκεῖναι*] (seven times elsewhere in the book).

xvi. 18; xx. 9, 11; xxvii. 20; xxviii. 6. *ἐπί* c. acc. temp. (eight times elsewhere in the book).

xxvii. 27. *κατὰ* c. acc. temp. (seven times elsewhere in the book).

xvi. 13. *ἡ ἡμέρα τῶν σαββάτων* (*vide* xiii. 14).

xx. 6. *αἱ ἡμέραι τῶν ἀζύμων* (*vide* xii. 3).

xx. 16. *ἡ ἡμέρα τῆς πεντηκοστῆς* (*vide* ii. 1).

xxi. 16. Mnason is an *ἀρχαῖος μαθητής* (*vide* xv. 7: *ἀφ' ἡμερῶν ἀρχαίων*—had God commanded the reception of the Gentile Cornelius).

xx. 7. *μεσονύκτιον* (*vide* xvi. 25).

xxi. 13. And three times elsewhere in the we-sections *τότε* (the same use seventeen times elsewhere in the book).

xvi. 10. *εὐθέως* (nine times elsewhere in the book).

xxvii. 22. *τὰ νῦν* (also iv. 29, v. 38, xvii. 30, xx. 32). Ὡς temp. eight times in the we-sections (twenty-one times elsewhere scattered through the whole work).[1]

All the chronological notices occurring in the we-sections

[1] Apart from the Lukan writings and the Gospel of St. John, ὡς temp. is very rare in the New Testament. It does not occur in St. Matthew (xxviii. 9 *init.* is not genuine); it is found once in St. Mark (ix. 21), once in the thirteen Pauline epistles (Gal. vi. 10), never in Hebrews, the Catholic epistles, and the Apocalypse.

—and among them some which are unusual, some indeed which do not occur elsewhere in the New Testament—are found again distributed throughout the other parts of the book ; with the exception only of τῇ ἑτέρᾳ, *scil.* ἡμέρᾳ (**xx. 15, xxvii. 3**), ἄχρι αὐγῆς (**xx. 11**) and δευτεραῖοι (in the sense of "two days," **xxviii. 13**).

Only a few chronological terms of constant occurrence not to be found in the we-sections can be discovered in the remaining parts of the book. One can point to ἐξαυτῆς (x. 33, xi. 11, xxi. 32, xxiii. 30), a word which is not of frequent occurrence in other Greek writers, to παραχρῆμα (iii. 7, v. 10, xii. 23, xiii. 11, xvi. 26, 33), to κατ' ἐκεῖνον τὸν καιρόν (xii. 1, xix. 23), to ποιήσας χρόνον (xv. 33, xviii. 23), to τεσσαρακονταετὴς χρόνος (vii. 23, xiii. 18), to διετία and τριετία (xxiv. 27, xxviii. 30, xx. 31), words of infrequent occurrence elsewhere (yet see Deissmann, *Neue Bibelstudien*, s. 86), to ἡμέραν τάσσεσθαι (xii. 21, xxviii. 23); but the words and their quite scanty attestation (ἐξαυτῆς and παραχρῆμα excepted) show of themselves that they can scarcely be accounted to belong to the characteristic vocabulary of the author in the Acts.[1]

[1] The chronological notices in the gospel only partially admit of comparison ; yet *vide*—xiii. 33 τῇ ἐχομένῃ—vii. 11 ; ix. 37 τῇ [τῷ] ἑξῆς—viii. 27 ; xx. 9 χρόνοι ἱκανοί—(iv. 25) ; x. 35 ; xviii. 4 ἐπί c. acc. temp.—x. 31 κατά c. acc. temp. [only here]—ix. 8, 19 προφήτης τῶν ἀρχαίων—ii. 36 ἐν ἡμέραις πολλαῖς, xv. 13 μετ' οὐ πολλὰς ἡμέρας—iv. 42 ἡμέραν γίνεσθαι—i. 24; i. 39; vi. 12; xxiii. 7; xxiv. 18 αἱ ἡμέραι αὗται—iv. 16 ; xiii. 14 ; xiii. 16 ; xiv. 5 ἡ ἡμέρα τοῦ σαββάτου—xxiv. 1 τῇ μιᾷ τῶν σαββάτων—xxii. 7 ἡ ἡμέρα τῶν ἀζύμων—xi. 5 μεσονύκτιον—τότε only fourteen times in the gospel—εὐθέως only seven times in the gospel—i. 48; v. 10; xii. 50 ἀπὸ τοῦ νῦν (*vide* Acts xviii. 6)—ὡς temp. about nineteen times in the gospel, thus in about the same proportion as in the Acts.

We may thus conclude that there is absolutely no difference between the chronological terminology of the we-sections and that which is employed in the rest of the work, and that so far as chronological procedure is concerned the we-sections cannot be distinguished from the work as a separate source. Moreover, even apart from terminology, the character and the extent of the author's employment of chronology is quite similar and consistent throughout the whole work. If the author possessed written sources for the Acts, then—so far as we can judge from his procedure in regard to chronology—he has not pieced them together unskilfully and corrected them clumsily throughout, but has used them freely, just as one would use oral sources.

APPENDIX II

Chronological Information to be gained from the Acts

The careful reader of the Acts could derive from the book the following pieces of chronological information: From the gospel he knew that our Lord was born under Augustus, that He entered upon His public ministry in the fifteenth year of Tiberius Cæsar, and that He was crucified under the procurator Pilate and the tetrarch Herod Antipas. It was not difficult for him to ascertain that Tiberius died in the year A.D. 37, that Antipas was banished in A.D. 39, and that Pilate was recalled in the year A.D. 36. From Acts xi. 28, xii. 1, he would see that the foundation of the first Gentile Christian community (in

Antioch) fell in the time of Claudius, and that the first sanguinary persecution of the Apostles, recorded as contemporary with the former event (to be distinguished from the persecution of the Christian Hellenists in Jerusalem), took place under Herod Agrippa. Since the latter reigned from A.D. 41 to A.D. 44 it would be obvious that all which is recorded in the first twelve chapters of the Acts belonged to a period of eleven to thirteen (fourteen) years, and accordingly occupied the last years of Tiberius, the reign of Caligula, and the very first years of Claudius.

On reading further he would recognise from xviii. 2 that the narrative was still confined to the reign of Claudius, and that therefore all the events recorded from chap. xi. to chap. xviii. up to the arrival of St. Paul in Corinth must have fallen within the years A.D. 41(44)–54. When, however, in xxiii. 26 *ff.* the reader met with the name of the procurator Felix and then with that of Festus, and further learnt that St. Paul was cast into prison two years before the recall of Felix (xxiv. 27)—the entry into office of three procurators could have been ascertained without great difficulty at that time—; and seeing, lastly, that in the chapters xviii.–xxii. reference is again and again made to the succession of years, we can perceive that he must have derived from these notices sufficiently satisfactory chronological information, even if he could no longer ascertain with accuracy the year in which Claudius banished the Jews from Rome. Although it is not expressly stated in the book, he could have no doubt that it was Nero to whom St. Paul appealed and to whom the Apostle was sent,[1] and that his transport to Rome must have taken place in the first half of the reign of this emperor.

Moreover, the individual reader, who was better instructed in this or that direction, would derive yet more exact information from his study of the book. If he were a Jewish Christian and a native of Jerusalem he could orient himself in chronology from the statements that St. Paul had been a pupil of Gamaliel, that he appeared before the high-priest Ananias, and that St. Peter had been tried before the high-priest Annas and before Caiaphas. If he were acquainted with the history of the Roman rule in the provinces he could find out when Sergius Paulus was proconsul in Cyprus, and when Gallio, the brother of Seneca, was proconsul in Corinth. If he were a Jewish Christian of Rome he could easily ascertain in what year Claudius had decreed the banishment of the Jews. If he were an Ephesian Christian he would find much in the book relating to the ministry of

[1] Can it be that the name of Nero was purposely omitted? In after times his name was mentioned with reluctance. In xxv. 8, 10, 11, 12, 21; xxvi. 32, xxvii. 24, xxviii. 19, where Nero is meant we find only *ὁ Καῖσαρ;* and in xxv. 21, 25, *ὁ Σεβαστός*. On the contrary, Claudius is mentioned simply by name without any title (*vide supra*). Moreover, St. Luke never calls the emperor *ὁ βασιλεύς*, as was the custom with so many orientals (so also 1 Timothy, 1 Peter, and the Apocalypse, but not St. Paul). Only the Jews in Thessalonica who accuse St. Paul and the Christians before the judgment-seat are allowed to say that these people act contrary to the decrees of Cæsar, *βασιλέα ἕτερον λέγοντες εἶναι Ἰησοῦν*. It is even possible to deduce an important inference as to the date of the Acts from the author's reluctance to use the title, seeing that *ὁ βασιλεύς* as a title for the emperor very quickly established itself in the East, indeed completely since the time of Domitian.

St. Paul in Ephesus that would direct him to a definite period of time. Indeed, if we only refrain from criticising the book according to our modern standards, we find that it satisfies even more exacting requirements in relation to chronology, and that when it gives definite information of this kind it proves itself trustworthy so far as we have the power of judging, however much we may deplore the absence of a guiding thread of systematic chronology running through the whole work. In short, the reader, even in regard to chronology, finds himself exceedingly well informed in a higher degree perhaps than the author himself consciously intended.

In conclusion, we would direct attention to the following point. The narratives of chaps. i.–v. and xiii.–xxviii. run in one direct line of strict succession of events.[1] We may with reason question whether everything in the succession i.–v. is in correct order, and in reference to chap. xv. this question has been already asked (*vide supra*). *But in the chaps. vi.–xii. the author follows many lines at once.* In the first place, he again and again directs his eye to the history of the Church of Jerusalem and of the Apostles (especially St. Peter and his missionary work). Secondly, in vi. 1 *ff.*, he starts upon a history of the Hellenistic Christians in Jerusalem and of the "Seven," which from its beginning leads up to the mission to the Gentiles and the foundation of the Church of Antioch. Thirdly, he traces the ministry of St. Philip in Samaria and in the coastlands, and treats it not as a part of the history of the Hellenists

[1] Only the episode of Apollos falls out of line.

and the "Seven," but as a history by itself. Fourthly and lastly, he relates the story of St. Paul up to his entry into the service of the youthful Church of Antioch. In the small space of seven chapters he follows all these lines and tries also to interweave them with one another, at the same time leading up to and picturing the great transit of the Gospel from the sphere of Judaism to that of Hellenism (for which one is in no way prepared in chaps. i.–v.). To us it seems as if in these seven chapters more gaps have been left than facts narrated, and that though the literary skill here shown is indeed commendable, it is nevertheless not very great. No wonder that for us these gaps give rise to numerous notes of interrogation which attach themselves to what is narrated. The question, however, whether the narrative of this part of the Acts really contains the leading events of the history and is essentially trustworthy forms a problem that has not yet been solved, nor will it probably ever be solved, seeing that we possess for its control such an extremely small quantity of parallel material.

APPENDIX III

The Chronological Note at the end of the Acts

The most difficult chronological statement in the book is the note at the end (xxviii. 30, 31): ἐνέμεινεν [*scil.* in Rome] δὲ διετίαν ὅλην ἐν ἰδίῳ μισθώματι καὶ ἀπεδέχετο πάντας τοὺς εἰσπορευομένους πρὸς αὐτόν, κηρύσσων τὴν βασιλείαν τοῦ θεοῦ καὶ *διδάσκων τὰ περὶ τοῦ κυρίου Ἰησοῦ Χριστοῦ μετὰ πάσης παρρησίας ἀκωλύτως.*

We must first ascertain that the construction of this passage fully coincides with that of other statements made by the author concerning the character and duration of the ministry of the Apostle in the great centres of his missionary field (*vide supra*). Concerning Antioch we read that St. Paul was there *ἐνιαυτὸν ὅλον—καὶ διδάξαι ὄχλον ἱκανόν* (xi. 26), of Corinth, that he stayed there *ἐνιαυτὸν καὶ μῆνας ἕξ διδάσκων ἐν αὐτοῖς τὸν λόγον τοῦ θεοῦ* (xviii. 11); of Ephesus that he first worked in the synagogue *ἐπὶ μῆνας τρεῖς διαλεγόμενος καὶ πείθων τὰ περὶ τῆς βασιλείας τοῦ θεοῦ* (xix. 8), then for two years more in the school of Tyrannus *καθ' ἡμέραν διαλεγόμενος, ὥστε πάντας τοὺς κατοικοῦντας τὴν Ἀσίαν ἀκοῦσαι τὸν λόγον τοῦ κυρίου* (xix. 10); lastly of Cæsarea, that he was there a *διετία*, and that Felix commanded the centurion *μηδένα κωλύειν τῶν ἰδίων αὐτοῦ ὑπηρετεῖν αὐτῷ* (xxiv. 27, 23). Comparison, therefore, teaches us that the author when he wrote of Rome would necessarily have been most concerned to record the duration and the character of St. Paul's ministry in that city. We learn, moreover, that what seems at first sight so strange—namely, the scantiness of the information concerning the ministry of St. Paul in Rome—is not out of character with the whole plan of the book; for St. Luke's procedure is not otherwise in his treatment of the ministry of St. Paul in Antioch, Corinth, and Cæsarea; he has contented himself with a few quite general touches. Only in the case of Ephesus has he imparted some detailed information. The inner life and growth of the Churches had evidently no interest for him so far as the scope of the task he had set himself was concerned, unless the hostility of the Jews came into play or the authorities intervened (*vide supra*). The difficulty of the passage, therefore, lies by no means in the statement itself, but simply in the fact that the book breaks off at this point. And this fact is doubly strange; firstly, in that the author breaks off just at this place; and secondly, in that in breaking off, *he at the very same moment hints that the history of St. Paul had a further continuation;* for Blass and other scholars are justified in deciding that the aorist ἐνέμεινεν, taken together with the chronological note, implies that after two years this situation was brought to an end by St. Paul's leaving Rome altogether or by his exchanging a condition of comparative freedom for one of closer confinement. It is indeed scarcely probable that the latter alternative is meant; for if this situation of closer confinement lasted only a very short time and led to the execution of the Apostle, it is difficult to see why his death is not recorded; if, however, it lasted for a longer time, we ask in vain why this time was not included in the period of his residence in Rome. *We are therefore left with the hypothesis—and this the most probable—that the Apostle again left Rome;* [1] for the hypothesis that St. Luke for political reasons did not *wish* to recount the fatal issue of the trial of St. Paul is not suggested by his attitude throughout

[1] That this hypothesis is supported by the historical notices concerning the Apostle in the second Epistle to Timothy may here be only mentioned without further examination.

the whole book (and is incredible in itself); and the other hypothesis, that St. Luke composed his book at the conclusion of this διετία must likewise be rejected, for in that case he must have written, "Paul has now been in Rome two full years"; instead of which, he has quite clearly described the residence in the hired lodging at Rome as a closed episode.

The problem, therefore, takes the following form: Why is it that St. Luke, who in the last quarter of this book has described the fortunes of St. Paul in such detail, has not proceeded further with his narrative of the history of the Apostle, but has concluded his account with the two years' residence in Rome—which he, moreover, disposes of in the same cursory fashion that he disposes of similar visits which are recorded elsewhere in the book (arrival; duration of the visit; relations with Judaism, xxviii. 17 *ff.*; relations with the authorities, xxviii. 31 [ἀκωλύτως]; the content of the Apostle's teaching)? Why has he not related what happened to St. Paul, and what he did after he had again left Rome?

Proposed in this form the problem is, in my opinion, capable of solution if one rightly discerns the aim and method of the book, while it remains insoluble if one follows the hypothesis, not suggested by the form of the concluding verse, that in the mind of the author the διετία closed with the execution of the Apostle, concerning which nothing is said. In spite of first impressions the book, even in its second half, does not profess to narrate the history of St. Paul, but to describe the way in which, according to the predestined purpose of God, Salvation passed to the Gentiles from the Jews, who had lost it (*cf. supra*, pp. xxi. *ss.*). Chap. xxviii. 25–28 forms both the true conclusion and the true key to the book. The fact here stated in impressive fulness of language, and with the trumpet-blast of Isaiah's prophetic utterance here proclaimed in the sentence: *γνωστὸν οὖν ἔστω ὑμῖν ὅτι τοῖς ἔθνεσιν ἀπεστάλη τοῦτο τὸ σωτήριον τοῦ θεοῦ· αὐτοὶ καὶ ἀκούσονται*, has been before expressly, even if not so loudly, declared in various passages of the work (from xiii. 46 onwards; *vide* xviii. 6, &c.). Certainly from vi. 1 *ff.* onwards it forms the leading thought in the whole economy of the book; while even earlier it probably lies at the background of the great list of nations in chap. ii. Now at the close this leading thought again comes to the front and holds the field with sovereign power. As he writes these concluding words the author plainly declares that he must now leave St. Paul as he before left St. Peter—the difficulty is the same in both cases, even if the disappearance of St. Peter is not half so strange—for the Divine plan of salvation is fulfilled! *Soli Deo gloria!* The author is concerned not with Peter nor with Paul, but with the grand development of the Divine purpose whereby Jewish hearts were hardened, whereby the gospel was proclaimed among the Gentiles from Antioch to Ephesus and Corinth and finally in Rome, whereby also Gentile hearts were made receptive of the message:[1] *αὐτοὶ καὶ ἀκούσονται!* According to St. Luke it was not St. Paul who began the mission to the Gentiles; others had preceded him; only with

[1] *Vide e.g.* xvi. 14: *ὁ κύριος διήνοιξεν τὴν καρδίαν τῆς Λυδίας.*

excelling power he had thrown himself into the work which had been already commenced.

And yet, after all, we may ask how the author could have had the heart not to tell us of the death of St. Paul (and of St. Peter). Even so early as the second century this question was asked, and the psychological problem herein presented is in truth sufficiently difficult. The hypothesis that St. Luke intended to write a τρίτος λόγος does not, in my opinion, receive any firm support from Acts i. 1; it is a makeshift that has little to commend it, because in accepting it we are almost compelled, against all likelihood, to suppose that St. Luke intended the second part of his work to be a history of (St. Peter and) St. Paul. What could St. Luke have purposed to narrate in this supposed third part if not the history of the last days of St. Peter and St. Paul? But coming after the history of our Lord and of the hardening of the heart of the Jewish nation and of the conversion of the Gentiles from Cæsarea to Rome, the story of the last days of the two apostles would have formed a finale which could scarcely have made up a complete book, and which in importance would not have reached the level of the first two parts, indeed would have been quite incongruous with them. We must therefore be content to assume that St. Luke could so concentrate himself upon the main subject of his work that he could allow himself to break off the thread of the story of St. Paul at the end of the two years' ministry in Rome, because the aim of the book had been now attained. We cannot indeed imagine his doing this if the two years' ministry had immediately preceded the gaining of the martyr's crown. If this had been so, the omission of the story of the martyrdom would have involved on the part of the author a piece of self-sacrifice which would have been quite useless, and which is, moreover, psychologically unintelligible. Neither does the text demand such an hypothesis; on the contrary, it almost excludes it. Between the end of the "διετία ὅλη" in Rome and the death of St. Paul there must have lain a fairly long period during which the Apostle continued his ministry, though this ministry was no longer of high importance in the grand progress of the mission.

APPENDIX IV

Special Readings of a Chronological character in the so-called β-recension

The so-called β-recension presents a series of interpolations and variant readings, some of which are chronological in character:—

1. ii. 1. D: *καὶ ἐγένετο ἐν ταῖς ἡμέραις ἐκείναις τοῦ συμπληροῦσθαι* (instead of *καὶ ἐν τῷ συμπλ.*), not received by Blass into the β-recension. The meaning of the passage is essentially altered by this interpolation; for we may now probably translate, "It happened in those days, when the day of Pentecost was fulfilled," *i.e.* the fulfilment is no longer to be understood simply in a temporal sense. At all events the reading is secondary and in its phraseology an imitation.

2. iii. 1. Dp: Ἐν (δὲ) ταῖς ἡμέραις ταύταις Πέτρος (instead of Πέτρος δέ); not received by Blass into the β-recension. It was intended to mark a new paragraph (*vide* ii. 1).

3. iii. 1. D: τὸ δειλινόν, received by Blass into the β-recension; perhaps original, but probably a descriptive interpolation.

4. v. 1. E: ἐν αὐτῷ δὲ τῷ καιρῷ ἀνήρ τις (instead of simply ἀνὴρ δέ τις), not received by Blass into the β-recension; *vide* ii. 1, iii. 1.

5. ix. 40. Egp Ps-August(sah): ἡ δὲ παραχρῆμα ἤνοιξεν (instead of ἡ δὲ ἤν.), not received into the β-recension by Blass. Concerning παραχρῆμα in St. Luke, *vide supra* and xxii. 29.

6. xi. 2. Dspw: ὁ μὲν οὖν Πέτρος διὰ ἱκανοῦ χρόνου ἠθέλησαν πορευθῆναι εἰς Ἱερουσόλυμα, an interpolation received by Blass into the β-recension. For ἱκανὸς χρόνος *vide* viii. 11, ix. 23 (ἡμέραι ἱκαναί), ix. 43 (ἡμ. ἱκ.), xiv. 3, xviii. 18, xxvii. 7 (ἱκ. ἡμ.), xxvii. 9. Feeble imitation.

7. xiv. 2. Dsgpw (E): ὁ δὲ κύριος ἔδωκεν ταχὺ εἰρήνην, an interpolation accepted by Blass; ταχύ does not occur elsewhere in the Acts.

8. xiv. 20. f sah: ἑσπέρας ἀναστάς (in place of ἀναστάς), accepted by Blass; probably due to imitation, *vide* iv. 3.

9. xvi. 11. DMs: τῇ δὲ ἐπαύριον ἀναχθέντες (*vide* ἀναχθέντες οὖν), to compensate for the omission of εὐθέως in verse 10; also due to imitation; accepted by Blass.

10. xvii. 19. DMs: μετὰ δὲ ἡμέρας τινὰς ἐπιλαβόμενοι (in place of ἐπιλαβόμενοι), interpola-

tion due to reflection; accepted by Blass; due to imitation.

11. xviii. 19. DfMs sah: τῷ ἐπιόντι σαββάτῳ εἰσελθών (in place of εἰσελθών); interpolation due to reflection; accepted by Blass; due to imitation.

12. xviii. 21. DHLP Syri gw al lat.: (εἶπεν)· δεῖ με πάντως τὴν ἑορτὴν τὴν ἐρχομένην ποιῆσαι εἰς Ἱεροσόλυμα, an interpolation inserted because it was thought that a journey to Jerusalem was referred to in verse 22; received by Blass into the β-recension. In xiii. 44 the right reading is perhaps τῷ ἐρχομένῳ (ἐχομένῳ?) σαββάτῳ.

13. xix. 9. Dsgw: (διαλεγόμενος ἐν τ. σχολῇ Τυράννου) ἀπὸ ὥρας πέμπτης ἕως δεκάτης, received by Blass into the β-recension; perhaps original (*vide supra* the passages where hours are noted in the Acts).

14. xx. 18. D[1]: ὡς τριετίαν ἢ καὶ πλεῖον, received by Blass into the β-recension; a proleptic repetition from xx. 31, with the enigmatic or rather incorrect addition ἢ καὶ πλεῖον.

15. **xxi. 5.** d: τῇ δὲ ἑξῆς ἡμέρᾳ, received by Blass into the β-recension (in place of ὅτε δὲ ἐγένετο ἐξαρτίσαι ἡμᾶς τὰς ἡμέρας); a careless and unsuitable correction, due to the constant occurrence of the phrase in the context.

16. **xxi. 15.** D: μετὰ δέ τινας ἡμέρας ἀποταξάμενοι (for μετὰ δὲ τὰς ἡμέρας ταύτας ἐπισκευασάμενοι); evidently a secondary reading;

received by Blass into the β-recension. Due to imitation.

17. xxi. 26. D: τῇ ἐπιούσῃ (for τῇ ἐχομένῃ), received by Blass into the β-recension; insignificant variant, due to imitation.

18. xxi. 27. D (g sch): συντελουμένης δὲ τῆς ἑβδόμης ἡμέρας (for ὡς δὲ ἔμελλον [αἱ] ἑπτὰ ἡμέραι συντελεῖσθαι), received by Blass into the β-recension; insignificant variant; due to imitation of the gen. abs., not infrequent in the Acts.

19. xxii. 29. Ms sah: καὶ παραχρῆμα ἔλυσεν αὐτόν, received by Blass into the β-recension; unsuitable interpolation. For παραχρῆμα *vide* ix. 40.

20. **xxvii. 1.** fgs: τῇ ἐπαύριον, received by Blass into the β-recension; really part of a more extensive interpolation.

21. **xxvii. 5.** f: καὶ μετὰ ταῦτα, received by Blass into the β-recension; really part of a more extensive interpolation.

22. **xxvii. 5.** Msf: δι' ἡμερῶν δεκαπέντε, received by Blass into the β-recension; perhaps original.

To treat these variants as homogeneous and related to one another, and to include them in a single recension, is a fundamental error. The tradition of the text itself protests against such a procedure. The numbers 1, 3, 14, 15, 16, 17, 18, as pure D readings, may perhaps be regarded as related to one another; a second group is formed by [2], 6, 7, 9, 10, 11, 12, 13; a third group by 8, 20, 21, 22. The numbers 4, 5, 19 stand in isolation. The text of the Acts has accordingly been corrected by various hands from a chronological point of view—among others—and in accordance with its own style. The second group is the most important; it alone has a claim to be regarded as a relic of a very ancient recension. To it also may be assigned the passage x. 41 overlooked in the preceding list, where D sah Egsw and Const. App. vi. 30 insert ἡμέρας τεσσαράκοντα in accordance with i. 3. We ought perhaps also to mention ix. 30, where διὰ νυκτός is inserted by E minusc. 180 sgp (in imitation of numerous passages *vide supra*).

It is improbable that St. Luke himself formally published the Acts of the Apostles (so also Ewald, *cf.* Wellhausen, *loc. cit.* s. 19 *f.*); for (1) many instances of roughness suggest the absence of a last careful revision by the author; (2) the history of the text of the book teaches that from the earliest times several, or at least two, editions of the book were in currency. The very fact that the book was not published by the author himself made it possible for different editions to establish themselves. One does not, however, in matters of chronology miss the revising hand of the author (contrary to Ramsay). There is not, in my opinion, a single passage in this book where a developed chronological notice (like that of St. Luke iii. 1, 2) would have been in place.

CHAPTER II

LANDS, NATIONS, CITIES, AND HOUSES

I.—*Terms of more General Significance.*

(Ἔθνος about forty-four times in the Acts).

Most frequently as *τὰ ἔθνη* meaning the *Gentile* nations, *i.e.* those who were not Jews (LXX); so also in **xxi. 11**;[1] more rarely in a quite neutral sense, as in ii. 5: *ἀπὸ παντὸς ἔθνους τῶν ὑπὸ τὸν οὐρανόν*, x. 35, xvii. 26: *πᾶν ἔθνος ἀνθρώπων*, viii. 9: *τὸ ἔθνος τῆς Σαμαρίας*, xiii. 19, &c. In the former signification it has been already so affected by the Judæo-Hellenic use of the word, that the Gentile inhabitants of a city are called *τὰ ἔθνη* (xiii. 48, xiv. 2); xv. 23: *ἀδελφοῖς τοῖς ἐξ ἐθνῶν*, xxi. 25: *περὶ τῶν πεπιστευκότων ἐθνῶν* = "the Gentile Christians." It is placed in contrast with its antithesis (the Jewish nation) in iv. 27 (*σὺν ἔθνεσιν καὶ λαοῖς Ἰσραήλ*), ix. 15 (*ἐνώπιον ἐθνῶν τε καὶ βασιλέων υἱῶν τε Ἰσραήλ*), xiv. 5 (*ὁρμὴ τῶν ἐθνῶν τε καὶ Ἰουδαίων*), xxi. 21 (*τοὺς κατὰ τὰ ἔθνη πάντας Ἰουδαίους*), xxvi. 17 (*ἐξαιρούμενός σε ἐκ τοῦ λαοῦ* [*i.e.* the Jewish nation] *καὶ ἐκ τῶν ἐθνῶν*), xxvi. 23 (*καταγγέλλειν τῷ τε λαῷ καὶ τοῖς ἔθνεσιν*). Nevertheless, the word is not yet absolutely secularised: in x. 22 we read that the Gentile centurion Cornelius was held in good repute

[1] References to the we-sections are in bolder type.

ὑπὸ ὅλου τοῦ ἔθνους τῶν Ἰουδαίων, St. Paul speaks (xxiv. 17; xxvi. 4; xxviii. 19) of the Jewish nation as ἔθνος μου, and the Jewish orator Tertullus (xxiv. 3) as well as St. Paul (xxiv. 10) call the Jewish nation τὸ ἔθνος τοῦτο. But in all these six instances it is to be noticed that we are dealing with discourses, or rather with the reports of discourses, in which the *official* terminology, such as was customary before a Gentile tribunal, would naturally be used. These passages only show how carefully St. Luke handled matters of style.

No difference can be distinguished between different parts of the book in the use of this word.

Λαός (about forty-eight times, including twenty-four times in the first seven chapters).

Ὁ λαός is, as a rule, the designation for the Jewish nation in the religious or political sense (*cf.* especially xxi. 28: οὗτός ἐστιν ὁ ἄνθρωπος ὁ κατὰ τοῦ λαοῦ κ. τοῦ νόμου κ. τοῦ τόπου τούτου διδάσκων, xxviii. 17); further for the community of the Jews at a definite place (*e.g.* Jerusalem). Often—but only in discourse of an exalted character—it is combined with the epithet Ἰσραήλ (iv. 10; iv. 27 [here λαοὶ Ἰσραήλ after the LXX]; xiii. 17, 24); only once (xii. 11) with τῶν Ἰουδαίων. Not infrequently it partakes of the meaning of our phrase "all the people" (in a city, *cf.* xxi. 36: τὸ πλῆθος τοῦ λαοῦ); or of the people in distinction from their leaders (*e.g.* iv. 17, 21; v. 13); or of a collection of people (*e.g.* v. 37). Only in a quotation from the Old Testament λαοί = ἔθνη (iv.

25). Λαός, as a rule, has as its antithesis τὰ ἔθνη, and so in xxvi. 17, 23 they are expressly opposed to one another (ἐκ τοῦ λαοῦ καὶ ἐκ τῶν ἐθνῶν—τῷ τε λαῷ καὶ τοῖς ἔθνεσιν, *cf.* iv. 27). Only in one passage does λαός signify Christians, namely, in xv. 14 (λαβεῖν ἐξ ἐθνῶν λαόν), the word as it occurs in xviii. 10 (διότι λαός ἐστί μοι πολὺς ἐν τῇ πόλει ταύτῃ) can scarcely be regarded as approaching this use.

No distinction can be drawn between the different parts of the book in regard to the use of the word. Its absence from the we-sections is accidental. In his use of τὰ ἔθνη and ὁ λαός St. Luke, the Gentile Christian, has kept quite closely to the idiom of the Septuagint. The fact that in the book the Christians are never called ὁ λαός is a strong argument for its high antiquity.

Ἕλληνες (ten or eleven times) and Ἑλληνισταί (twice).

The former word, which is wanting in the synoptic gospels (it occurs, however, thrice in St. John), appears five times in the Acts in the combination—frequently met with after St. Paul—Ἰουδαίων τε καὶ Ἑλλήνων (xiv. 1; xviii. 4; xix. 10, 17; xx. 21)—in the first four places the author is speaking, in the fifth St. Paul. By its combination with Ἰουδαῖοι the word received a wider significance, so that it almost coincides with τὰ ἔθνη (it is not, however, till the fourth century that the process is completed and οἱ Ἕλληνες = the Gentiles). Apart from combination with Ἰουδαῖοι the word occurs again xi. 20 (dispersed Christians of Jerusalem preach to the Hellenes in Antioch), xvi. 1, 3 (the father of Timothy of Lystra was a Hellene), xvii. 4 (the σεβόμενοι Ἕλληνες in Thessalonica, *i.e.* the proselytes), and xxi. 28 (St. Paul is supposed to have introduced Hellenes into the Temple[1]). It cannot therefore be proved that St. Luke uses the word only in reference to particular regions and excludes it from others. We find once Ἑλληνίδες γυναῖκες (xvii. 12 in Berœa of Macedonia), once Ἑλληνιστί (xxi. 37[2]), and twice[3] (vi. 1 and ix. 29) Ἑλληνισταί, only Jews of the Diaspora dwelling in Jerusalem and speaking Greek are so called (antithesis: οἱ Ἑβραῖοι), and are still so called after they have become Christians. The word is not found elsewhere in the New Testament, and is altogether very rare. By the expression Ἰουδαῖοι τε καὶ Ἕλληνες St. Luke is characterised as belonging to the Pauline school.

Ἑβραῖοι (once).

St. Luke again coincides with St. Paul in his sparing use of Ἑβραῖος and in the way in which he uses it. St. Paul, as is well known, uses the word only twice (2 Cor. xi. 22; Philipp. iii. 5) to express the fact that he was fully a Jew by birth (in spite of his birth in the Diaspora); similarly Ἑβραῖοι is used in vi. 1 in contrast to Ἑλληνισταί (*vide supra*). Every Hebrew is a Jew, but not every Jew is a Hebrew. As this distinction between Ἰουδαῖοι and Ἑβραῖοι was

[1] In xviii. 7 the word Ἕλληνες is of doubtful authority.

[2] Elsewhere only in St. John xix. 20.

[3] In xi. 20 we must read Ἕλληνες (*vide supra*).

not universal[1] (*vide* Heinrici on 2 Cor. xi. 22) there exists here a relationship in the use of language between the two missionaries.

Three times in the Acts we find the phrase τῇ Ἑβραΐδι διαλέκτῳ (xxi. 40; xxii. 2; xxvi. 14; nowhere else in the New Testament). This can only mean Aramaic, which has the same name in St. John, and is elsewhere described even by born Jews as "Hebrew" (*vide* Zahn, *Einl.*,[1] I. s. 5, 18).[2]

Ἰουδαῖοι (about eighty-two times).

While Ἰουδαῖοι is found in the three synoptic gospels only seventeen times (including five times in St. Luke), it occurs in St. John about seventy-one times and in the Acts about eighty-two times! And it is most noteworthy that in the first eight chapters of the Acts it is found only thrice; these chapters also in other respects partake of the linguistic characteristics of the gospel.

The connections in which the word occurs in the Acts are very manifold: (1) it stands in combination with Ἕλληνες, λαός, and ἔθνη (*vide supra*); (2) in combination with proselytes (ii. 10; xvii. 17); (3) pleonastically side by side with συναγωγή[3] and νόμος[4] (xiii. 5; [xiii. 42]; xiv. 1; xvii. 1, 10; xxv. 8); (4) in the vocative; (5) as an adjective (x. 28; xxii. 3 ἀνὴρ Ἰουδαῖος, xiii. 6 ψευδοπροφήτης, xvi. 1; xxiv. 24

[1] Yet Jews avoided the word Ἑβραῖοι; it is also wanting in the gospels and the Apocalypse. The name of honour, which was therefore preferred, was Ἰουδαῖοι.

[2] τῇ ἰδίᾳ διαλέκτῳ stands in i. 19; ii. 6, 8.

[3] Generally, however, it is wanting with this word.

[4] Yet only in the speech of St. Paul before Festus.

γυνή, xix. 13 ἐξορκισταί, xix. 14 ἀρχιερεύς); (6) as a designation of the Jewish population of a land or a city (xiv. 19 ἀπὸ Ἀντιοχείας καὶ Ἰκονίου Ἰουδαῖοι, xvii. 13 οἱ ἀπὸ Θεσσαλονίκης Ἰουδ., xxi. 27 οἱ ἀπὸ τ. Ἀσίας Ἰουδ., *cf.* xxiv. 18; xxi. 39 Ἰουδαῖος Ταρσεύς, xxv. 7 οἱ ἀπὸ Ἱερουσ. καταβεβηκότες Ἰουδ., see also xviii. 2 εὑρών τινα Ἰουδ., xviii. 24 Ἰουδαῖος δέ τις Ἀπολλώς, xix. 34; strange [*vide infra*] but yet correct ii. 5: ἦσαν [ἐν] Ἱερουσαλὴμ κατοικοῦντες Ἰουδαῖοι ... ἀπὸ παντὸς ἔθνους); (7) *vide* expressions such as οἱ πρῶτοι (xxv. 2; xxviii. 17) *vel* οἱ πρεσβύτεροι (xxv. 15) τ. Ἰουδαίων; ἡ χώρα τ. Ἰουδ. is found only once (x. 39), and then with Jerusalem. Most often, however, it occurs, as in St. John, as a designation for the whole nation; and in some passages, as so often in St. John, in a somewhat disparaging sense. To apply again and again the general name of a nation or of a religious society to a distinct group of the same is an unusual procedure. It may be very complimentary, it may, however, also be the opposite, and so it is here and there with St. Luke. It is important that in the passage of the we-sections where Ἰουδαῖοι occurs (xxi. 11) it has just this disparaging significance: τὸν ἄνδρα οὗ ἐστιν ἡ ζώνη αὕτη οὕτως δήσουσιν ἐν Ἱερουσαλὴμ οἱ Ἰουδαῖοι καὶ παραδώσουσιν εἰς χεῖρας ἐθνῶν. Thus the whole nation is made responsible, and the prophet Agabus, who himself was sprung from among the Jews, speaks of the members of his own nation as οἱ Ἰουδαῖοι, *cf.* 1 Thess. ii. 14.[1]

[1] It is noteworthy that in xxviii. 21 and xxii. 5 the Jews address one another—and that in official discourse—as ἀδελφοί. St. Luke must have heard them speak thus. The use of this term by Christians in addressing one another seems therefore to have been borrowed.

Ἰσραήλ (about fifteen times), Ἰσραηλῖται (five times).

Both words belong almost exclusively to the first half of the book, but in the second half they occur each once (xxviii. 20 τῆς ἐλπίδος τ. Ἰσραήλ, xxi. 28 ἄνδρες Ἰσρ. βοηθεῖτε). Ἰσραήλ is used in the same connections in which it would also stand in the Old Testament (with βασιλεία, πᾶς οἶκος, λαός, υἱοί); it stands by itself only in v. 31 and xiii. 23 (as so often in the Pauline epistles). Ἰσραηλῖται only occurs with ἄνδρες in the vocative; elsewhere in the New Testament it is found only in St. Paul (thrice) and once in St. John (i. 48).

βάρβαροι (twice).

The word only occurs in St. Paul (twice)[1] and in St. Luke of the writers of the New Testament,—and in contrast to Ἕλληνες; but while St. Paul uses it, so to say, objectively, as indeed every Jew could use it, St. Luke in applying it to the inhabitants of Malta who could not speak Greek (xxviii. 2, 4),[2] uses it subjectively, and thereby declares his own Greek descent.

Οἱ κατοικοῦντες = the inhabitants (thirteen times).

This term for "inhabitants"[3] imitated from the LXX is found in all parts of the book, usually the

[1] The passage 1 Cor. xiv. 11 does not belong here.

[2] Mommsen was therefore not justified in thinking this strange.

[3] Elsewhere in the New Testament it is found in St. Luke xiii. 4, and often in the Apocalypse.

place (the land) is put in the accusative (but in ii. 5; ix. 22; xi. 29; xiii. 27 ἐν is used). It is combined with Jerusalem [1] in i. 19; ii. 5, 14; iv. 16; xiii. 27; with Damascus in ix. 22; xxii. 12, with Lydda in ix. 32, 35, with Ephesus in xix. 17, with Mesopotamia in ii. 9, with Asia in xix. 10, with Judæa in xi. 29.[2]

Γῆ (about thirty-four times), Χώρα (eight times; ἡ περίχωρος once), Πόλις (about forty-three times), Κώμη (once), Τόπος (eighteen times).

In the great majority of passages γῆ is used either of the land, or of the world, or of the earth in distinction from the heavens, or in quotations from the Old Testament. It signifies a particular land in vii. 4 (γῆ Χαλδαίων and ἡ γῆ αὕτη = Palestine), vii. 36, 40;

[1] While in ii. 14 we read: Ἄνδρες Ἰουδαῖοι καὶ οἱ κατοικοῦντες Ἱερουσαλήμ, in ii. 5 it is the Jews of the Diaspora dwelling in Jerusalem who are termed κατοικοῦντες. But this is not inadmissible (as say Blass, who in ii. 5 omits Ἰουδαῖοι with Cod. Sin., *Neue kirchl. Ztschr.* 1892, s. 826 *ff.*, and Joh. Weiss, who thinks that a καί must be inserted after Ἰουδαῖοι), rather it is demanded by the context. The author wished to say that the people described some verses later as Parthians, Medes, &c., who were dwelling at that time at Jerusalem, were nevertheless Jews, and this is quite correctly expressed by the words: ἦσαν δὲ ἐν Ἱερουσαλὴμ κατοικοῦντες Ἰουδαῖοι, ἄνδρες εὐλαβεῖς ἀπὸ παντὸς ἔθνους τῶν ὑπὸ τὸν οὐρανόν.

[2] Παροικία and πάροικος have not yet reached a technical significance in the Acts (παροικεῖν is altogether wanting) and are of very rare occurrence; they are only found in the speech of St. Stephen (vii. 6. 29) and in St. Paul's sermon at Antioch (xiii. 17), *thus* only in connection with Old Testament history. This is again a proof of the relatively high antiquity of the Acts; for these words became technical ecclesiastical terms before the end of the first century, *vide* 1 Peter i. 17; ii. 11; First Epistle of Clement, &c. In ii. 10 we find οἱ ἐπιδημοῦντες Ῥωμαῖοι and in xvii. 20 οἱ ἐπιδημοῦντες ξένοι. The word is wanting elsewhere in the New Testament.

xiii. 17 (γῆ Αἰγύπτου or Αἰγύπτῳ), vii. 29 (γῆ Μαδιάμ), xiii. 19 (γῆ Χαναάν, twice); this use is, however, confined to lands mentioned in the Old Testament, and is derived from the LXX; *St. Luke himself never uses this form of expression.* In the we-sections (**xxvii. 39, 43, 44**) γῆ is the dry land (so also in iv. 24; xiv. 15, where it occurs together with θάλασσα).

Χώρα occurs only once in the plural (viii. 1) and there is used like "agri" to signify villages. The Christian Hellenists driven by persecution from Jerusalem are scattered over the villages of Judæa and Samaria; and so we read (viii. 25) πολλάς τε κώμας τῶν Σαμαρειτῶν εὐηγγελίζοντο. Apart from this passage the extension of the movement over a country (the villages) appears to be distinctly mentioned only once again. In xiii. 49 we read that the word of the Lord spread abroad from Antioch in Pisidia δι' ὅλης τῆς χώρας. But (*vide infra*) it is possible that here χώρα = "regio" in the official sense. In the sense of an undefined land as distinguished from the sea it is found in **xxvii. 27.** In the sense of a definite land it is combined in x. 39 with τῶν Ἰουδαίων, in xxvi. 20 with τῆς Ἰουδαίας, in xvi. 6 and xviii. 23 with Γαλατική; in xii. 20 it signifies the region of Tyre and Sidon. It does not occur in other passages of the book. Seeing that the word is so rarely used in the book, though so many lands are mentioned therein, the question must be asked whether in all these passages (with the exception of xii. 20) χώρα is not purposely used to indicate that the whole country-side is meant. In chapter x. 39 we read: ἡμεῖς μάρτυρες πάντων ὧν ἐποίησεν ἔν τε τῇ χώρᾳ τῶν Ἰουδαίων καὶ [ἐν] Ἱερουσαλήμ, and in xxvi. 20: ἀλλὰ τοῖς ἐν Δαμάσκοις πρῶτόν τε καὶ Ἱεροσολύμοις εἰς πᾶσάν τε τὴν χώραν τῆς Ἰουδαίας [Blass unnecessarily proposes Ἰουδαίοις], καὶ τοῖς ἔθνεσιν ἀπήγγελον. Why does St. Luke not here simply write ἡ Ἰουδαία, as he so often does? Evidently he wishes to emphasise the fact that St. Paul's preaching extended to the country folk of Judæa. Again it is of additional importance that the author in the only two places where he mentions Galatia uses the expression ἡ Γαλατικὴ χώρα,[1] while elsewhere when speaking of Roman provinces he always names them Asia, Phrygia, Cilicia, and so forth. We may assert that he so speaks because Galatia was poor in cities, and because in official terminology the word "regiones" was also used of this province. It then further follows that in the much discussed question where the Galatia of St. Paul is to be found, we may not claim St. Luke as a witness in favour of the South-Galatian theory; rather we must regard him as a witness to the contrary. The word περίχωρος, sometimes found in the synoptic gospels, occurs only once in the Acts (xiv. 6): εἰς τὰς πόλεις τῆς Λυκαονίας Λύστραν καὶ Δέρβην καὶ τὴν περίχωρον.

The use of the word χώρα in the Acts, though it is so rare, again shows the consistency of the author.[2]

The word πόλις is added to the name of a city

[1] Some exegetes think that χώρα (xvi. 6) is also connected with Φρυγίαν, but Φρυγίαν cannot be adjectival; moreover, in xviii. 23 we read: διερχόμενος καθεξῆς τὴν Γαλατικὴν χώραν καὶ Φρυγίαν, here Φρυγίαν is certainly a substantive.

[2] Χωρίον (field) is found in Acts i. 18, 19; iv. 34; v. 3, 8; xxviii. 7.

twice in the we-sections (**xvi. 14**; **xxvii. 8**: πόλεως Θυατείρων, πόλις Λασαία) and once in the rest of the book (xi. 5: ἐν πόλει Ἰόππῃ); in all other numerous instances where a town is mentioned the name stands without πόλις. The phrase: ἡ Ἐφεσίων πόλις (xix. 35)[1] occurs once in a speech to the Ephesians in order to flatter their pride. Samaria is introduced in viii. 5 without closer definition as "ἡ πόλις τῆς Σαμαρίας"—scarcely because the author assumed that his readers knew what city was meant, but because he wanted to let us know that the Gospel, when it was carried from Judæa to Samaria, made its entrance at once into the capital city of that country.

Sometimes the author adds the name of the province to the name of the city. His reasons for this procedure are not always the same, and are not always clearly discernible; as a rule, however, we may assume that it is because he wishes to draw attention to the fact that the Gospel had now made its way into the particular province mentioned—youthful missionary religions count their conquests by provinces!—perhaps also because he wishes to determine more accurately the geographical situation of the city and to

[1] Like a true Hellene St. Luke likes to describe persons by the cities from which they sprang. He speaks not only of Romans and Athenians (xvii. 21, 22), but he also writes Ναζωραῖος (often), Τύριος (xii. 20), Σιδώνιος (xii. 20), Ταρσεύς (ix. 11; xxi. 39), Ἀντιοχεύς (vi. 5), Ἀλεξανδρεύς (vi. 9; xviii. 24), Δερβαῖος (xx. 4), Θεσσαλονικεύς (xx. 4; **xxvii. 2**), Βεροιαῖος (xx. 4), Κορίνθιος (xviii. 8), Ἐφέσιος (xix. 28, **34**, 35; xxi. 29), Λυδία πόλεως Θυατείρων (**xvi. 14**). *Cf.* also the terms Ποντικός (xviii. 2), Ἀσιανός (xx. 4), Κύπριος (iv. 36; xi. 20; **xxi. 16**), Κυρηναῖος (vi. 9; xi. 20; xiii. 1), Αἰθίοψ (viii. 27), Μακεδών (**xvi. 9**; xix. 29; **xxvii. 2**), Αἰγύπτιος (xxi. 38), Σαμαρείτης (viii. 25), &c.

avoid by this means any confusion with another city of the same name. St. Luke writes:—

Πέργη τῆς Παμφυλίας (xiii. 13).
Ἀντιόχεια τῆς Πισιδίας (xiii. 14).[1]
Λύστρα καὶ Δέρβη, πόλεις τῆς Λυκαονίας (xiv. 6).
Φίλιπποι, ἥτις ἐστὶν πρώτη τῆς μερίδος Μακεδονίας πόλις (xvi. 12).
Ταρσεὺς τῆς Κιλικίας (xxi. 39).
Ταρσὸς τῆς Κιλικίας (xxii. 3).
Μύρρα τῆς Λυκίας (xxvii. 5).

It is most extraordinary that the epithet "of Cilicia" is twice added to the large and well-known city of Tarsus. One is almost tempted to recollect that there was another Tarsus in Bithynia, and that St. Luke, according to the very ancient preface to his gospel, is reported to have died in Bithynia. It is better to remember that it belonged to the style of the registers—a style that would naturally be adopted by a man giving formal account of himself—to give the name of the province, however well known the city might be.

St. Luke exhibits great acuteness and delicacy of perception when in xxi. 39 he makes St. Paul add to Ταρσεύς the words "οὐκ ἀσήμου πόλεως πολίτης"[2] in order that by this reference to Eurip. Ion. 8 (οὐκ ἄσημος Ἑλλήνων πόλις) he might show himself, in the face of the Chiliarch's mistake, to be a man of

[1] Εἰς Ἀντιοχείαν τὴν Πισιδίαν has almost unanimous attestation; but Πισιδίαν cannot be an adjective; we must therefore probably read Πισιδίας with D.

[2] Πολίτης occurs only here in the Acts, but is found elsewhere in the New Testament in St. Luke xv. 15; xix. 14 (in the Hebrews in a quotation).—Πολιτεία = Roman citizenship only in Acts xxii. 28.

Hellenic culture. Similar phrases occur in inscriptions found in Asia Minor, for instance in the famous inscription of Abercius: Ἐκλεκτῆς πόλεως ὁ πολίτης.—In connection with the use of the word πόλις the following additional remarks are perhaps worthy of note.[1] The mission was for the most part carried on in the cities, as also the Jews

[1] Let me here point out another small detail which is nevertheless of importance in reference to the author's consistency of style. In general he does not use the article with names of cities. It is found only in 23 (24) out of about 250 instances, if I have not overlooked any; in xxvi. 12 the article is not quite certain (among the 59 instances where Jerusalem is named the article only occurs once in v. 28). In 13 of these instances the reason of the addition of the article is obvious (ix. 3, 38; x. 8; xiii. 14; xvii. 13, 16; xviii. 1, 21; xix. 17; **xx. 6**; xx. 17; xxii. 6; xxiii. 31); for the city has been mentioned just before and is now repeated with the article (in many cases of course this is not done in spite of the repetition). The instance in xiv. 21 also belongs to this group, indeed the passage is especially characteristic: ὑπέστρεψαν εἰς τὴν Λύστραν καὶ εἰς Ἰκόνιον καὶ εἰς Ἀντιόχειαν. The stay in Lystra had been shortly before described in detail, therefore the article stands only with this city. But there remain yet nine instances which do not admit of this explanation. Of these xviii. 2 ἀπὸ τῆς Ῥώμης and **xxviii. 14** εἰς τὴν Ῥώμην are sufficiently explained by the fame and importance of the city (and besides in **xxviii. 14** it is implied that St. Paul had at last reached the goal of his ministry; afterwards in verse 16 we read: εἰς Ῥώμην). The article before Ἀντιόχειαν (xv. 23) is sufficiently explained by the circumstance that Syria and Cilicia come afterwards. Of the six instances still remaining four may be explained from the circumstance that they mark the necessary direction of the determined route which the Apostle took (*vide* Blass); they occur in xvii. 1; **xx. 13, 14**; xxiii. 31 (notice again the agreement of the we-sections with the whole work). The force of the article in v. 28 (τὴν Ἰερουσαλήμ) and in xx. 16 (τὴν Ἔφεσον) is somewhat obscure; but the author may very well have once written ἡ Ἔφεσος for the same reason that he wrote ἡ Ῥώμη, and the article with Jerusalem in the mouth of the high-priest is probably intended to signify: "this Jerusalem of ours."

of the Diaspora were chiefly settled in the cities. Hence we read in viii. 40 of St. Philip: εὐηγγελίζετο τὰς πόλεις πάσας (*scil.* of Philistia); again St. James says (xv. 21) that Moses has κατὰ πόλιν ἐν ταῖς συναγωγαῖς τοὺς κηρύσσοντας αὐτόν, and St. Paul admits (xxvi. 11) that he persecuted the Christians not only in Jerusalem, but also followed them up even εἰς τὰς ἔξω πόλεις; St. Paul and Silas pass through (xvi. 4) τὰς πόλεις and revisit (xv. 36) κατὰ πόλιν πᾶσαν the communities that were founded on the first journey; St. Paul declares that the Spirit κατὰ πόλιν prophesied sufferings that were about to come upon him (xx. 23), and τὸ πλῆθος τῶν πέριξ πόλεων Ἱερουσαλήμ crowded into the city (v. 16) to be healed by the apostles. It is characteristic of the exactness of the author that he often marks the fact that something took place outside the city. Stephen was stoned ἔξω τῆς πόλεως[1] (vii. 58); the temple of Zeus in Lystra was situated πρὸ τῆς πόλεως (xiv. 13); St. Paul was dragged ἔξω τῆς πόλεως (xiv. 19); the place of prayer in Philippi lies ἔξω τῆς πύλης (xvi. 13); and the brethren and sisters in Tyre accompany St. Paul ἕως ἔξω τῆς πόλεως (xxi. 5). Lastly, it is a fine proof of the precision of the author that in xiii. 50 he speaks of the πρῶτοι τῆς πόλεως (in Antioch of Pisidia), in xxv. 23 of those κατ' ἐξοχὴν τῆς πόλεως (in Cæsarea of Palestine), and elsewhere of the rulers of cities, but in the case of Philippi alone does he call the magistrates of the city "στρατηγοί" (xvi. 20 *ff.*), and in the case of Thessalonica alone

[1] Among both Jews and Gentiles executions took place as a rule outside the city, *vide* Heb. xiii. 12, 13.

πολιτάρχαι (xvii. 6, 8), while he calls the governor of Malta (xxviii. 7) ὁ πρῶτος τῆς νήσου. These names are correct, for in the Roman colony Philippi prætors (duumviri) held sway, the title "Politarch" is vouched for in Thessalonica by inscriptions, and the title πρῶτος Μελιταίων is found in an inscription discovered in Malta (Inscr. Græc. Ital. et. Sicil. 601); a certain Prudens an *eques Romanus* is there so described. We also learn from inscriptions that the part which the official described as ὁ γραμματεύς (town-clerk) plays in Ephesus (xix. 35 *f.*) suits the γραμματεύς in Ephesus, though it would not at all suit the official of the same name in every other city.[1]

The use of τόπος is most varied, and yet even

[1] All the other official titles in the book are correct. The monarch is called, as in Phil. iv. 22, simply ὁ Καῖσαρ (xvii. 7 ; xxv. 8–12, 21 ; xxvi. 32 ; xxvii. 4 ; xxviii. 19) or ὁ Σεβαστός (xxv. 21, 25), or is simply described by *one* of his own names (xi. 28 ; xviii. 2). He is never called Βασιλεύς, a title, however, rightly applied to Herod (xii. 1, 20) and to Agrippa (xxv. 13, 14, 24 ; xxvi. 2, 7, 13, 19, 26, 27, 30). Sergius Paulus in Cyprus and Gallio in Corinth are rightly called ἀνθύπατοι (xiii. 7, 8, 12 ; xviii. 12 ; [xix. 38]) ; on the other hand this title is wanting, and rightly wanting, in the cases of Felix and Festus ; each of these is called, as also in Josephus, ἡγεμών (xxiii. 24, 26, 33, 34 ; xxiv. 1, 10 ; xxvi. 30). The term ἐπαρχία (="provincia") is found only in the mouth of Felix in his question concerning St. Paul : ἐκ ποίας ἐπαρχίας (xxiii. 34) and in the clause (xxv. 1) : Φῆστος ἐπιβὰς τῇ ἐπαρχίᾳ [a strange use of dative just as in xxvii. 2 : ἐπιβάντες πλοίῳ] elsewhere it is avoided. The titles ἑκατοντάρχης (x. 1, 22 ; xxi. 32 ; xxii. 25, 26 ; xxiii. 17, 23 ; xxiv. 23 ; xxvii. 1, 6, 11, 31, 43 ; xxviii. 16) and χιλίαρχος (xxi. 31–37 ; xxii. 24–29 ; xxiii. 10–22 ; xxiv. 7, 22 ; xxv. 23) are correctly used. It is uncertain whether the Stratopedarch of xxviii. 16 is original. The epithet "κράτιστος" is only employed in addressing Felix and Festus (xxiii. 26 ; xxiv. 3 ; xxvi. 25), and its use in this instance is correct.

here one can establish the homogeneity of the author's style.[1] It is used metaphorically in i. 25 (*λαβεῖν τὸν τόπον τῆς διακονίας*) and in xxv. 16 (*τόπον ἀπολογίας λαβεῖν*); the Temple is called in vi. 13 and xxi. 28 *ὁ ἅγιος τόπος*, and in vi. 14 and xxi. 28 *ὁ τόπος οὗτος*, in vii. 7 *ὁ τόπος οὗτος* is to be understood as referring to the Holy Land. In xvi. 3 *οἱ τόποι ἐκεῖνοι* describes the region round Lystra and Iconium; likewise we read in **xxvii.** 2 *εἰς τοὺς κατὰ τὴν Ἀσίαν τόπους* and similarly in **xxviii.** 7 *τά περὶ τὸν τόπον ἐκεῖνον*. The word has a mysterious sound in i. 25: *ἀπὸ τῆς ἀποστολῆς παρέβη Ἰούδας πορευθῆναι εἰς τὸν τόπον τὸν ἴδιον*, and even in xii. 17: *Πέτρος ἐξελθὼν ἐπορεύθη εἰς ἕτερον τόπον* (for *τόπος* = place, city, *vide* **xxvii.** 8 *ἤλθομεν εἰς τόπον τινὰ καλούμενον Καλοὺς λιμένας*). Only once (**xxi.** 12) are the native inhabitants of a city called *οἱ ἐντόπιοι* (the word is found in Plato; it is not one that is often met with).

Γένος (nine times).[2]

The use of the word in iv. 36 *Κύπριος τ. γένει*, xviii. 2 *Ποντικὸς τ. γένει*, xviii. 24 *Ἀλεξανδρεὺς τ. γένει*, vii. 19 *τὸ γένος ἡμῶν* shows the consistency of style in both halves of the book. The remaining passages where the word occurs give it the significance

[1] The passages (iv. 31; vii. 33, 49; **xxvii.** 29, 41) are neutral.

[2] Similar words, which occur only rarely or only once, and are therefore not fitted for use in comparison, are *τὰ ὅρια* (for a region, xiii. 50), *ἡ ἐπαρχία* (xxiii. 34; xxv. 1), *ἡ οἰκουμένη* (xi. 28; xvii. 6, 31; xix. 27; xxiv. 5), &c. The use of *τὰ μέρη* is, however, worthy of note. In ii. 10 we read *τὰ μέρη τῆς Λιβύης*, in xix. 1 *Παῦλος διελθὼν τὰ ἀνωτερικὰ μέρη*, and likewise in xx. 2 *διελθὼν τὰ μέρη ἐκεῖνα* (said of Macedonia)

of race, not in the sense of nationality but of descent (iv. 6; vii. 13; xiii. 26; xvii. 28, 29).

II.—*Terms of more Special Significance.*

The list of nations in chapters ii. 5, 9–11 and in vi. 9.

ἦσαν δὲ ἐν [εἰς] Ἱερουσαλὴμ κατοικοῦντες Ἰουδαῖοι, ἄνδρες εὐλαβεῖς ἀπὸ παντὸς ἔθνους τῶν ὑπὸ τὸν οὐρανόν . . . Πάρθοι καὶ Μῆδοι καὶ Αἰλαμῖται καὶ οἱ κατοικοῦντες τὴν Μεσοποταμίαν [Ἰουδαίαν? Ἀρμενίαν? Συρίαν? Ἰνδίαν?] τε καὶ Καππαδοκίαν, Πόντον καὶ τὴν Ἀσίαν, Φρυγίαν τε καὶ Παμφυλίαν, Αἴγυπτον καὶ τὰ μέρη τῆς Λιβύης τῆς κατὰ Κυρήνην, καὶ οἱ ἐπιδημοῦντες Ῥωμαῖοι, Ἰουδαῖοί τε καὶ προσήλυτοι [Κρῆτες καὶ Ἄραβες].

After the first three national names St. Luke continues with *οἱ κατοικοῦντες*, because there was no national name for Mesopotamia; but this has led to a formal discrepancy with the preceding clause. St. Luke is speaking simply of such persons as were resident in Jerusalem (not of pilgrims for the feast), yet he describes them most awkwardly as *κατοικοῦντες τὴν Μεσοποταμίαν κ.τ.λ.* after their former place of abode. In its significance, therefore, the second *κατοικοῦντες* must be regarded as pluperfect. Moreover, seeing that from Pontus onwards the author gives the names in pairs and that *Ἰουδαίαν*—though the reading of all MSS.—is senseless, while *Ἀρμενίαν* (Tertullian, and once in Augustine), as well as *Συρίαν* (Hieron.), are evidently only attempts to clear away a difficulty which was felt already at an early date; we must therefore delete Ἰουδαίαν.[1] We can of course give no satisfactory explanation for the interpolation of this word. The irregularity of the use of the article in this section is surprising, so also the appended Κρῆτες καὶ Ἄραβες,—here also we must assume an ancient gloss, for both the special mention of these people and their combination together is extraordinary. The assumption of an interpolation becomes yet more probable if the preceding words "Ἰουδαῖοί τε καὶ προσήλυτοι" belong not only to "οἱ ἐπιδημοῦντες Ῥωμαῖοι," but to all the foregoing national names, as is almost certainly the case. The author had said at the beginning of the list that he was concerned with those *Jews* now dwelling in Jerusalem who had before lived in Parthia, Media, &c. At the conclusion he says more exactly that these included both Jews by birth and proselytes, and this without doubt answered to the truth, and did not apply only to Rome. Strange, lastly, is the epithet "ἐπιδημοῦντες" applied to οἱ Ῥωμαῖοι. In my opinion it finds its explanation in the fact that οἱ Ῥωμαῖοι could be understood as meaning "Roman citizens" (*vide* Acts xvi. 37, 38; xxii. 25, 26, 27, 29; xxiii. 27). St. Luke wishes to avoid this ambiguity. Instead of οἱ ἐπιδημ. Ῥωμ. he might also have written οἱ κατοικοῦντες τὴν Ῥωμην (as in verse 9); but he wished at the close to remind us that the people in question throughout *now* dwelt in Jerusalem, though

[1] Mesopotamia and Cappadocia could very well be mentioned together for they are contiguous, and as the counting is from East to West this order is specially appropriate (*vide infra* another reason for the omission).

they were properly at home in other lands. Thus "οἱ ἐπιδημοῦντες Ῥωμαῖοι" does not mean "Romans settled in Rome" (as Wendt and others would interpret), but "Romans who had migrated to Jerusalem and had settled in that city" (so Overbeck). The circumstance that after striking out Ἰουδαίαν, Κρῆτες, and Ἄραβες we are left with a list of twelve nations confirms the omission; *i.e.* the author perhaps intended to indicate that each apostle spoke in one of these tongues. It is true that according to ii. 1 we must suppose that the Holy Spirit descended upon all the Christians in Jerusalem; but nevertheless, according to ii. 7, it is the Apostles alone who are thought of. If we do not choose to accept this hypothesis, it still follows that the number twelve of the nations was purposely chosen.

The list begins with the nations in the remotest East, where the tribes that had not returned to Palestine were settled; with Cappadocia it reaches Asia Minor, which is described first from north to west (Pontus and Asia); then—in a parallel line—from the centre (Phrygia) to the south (Pamphylia). Then the author passes to the real south of the empire, and names—again from east to west—Egypt and the parts of Libya about Cyrene.[1] Rome, as the representative of the West, closes the list.

It is possible to argue with the author concerning his reasons for naming one region and passing over another, but it will be difficult to make any point against him.

[1] With κατὰ Κυρήνην compare St. Luke x. 32: Λευείτης κατὰ τὸν τόπον ἐλθών, and **Acts xxvii. 5**: τὸ πέλαγος τὸ κατὰ τὴν Κιλικίαν καὶ Παμφυλίαν.

With relative completeness he begins with "Parthians, Medes, and Elamites," because these nations were far distant and dwelt outside the Roman Empire—it was the more important for him that their representatives heard the new message! These are followed most appropriately by Mesopotamia and Cappadocia. He naturally passed over Syria because it lay too near, and because it was self-evident that numerous Syrians were to be found in Jerusalem. Besides, their language was so nearly allied to that spoken in Jerusalem that for them the miracle, which the author intends, was scarcely a miracle at all. If in the case of Asia Minor the four countries, Pontus, Asia, Phrygia, and Pamphylia, are chosen for mention, one cannot but approve of the choice, seeing that Cappadocia had been already mentioned: the chief province in the north, the west, the centre, and the south is thus marked. Could any one proceed on a better plan? With equal appropriateness he now mentions Egypt and Cyrene and closes with Rome. In the two former regions it was a matter of common knowledge that the Jews had settled in especially compact bodies; and that the whole West should be represented by Rome is not strange but rather what one would expect in a Greek writer of the East. The omission of the Balkan peninsula is less intelligible. It has been said that the author has not included purely Greek regions in his list, because for Greeks with their universally-spoken language the miracle of Pentecost was no miracle at all,—at least they did not need such a miracle; this explanation is ingenious but scarcely correct. The disciples in their ecstasy spoke Aramaic, not Greek (v. 7: οὐχὶ ἰδοὺ ἅπαντες οὗτοί εἰσιν οἱ λαλοῦντες Γαλιλαῖοι;). The Balkan peninsula (Macedonia and Achaia) is passed over either because in this region, when compared with the others mentioned, the Jews were not specially numerous, or because the author passing naturally from Asia to Egypt and then to Cyrene had now come so far to the west that he concluded with Rome. Besides, he did not wish to exceed the number twelve (*vide supra*).

The formal construction of this passage is very skilful and superior to that of the list given by Philo (*Agrippæ ep. ad Caligulam, Legat. ad Caium*, § 36), which contains double the number of nations. The author begins with the sonorous triplet, "Parthians, Medes, and Elamites"; then he follows with 4 × 2 nations, and the "οἱ ἐπιδημοῦντες Ῥωμαῖοι, *i.e.* the great Capital of the World, standing by itself, brings the twelve to a very impressive conclusion.[1] We trace here the literary skill of the Hellene. But how much greater still does this skill appear when we place this list of nations in the light of the aim which dominates the whole work! Ἔσεσθέ μου μάρτυρες ἔν τε Ἱερουσαλὴμ καὶ ἐν πάσῃ τῇ Ἰουδαίᾳ καὶ Σαμαρίᾳ καὶ ἕως ἐσχάτου τῆς γῆς! (i. 8). Θάρσει· ὡς γὰρ διεμαρτύρω τὰ περὶ ἐμοῦ εἰς Ἱερουσαλήμ, οὕτω σε δεῖ καὶ εἰς Ῥώμην μαρτυρῆσαι (xxiii. 11). Γνωστὸν οὖν ἔστω ὑμῖν ὅτι τοῖς ἔθνεσιν ἀπεστάλη τοῦτο τὸ σωτήριον τοῦ θεοῦ· αὐτοὶ καὶ ἀκούσονται (xxviii. 28). On the very threshold of a work, which was intended to

[1] *Cf. Herm. Simil.* ix.: the twelve hills = the twelve nations of the world.

describe the realisation of this aim, is placed this list of the nations of the known World, and we are told how this great promise was at once fulfilled for their representatives! Could anything be more impressive? How many are there who could measure their art against this writer? And yet more, the barriers of language are seen to be overthrown! All understand the ecstatic speech inspired by the Spirit! The racial divisions of mankind are now abolished; in the new religion the consequences of the building of the Tower of Babel are seen to be annulled! True, this grand picture cannot stand investigation in cold blood. The people of course all understood Aramaic; moreover, it is not even Aramaic alone which is in question, but also a language of enthusiasm which works by suggestion. But one does not think of this at first. St. Luke takes up two facts of actual history—that Jews and proselytes out of all countries of the world were resident in Jerusalem, and that on a certain day, the day of Pentecost or shortly beforehand, a great multitude were won over to the Gospel owing to a sudden outbreak of rapturous enthusiasm, accompanied by ecstatic speaking, among the disciples of Jesus—these two facts the author works up with consummate skill, so that they form as it were a grand flourish of trumpets heralding the appearance of the great theme of his work.

We have yet to compare this list of nations with the statement of chapter vi. 9. Here we are told of Libertines, men of Cyrene, of Alexandria, of Cilicia and Asia, dwelling in Jerusalem. Unfortunately we cannot gain a quite clear conception of the meaning of the words; for St. Luke has not expressed himself with precision.[1] They are, however, important on this account, because here in a context dealing with a simple succession of events—not a worked-up description—witness is borne to some representatives of the nations mentioned in ii. 9 *ff.*, namely men of Cyrene, Alexandria (Egypt), and Asia. Hence Jews and proselytes from these regions were really settled in Jerusalem, a circumstance which is moreover probable in itself.

Palestine (Galilee, Judæa, the Philistian cities, Samaria and Phœnicia).

If St. Luke, the author of the we-sections, was also the author of the Acts of the Apostles, we learn from his own account that he accompanied the Apostle St. Paul to Jerusalem (chap. xxi.), and that about two and a half years later he journeyed with him

[1] The words run: *ἀνέστησαν δέ τινες τῶν ἐκ τῆς συναγωγῆς τῆς λεγομένης Λιβερτίνων καὶ Κυρηναίων καὶ Ἀλεξανδρέων καὶ τῶν ἀπὸ Κιλικίας καὶ Ἀσίας συνζητοῦντες τῷ Στεφάνῳ.* According to the simplest interpretation only one combined synagogue of Libertines and of men of Cyrene and Alexandria, and in addition Jews of Cilicia and Asia are here spoken of (the Libertines are usually explained to be Jews who were once Roman captives taken in war, and who then [either themselves or their descendants] had returned to Jerusalem; this explanation cannot be regarded as satisfactory). But the combination, "Libertines, men of Cyrene and of Alexandria," is very strange. It has therefore been supposed that St. Luke has not expressed himself with accuracy; and that three different synagogues are intended. Some indeed think of four synagogues in that they conceive of the men of Cilicia and Asia as also belonging to a synagogue. Others again think of one synagogue of the Libertines alone, leaving *Κυρηναίων κ.τ.λ.* to depend upon *τινες*.

from Cæsarea to Rome (chaps. xxvii. xxviii.). It is more than doubtful whether he was with the Apostle between these two dates, for the "we" breaks off directly after the arrival in Jerusalem, and first appears again at the departure from Cæsarea. The explanation that the "we" does not appear in the chapters in question (xxi. 19–xxvi. 32), because St. Luke had nothing to relate in which he himself took part as eye-witness is most improbable; for he himself relates that St. Paul when in Cæsarea could receive his friends without hindrance, and that they were allowed to minister to him (xxiv. 23). There must have been opportunity enough for St. Luke not only to have visited the Apostle, but also to have shared in experiences of his that were worthy of record. Besides this he could have attended on the various occasions when St. Paul appeared before the procurator; even here, however, he has not written as an eye-witness. We may therefore assume that St. Luke set foot indeed upon the soil of Palestine and Jerusalem in company with the Apostle, but that he left it again very soon. We accordingly expect that he will show the amount of information concerning the country and city which a traveller is wont to acquire after a short residence. And this is just what we find in the work itself. Here, however, we can only show that this is so in the case of the information he gives us on geographical, topographical, and ethnographical points.

Ὑμεῖς οἴδατε τὸ γενόμενον ῥῆμα καθ' ὅλης τῆς Ἰουδαίας, ἀρξάμενος ἀπὸ τῆς Γαλιλαίας μετὰ τὸ βάπτισμα ὃ ἐκήρυξεν Ἰωάννης (x. 37): the movement started from Galilee (xiii. 31: ὤφθη τοῖς συναναβᾶσιν αὐτῷ ἀπὸ τῆς Γαλιλαίας εἰς Ἰερουσαλήμ) and first spread over the whole of Judæa. Jesus is ὁ ἀπὸ Ναζαρέθ,[1] and the eleven apostles are addressed (i. 11) as ἄνδρες Γαλιλαῖοι; St. Luke at the same time knows that the Galilæans could be distinguished by their dialect (ii. 7 οὐχὶ ἰδοὺ ἅπαντες οὗτοί εἰσιν οἱ λαλοῦντες Γαλιλαίοι; *cf.* St. Mark xiv. 67, 70; St. Matt. xxvi. 71, 73). When intending to give the boundaries of Christendom in the first years after its foundation, he says (ix. 31): ἡ ἐκκλησία καθ' ὅλης τῆς Ἰουδαίας καὶ Γαλιλαίας καὶ Σαμαρίας. A few times, when we should have expected Galilee to be mentioned with Judæa, it is wanting, possibly because it is included in Judæa. Galilee plays no part in the narrative of St. Luke—it is merely a reminiscence—this, however, in all probability answers to actual history. St. Paul never mentions Galilee and the Galilean Christian communities in his epistles. Jerusalem the capital became the exclusive determining

[1] Thus only once in the book (x. 38), on the other hand six times Ἰησοῦς (Χριστὸς) ὁ Ναζωραῖος (ii. 22; iii. 6; iv. 10; vi. 14; xxii. 8; xxvi. 9); it is probable in itself—but that single passage is decisive—that ὁ Ναζωραῖος means one who was a native of Nazareth. It is noteworthy that St. Paul never uses the expression, and that it occurs only in the first half of the Acts, or rather the only two passages in the second half where it occurs really belong, so far as their subject is concerned, to the first half. The designation "Jesus the Nazarene" is thus Palestinian, and is only used by St. Luke in order to give the right colouring to the first half of his book. His procedure, as is well known, is similar elsewhere. It is only in the mouth of the Jewish orator Tertullus (xxiv. 5) that the Christians are disdainfully called ἡ τῶν Ναζωραίων αἵρεσις. A like feeling is expressed in St. John i. 45 *f.*: Ἰησοῦν τὸν ἀπὸ Ναζαρέτ ... καὶ εἶπεν αὐτῷ Ναθαναήλ· ἐκ Ναζαρὲτ δύναταί τι ἀγαθὸν εἶναι.

centre of the movement soon after the Crucifixion of our Lord.[1]

Judæa is more frequently mentioned in the book. There, and indeed *ἐν πάσῃ τῇ Ἰουδαίᾳ*, the disciples are to bear witness (i. 8). The adherents of Stephen are scattered *κατὰ τὰς χώρας τῆς Ἰουδαίας* (viii. 1), *i.e.* throughout the Holy Land (*vide supra sub χώρα*). With the phrases *ἐκκλησία καθ' ὅλης τῆς Ἰουδαίας* (ix. 31),[2] and *ἀδελφοὶ οἱ ὄντες κατὰ τὴν Ἰουδαίαν* (xi. 1), and *κατοικοῦντες ἐν τῇ Ἰουδαίᾳ ἀδελφοί* (xi. 29), we may compare Gal. i. 22: *αἱ ἐκκλησίαι τῆς Ἰουδαίας* and 1 Thess. ii. 14: *αἱ ἐκκλησίαι αἱ οὖσαι ἐν τῇ Ἰουδαίᾳ*. It is noteworthy that St. Luke realises that Cæsarea does not belong to Judæa in the proper sense of the word; in xii. 19 and xxi. 10 he writes *κατελθὼν ἀπὸ τῆς Ἰουδαίας εἰς Καισαρίαν* and *κατῆλθέν τις ἀπὸ τῆς Ἰουδαίας προφήτης* [*εἰς Καισαρίαν*] respectively—note the coincidence here; xxi. 10 stands in a we-section—; but already, from viii. 26–40; ix. 32 *ff.* one recognises that St. Luke did *not* count Cæsarea and the whole belt of Philistian cities as belonging to Judæa, and yet he has no inclusive name for the region; in viii. 40 he writes:

[1] In the history of the Church the expectation of the near approach of the "Kingdom" has always had as a corollary the assembling of believers at one single place. We may accordingly assume that after the first appearances of our Lord in Galilee all or almost all of His adherents betook themselves to Jerusalem, where it was expected that the "Kingdom" would be revealed. Hence Galilee passed at once quite into the background (St. Paul speaks only of Churches in Judæa), and hence it is also explained why it happened that the first appearances of the Risen Christ in Galilee were replaced by appearances in Jerusalem. It was afterwards that churches gradually formed themselves in Galilee.

[2] The same expression: *καθ' ὅλης τῆς Ἰουδαίας* occurs also in x. 37.

Φίλιππος εὑρέθη εἰς Ἄζωτον, καὶ διερχόμενος εὐηγγελίζετο τὰς πόλεις πάσας ἕως τοῦ ἐλθεῖν αὐτὸν εἰς Καισαρίαν, and in ix. 32: ἐγένετο Πέτρον διερχόμενον διὰ πάντων [*scil.* all the brethren in the cities of the Philistian coast] κατελθεῖν καὶ πρὸς τοὺς ἁγίους τοὺς κατοικοῦντας Λύδδα.

Judæa occurs in some passages where we should expect Jerusalem, and *vice versâ*; but this is scarcely due to inaccuracy. That the Christian communities of Judæa in the first days, and for some considerable time, were only relatively independent, indeed were for the most part dependent upon the Church of Jerusalem, and were, one might say, really identical with that Church, is a fact which can be deduced from the Pauline epistles, and which answers to the natural course of development of all such organisations: the mother community remained at first "the Church," the rest were only in dependent filial relationship to her. St. Luke thus shows himself well-informed when in the cases in question he writes Jerusalem for Judæa, and *vice versâ*.

It is, however, believed that it can be proved that the author has made a mistake in writing Judæa in xxvi. 20: St. Paul did not preach, as St. Luke makes him say, in Judæa, not at least ἐν πάσῃ τῇ χώρᾳ τῆς Ἰουδαίας. It cannot, in fact, be proved that he did preach in Judæa, and before the time mentioned in Gal. i. 22 he cannot have done so; but why may he not have proclaimed the Gospel in this region on the occasion of later visits when he was journeying from Antioch or Cæsarea to Jerusalem? For this ministry days, not weeks, were quite sufficient, and he himself says (Rom. xv. 19): *ὥστε με ἀπὸ Ἱερουσαλὴμ . . . πεπληρωκέναι τὸ εὐαγγέλιον τοῦ Χριστοῦ.*

The centre of Judæa and of Christendom is Jerusalem. Here the name given to the city by St. Luke is of itself a matter of the deepest interest.[1] As is well known St. Mark uses *without exception* the name Ἱεροσόλυμα, so also St. Matthew (for the single passage where Ἱερουσαλήμ occurs [xxiii. 37] belongs to a quotation),[2] and St. John. On the other hand, St. Paul and St. Luke use sometimes Ἱεροσόλυμα and sometimes Ἱερουσαλήμ[3]—again a proof of their mutual relationship. In St. Paul's case we can without difficulty discern the rule which guides his use of the respective names: where Jerusalem has religious significance (Gal. iv. 25, 26), and in passages of special solemnity where the Apostle thinks of the "saints" in Jerusalem (Rom. xv. 25, 26, 31; here Jerusalem is everywhere combined with οἱ ἅγιοι) he writes Ἱερουσαλήμ, *i.e.* he chooses the *Hebrew* name, elsewhere he writes Ἱεροσόλυμα (Gal. i. 17: ἀνῆλθον εἰς Ἱεροσ., likewise i. 18; ii. 1 ἀνέβην εἰς Ἱεροσ.). Two instances only are left which do not seem to conform to the rule. In Rom. xv. 19 we read: *ὥστε με ἀπὸ Ἱερουσαλὴμ καὶ κύκλῳ μέχρι τοῦ Ἰλλυρικοῦ πεπληρωκέναι τὸ εὐαγγέλιον*, and 1 Cor. xvi. 3: *οὓς ἂν δοκιμάσητε δι' ἐπιστολῶν τούτους πέμψω ἀπενεγκεῖν τὴν χάριν ὑμῶν* [the alms that had been collected] *εἰς Ἱερουσαλήμ.* But in the second instance St. Paul is thinking of the

[1] *Cf.* Ramsay in *The Expositor*, 1907, p. 110 *ff.*

[2] *Vide* my work "The Sayings of Jesus," Williams & Norgate, 1908, pp. 29, 143, 103 *f.*, 168 *ff.*

[3] In the Apocalypse only Ἱερουσαλὴμ is found (iii. 12; xxi. 2, 10). So also in Hebrews (xii. 22).

saints in Jerusalem, and has therefore chosen the more sacred name; and in the first instance his feeling of reverent wonder at the grandeur of the work that had been accomplished through him may have led him to write the name Ἱερουσαλήμ.

In regard to St. Luke's usage in the Acts the matter is not quite so simple. First let us give a statistical summary of the occurrences of the two names:[1] —

Chaps. i.–vii. — Ἱεροσόλυμα once; Ἱερουσαλήμ eleven times.

Chaps. viii.–xv.—Ἱεροσόλυμα five times; Ἱερουσαλήμ fifteen times.

Chaps. xvi.–xxi. (without the we-sections).—Ἱεροσόλυμα twice; Ἱερουσαλήμ twice.

The we-sections.—Ἱεροσόλυμα four times; Ἱερουσαλήμ three times.

Chaps. xxii.–xxviii.—Ἱεροσόλυμα ten times; Ἱερουσαλήμ six times.

Here the first thing to notice is that St. Luke uses Ἱερουσαλήμ (thirty-seven times) very much more frequently than Ἱεροσόλυμα (twenty-two times). Seeing, however, that in his gospel he has written Ἱεροσόλυμα only four times (ii. 22; xiii. 22; xix. 28; xxiii. 7) while he writes Ἱερουσαλήμ twenty-six times, and seeing that almost the same ratio obtains in the first half of the Acts (Ἱεροσόλυμα six times, Ἱερουσαλήμ twenty-six times), it is at once evident

[1] The manuscripts of course vary, yet in each particular case it is possible with the highest degree of probability to ascertain which form St. Luke chose. We here leave D out of consideration.

that the author who, even as a Hellene, loved to imitate the antique style of sacred literature, had an especial affection for Ἱερουσαλήμ. In his gospel and in Acts i.–xv. taken together, Ἱερουσαλήμ occurs fifty-two times, Ἱεροσόλυμα only ten times.

The second thing to notice is that the problem is the same for the we-sections as for the whole book. If the author of the we-sections is not identical with St. Paul we should have to assume *three* writers who varied between Ἱεροσόλυμα and Ἱερουσαλήμ—unless indeed we assume that St. Luke has carefully worked through his source correcting it and bringing it into conformity with the rest of his work even in this point! But who will believe this!

In regard to the rule which governs the use of these two forms of the name in the Acts of the Apostles, something can be learned from the gospel. Here St. Luke in the parts which he has in common with St. Mark or St. Matthew, or with both, has in the first place written Ἱερουσαλήμ where these have Ἱεροσόλυμα; in the second place he has often inserted Jerusalem where they do not give the name of the city. Ἱεροσόλυμα *is only used by him in the gospel where he has no source before him, and in the purely geographical sense* (ii. 22: ἀνήγαγον αὐτὸν εἰς Ἱεροσ., xiii. 22: διεπορεύετο κατὰ πόλεις καὶ κώμας . . . πορείαν ποιούμενος εἰς Ἱεροσ.), xix. 28: ἐπορεύετο ἔμπροσθεν ἀναβαίνων εἰς Ἱεροσόλυμα, xxiii. 7: πρὸς Ἡρῴδην ὄντα καὶ αὐτὸν ἐν Ἱεροσ.). Ἱερουσαλήμ is thus for him the more sacred name, and, because almost the whole narrative of the gospel is noble and sacred, it is the proper word for constant use.

The same attitude towards the names is plainly discernible in chapters i.–vii. of the Acts and in the we-sections. In the former passage (chapters i.–vii.) the author has only *once* written Ἱεροσόλυμα (in the introduction i. 4), where he tells us that our Lord commanded His disciples not to depart at once from the place Jerusalem (ἀπὸ Ἱεροσολύμων μὴ χωρίζεσθαι); as for the rest of the passage everything in the early history of the Church is of so lofty a character that he only speaks of Ἱερουσαλήμ (eleven times). In the we-sections the reason of the variation between the two forms of the name is quite evident: in **xx. 16; xxi. 4, 15, 17** Ἱεροσόλυμα is written because the author is concerned simply with topographical notices (St. Paul wished to be in Jerusalem for Pentecost; St. Paul ought not to go up to Jerusalem; we took our journey up to Jerusalem; when, however, we arrived at Jerusalem). *But among these verses stands a saying of the prophet Agabus;* here we read in *oratio directa* (**xxi. 11**)*:* τὸν ἄνδρα . . . δήσουσιν ἐν Ἱερουσαλὴμ οἱ Ἰουδαῖοι, and now the bystanders take up this word Ἱερουσαλήμ (**xxi. 12**), and also St. Paul says (**xxi. 13**): ἀποθανεῖν εἰς Ἱερουσαλὴμ ἑτοίμως ἔχω. The Biblical form Ἱερουσαλήμ alone suited the solemnity of the whole scene. This may seem to us somewhat petty; and so it is. So ultra-refined was the feeling of the stylist St. Luke! Let there then be no doubt that he who wrote the gospel and Acts i.–vii. also wrote the we-sections! The manner in which the two forms of the name for Jerusalem are used is enough to show it.

At first sight the variation between the two forms

in chapters viii.–xxviii. (omitting the we-sections) appears to present greater difficulty. We are concerned with seventeen passages in which Ἱεροσόλυμα is read. Obviously Ἱεροσόλυμα is more frequently used since the narrative is no longer concerned with the earliest history of the Church of Jerusalem, and at the end, although the scene of action again returns to the soil of Palestine, Ἱερουσαλήμ is yet less frequently used than Ἱεροσόλυμα. But even in chapters xxii.–xxviii. where the former occurs only six times, while the latter occurs ten times, it is still possible to observe a peculiar and quite invariable rule. *In* xxii. 5, 17, 18; xxiii. 11; xxv. 3 *we read* Ἱερουσαλήμ, *for here Jerusalem is spoken of in Jerusalem itself; in* xxv. 1, 7, 9, 15, 20, 24; xxvi. 4, 10, 20; xxviii. 17 *we read* Ἱεροσόλυμα, *for Jerusalem is here spoken of in Cæsarea and* (xxviii. 17) *in Rome.* The *place* where the scene is located, not the speaker, makes the difference: St. Paul speaks in Jerusalem of Jerusalem, in Cæsarea and Rome of Hierosolyma.[1] There accordingly remain for consideration only seven more passages where Ἱεροσόλυμα is found, namely viii. 1, 14, 25; xi. 27; xiii. 13; xvi. 4, and xix. 21 (Ἱερουσαλήμ occurs seventeen times in these chapters, namely viii. 26, 27; ix. 2, 13, 21, 26, 28; x. 39; xi. 2, 22; xii. 25; xiii. 27, 31; xv. 2, 4; xx. 22; xxi. 31). Evidently Ἱερουσαλήμ is still the rule in this part of the Acts. The rule is broken where the scene

[1] In chapters xxii.–xxviii. (in sixteen instances) there is only *one* exception, namely xxiv. 11; here one would expect "Hierosolyma," yet we read "Jerusalem." But this exception proves the rule: St. Paul speaks of προσκυνεῖν in Jerusalem; this suggested the use of the sacred form (*cf.* viii. 27: προσκυνήσων εἰς Ἱερουσ.).

of action tends towards Samaria or is situated there (viii. 1, 14, 25); again when the narrator takes his stand in Antioch (xi. 27), in Perga (xiii. 13), in Lycaonia (xvi. 4), and in Ephesus (xix. 21); but seeing that in these sections St. Luke under the same conditions also speaks of Ἰερουσαλήμ, no fixed rule can be here established. We must confess that the variation in chapters viii.–xxi.—omitting the we-sections—is not to be explained, *i.e.* that St. Luke here (though he prefers Ἰερουσαλήμ) keeps to no rule; but in chapters i.–vii., in the we-sections, and in xxii.–xxviii. his rule can be clearly discerned. And yet the number of instances (where Ἰεροσόλυμα is used) where the rule is not clear is not more than seven.

In regard to the knowledge of Jerusalem and Judæa the passages wherein the author betrays a certain knowledge of his own are no less numerous in the Acts than in his gospel. The gospel contains an important body of traditions connected with Jerusalem and Judæa, and peculiar to St. Luke, which it is probable that the author acquired on the spot. One does not write in a gospel passages like: *κώμη ἀπέχουσα σταδίους ἑξήκοντα ἀπὸ Ἰερουσαλήμ, ᾗ ὄνομα Ἐμμαούς* unless one has been oneself on the spot. But we also read in the Acts (i. 12): *τότε ὑπέστρεψαν εἰς Ἰερουσαλὴμ ἀπὸ ὄρους τοῦ καλουμένου ἐλαιῶνος, ὅ ἐστιν ἐγγὺς Ἰερουσαλὴμ σαββάτου ἔχον ὁδόν*, again (i. 19): *ὥστε κληθῆναι τὸ χωρίον ἐκεῖνο τῇ διαλέκτῳ αὐτῶν Ἀχελδαμάχ, τοῦτ' ἔστιν χωρίον αἵματος*, again (viii. 26): *πορεύου κατὰ μεσημβρίαν ἐπὶ τὴν ὁδὸν τὴν καταβαίνουσαν ἀπὸ Ἰερουσαλὴμ εἰς Γάζαν· αὕτη ἐστὶν* ἔρημος.[1] The πέριξ πόλεις Ἰερουσαλήμ (v. 16) might also be mentioned here. St. Luke, moreover, knows of a definite ὑπερῷον in which the first disciples were wont to assemble;[2] he mentions the house of the mother of John and Mark (xii. 12: οὗ ἦσαν ἱκανοὶ συνηθροισμένοι καὶ προσευχόμενοι); he has a definite conception of the locality of the prison where St. Peter was confined and of its distance from the house just mentioned (xii. 10 *f.*: διελθόντες δὲ πρώτην φυλακὴν καὶ δευτέραν ἦλθαν ἐπὶ τὴν πύλην τὴν σιδηρᾶν τὴν φέρουσαν εἰς τὴν πόλιν . . . καὶ ἐξελθόντες προῆλθον ῥύμην μίαν . . . καὶ ὁ Πέτρος . . . ἦλθεν ἐπὶ τὴν οἰκίαν τῆς Μαρίας). Had he visited St. Paul in this same prison? He knows the gate of the Temple, which Josephus (Bellum, v. 5, 3) also calls the "Beautiful Gate" (iii. 2, 10: ἡ θύρα τοῦ ἱεροῦ ἡ λεγομένη ὡραία) and Solomon's Porch (iii. 11; v. 12: ἡ στοὰ ἡ καλουμένη Σολομῶντος), which is also mentioned in St. John (x. 23) and by Josephus ("Antiq.," xx. 9, 7).[3] He knows of the (priestly) στρατηγὸς τοῦ ἱεροῦ (iv. 1; v. 24, 26), likewise of the *cohors Romana auxiliaris*, which was stationed in the citadel Antonia (xxi. 31 *ff.*); he is acquainted with the situation of

[1] It can scarcely be meant that the road was deserted at the given time; for that κατὰ μεσημβρίαν means "mid-day," and not "towards the south," is not probable, in spite of Nestle (*Stud. u. Krit.*, 1892, s. 335 *f.*). The most probable meaning of the passage is that the road was always deserted, that is, passed through a desert region; in spite of this the Evangelist was to go along it. St. Luke, if he has added this note, must have known the road.

[2] He did not, however, know or did not think it necessary to tell us the exact locality in which the event recorded in ii. 1 *ff.* took place.

[3] Knowledge of the Temple is also presupposed in xxi. 30.

the *castra* in relation to the Temple, indeed even with the *ἀναβαθμοί* (xxi. 34, 37, 40). He has such correct knowledge of the Sadducees that he writes with precision (v. 17): *ὁ ἀρχιερεὺς καὶ πάντες οἱ σὺν αὐτῷ, ἡ οὖσα αἵρεσις τῶν Σαδδουκαίων.* Similarly, he shows himself well informed concerning the Pharisees; he knows that both parties were represented in the Sanhedrin (xxiii. 6); he knows the question on which the Pharisees and Sadducees were opposed (xxiii. 7): *Σαδδουκαῖοι μὲν γὰρ λέγουσιν μὴ εἶναι ἀνάστασιν μήτε ἄγγελον μήτε πνεῦμα, Φαρισαῖοι δὲ ὁμολογοῦσιν τὰ ἀμφότερα.* It is known to him that a considerable number (vi. 7: *πολὺς ὄχλος*) of both priests and also Pharisees (xv. 5) had joined the Christian community in Jerusalem, that the latter demanded that Gentile Christians in the Diaspora should be circumcised and observe the Law (*loc. cit.*), and that the Jewish Christians in Palestine, in spite of the decree of the Council of Jerusalem, all remained *ζηλωταὶ τοῦ νόμου* (xxi. 20). He knows that of the *γραμματεῖς* (iv. 5; vi. 12) a part belonged to the Pharisees and a part did not (xxiii. 9). He tells us that the Pharisee Gamaliel—*τίμιος παντὶ τῷ λαῷ*—interfered to a certain extent in favour of the Apostles (v. 34 *f.*), and that during the proceedings against St. Paul the Pharisees took his part against the Sadducees (xxiii. 9). It is not unknown to him (xxi. 27; xxiv. 18) that it was not so much native Jews, but Asiatic Jews, present in Jerusalem, who instigated the assault upon St. Paul in that city. It is not from St. Paul that we learn anything concerning the dispute between the "Hebrews" and the "Hellenists" in the Primitive Community, or concerning the choice of the "Seven" and their names, or concerning the heroic Stephen and his teaching against the Temple,[1] or concerning the gradual preparation for the transformation of Christian Judaism into Christianity which underlies all these events in the history of the Church of Jerusalem, but only from St. Luke (chaps. vi.–vii.); and it is St. Luke, not St. Paul, who, in the story of Ananias and Sapphira, has painted the shadows into the portrait of the "saints" of Jerusalem and makes us suspect many other shadows. All these things—in the first place, the topographical statements; in the second place, the more intimate acquaintance with the early history of the Church in Jerusalem—admirably agree with the information afforded by St. Luke himself, that he came to Jerusalem with St. Paul (and there shared with the Apostle the hospitality of an "old disciple, Mnason of Cyprus," xxi. 15, 16). We have already mentioned what other knowledge he had of Judæa. Let it be added that he knows that it took two days to travel from Jerusalem to Cæsarea by way of Antipatris (about 62 miles).[2] Of the cities on the coast Cæsarea and the towns lying to the south, the former is mentioned fifteen times in the book. St. Luke himself landed there (xxi. 8);

[1] Also chap. xxi. 28 is important from this point of view; here it is the Temple which is most thought of.

[2] Chap. xxiii. 31 *f.* This was not the first time that St. Paul had gone from Jerusalem to Cæsarea; already in ix. 30 we are told that the brethren escorted him thither from Jerusalem; in xviii. 22, however, we must not suppose that a journey from Cæsarea to Jerusalem and thence to Antioch is implied. Neither, on the other hand, was Cæsarea the goal of this journey; but the ship, in which St. Paul voyaged to the East, was bound for Cæsarea.

he knows it as the abode and centre of activity of the Evangelist St. Philip (*loc. cit.* and viii. 40); he speaks of the Church in that city (xviii. 22) and the brethren there (xxi. 16), also of the Prætorium which Herod the Great had built there (xxiii. 35); and he knows that St. Paul was confined there in mild imprisonment. That the σπεῖρα ἡ καλουμένη Ἰταλική was stationed in Cæsarea is, according to x. 1, quite probably meant by St. Luke; yet we cannot be certain that this was his meaning, and it is still less certain that St. Luke has here made a mistake (as Schürer contends, *Gesch. des jüd. Volks*, I.[3] s. 462 *f.*). The first missionary station of St. Philip in the southern cities seems to have been Azotus (viii. 40); thence he worked through the principal towns until he transferred his seat to Cæsarea (*loc. cit.*). Other places mentioned are Lydda (with Sharon) [1] and Joppa (ix. 32 *f.*, 36 *ff.*), with their Christian communities. They are specially mentioned because two great miracles were wrought in them by St. Peter. In spite of the exact statements that Lydda was nigh to Joppa (ix. 38), and that St. Peter dwelt in Joppa "in the house of one Simon a tanner, ᾧ ἐστιν οἰκία παρὰ θάλασσαν" (ix. 43; x. 6, 17)—tanning was an uncleanly trade [2]—the narratives do not give the impression that St. Luke himself had been in those parts. He speaks here on the strength of information the source of which was very near at hand. The first

[1] The plain of the coast stretching northwards from Lydda and Joppa is meant.

[2] If St. Peter enters into a house on the seashore and stays there a long time (ἡμέρας ἱκανάς, ix. 43), we may perhaps assume that his trade of fisherman influenced him. He was no tanner.

great success of the mission was not, however, in the parts of southern Palestine, but in Samaria. The Christian Hellenists dispersed by the persecution concerning Stephen and the same Philip who afterwards became the missionary of the Philistian cities, won over this region (viii. i. 5 *ff.*). The rejoicing concerning this first success is already reflected in i. 8 (ἐν πάσῃ τῇ 'Ιουδαίᾳ καὶ Σαμαρίᾳ, then follows at once ἔσχατον τῆς γῆς, *cf.* ix. 31: ἡ ἐκκλησία καθ' ὅλης τῆς 'Ιουδαίας . . . καὶ Σαμαρίας, also xv. 3), again in viii. 14: δέδεκται ἡ Σαμαρία τὸν λόγον τοῦ θεοῦ, and in the emphasis laid upon the fact that here the gospel had won its way into many villages (viii. 25); but even in the gospel of St. Luke we may trace a reflection of this conversion of Samaritans (ix. 52; x. 33; xvii. 11, 16, but see also St. John iv. 39 *f.*). Yet on the other hand, it is obvious that St. Luke had not himself seen the country so as to have a clear conception of its topography; he speaks only from second-hand information concerning "the city" (viii. 5), "the people" of Samaria (viii. 9), and the Church in that country. In reference to Tyre, Ptolemais, and Sidon (xxi. 3 *f.* 7; xxvii. 3) we hear that St. Luke, together with the Apostle, had learned something of the churches in these cities on flying visits. In Tyre their reception was especially hearty. The general name "Phœnicia" occurs thrice (xi. 19; xv. 3; xxi. 2) in the Acts. In the second passage it stands together with Samaria; in the first (according to viii. 1) Samaria is also to be supplied: διῆλθον [from Samaria] ἕως Φοινίκης καὶ Κύπρου καὶ 'Αντιοχείας—at that time the foundation of the Phœnician Church was laid by those who had been driven from Jerusalem; this Church, however, was at first according to xi. 19 purely Jewish-Christian—; the third passage is purely geographical. Phœnicia, like Judæa and Samaria, appears as an independent ecclesiastical "province," which cannot be said of the Philistian cities,[1] and to it we must also assign Damascus. Concerning this city St. Luke possesses special information, however improbable it is that he himself visited it. He knows that it had several synagogues (ix. 20), that one of its streets was called "ἡ εὐθεῖα" (ix. 11),[2] and that St. Paul took up his abode there in the house of a man named Judas.

Syria and Cilicia.

In the Acts Syria is mentioned three times purely geographically as the goal of the journeys of St. Paul (xviii. 18: ἐξέπλει εἰς τὴν Συρίαν, xx. 3: ἀνάγεσθαι εἰς τὴν Συρίαν, **xxi. 3**: ἐπλέομεν εἰς τὴν Συρίαν—notice here the consistency of expression, which was by no means a matter of course); in the two other passages, where it again occurs, it stands—just as in Gal. i. 21—together with Cilicia (xv. 23, 41), and here we learn that the two provinces in St. Luke's

[1] This answers to what we know of the later circumstances. The south-western cities of Palestine, including Cæsarea, did not form a proper ecclesiastical province, but were included with Judæa.

[2] Ἡ ῥύμη ἡ καλουμένη εὐθεῖα. This use of καλεῖσθαι is characteristic in regard to the consistency of St. Luke's style. It occurs about fifteen times in the gospel and likewise fifteen times in the Acts, including four times in the we-sections (**xxvii. 8, 14, 16**; **xxviii. 1**).

view formed a single ecclesiastical district.[1] It is the first great Gentile Christian district; in its centre stands Antioch and the church in that city. The foundation of this church forms the goal towards which the narrative tends even from vi. 1 *ff.*[2] St. Luke shows himself well informed concerning this community,[3] and regards it as, after Jerusalem, the second capital of Christendom.[4] He relates that

[1] This answers to the development in succeeding times, but also to the political situation in the time of St. Luke. Cilicia is yet again mentioned as the native country of St. Paul (xxi. 39; xxii. 3; xxiii. 34). In vi. 9 it stands together with Asia (Jews of Cilicia and Asia resident in Jerusalem), in **xxvii. 5** with geographical propriety together with Pamphylia (τὸ πέλαγος τὸ κατὰ τὴν Κιλικίαν καὶ Παμφυλίαν). Even in such small points St. Luke exhibits knowledge and conscientious care. This variation in the coupling of the province with other provinces is highly characteristic.

[2] In this connection it is also most significant, that the native place of only one of "the Seven" is mentioned (vi. 5: Νικόλαος προσήλυτος Ἀντιοχεύς).

[3] St. Luke knows nothing, or at least has told us nothing, of the Christian community in Tarsus. He only says that St. Paul came from that city and possessed the right of citizenship (Ταρσεύς) there (ix. 11; xxi. 39; xxii. 3), that the brethren of Jerusalem dispatched him thither by way of Cæsarea (ix. 30), and that after a seemingly long ministry St. Barnabas brought him thence to Antioch. The statement agrees admirably with Gal. i. 21.

[4] Of other Syrian cities St. Luke mentions only Seleucia, the haven of Antioch (xiii. 4), and that casually, without stating whether it possessed a Christian community. It is part of the author's literary custom to give the names of the havens, *cf.* the mention of Attalia (xiv. 25) of Neapolis (**xvi. 11**), of Cenchreae (xviii. 18). In xvii. 14 we read ἐξαπέστειλαν οἱ ἀδελφοὶ πορεύεσθαι ἕως ἐπὶ τὴν θάλασσαν. It may well be that St. Paul, in order to guard against plots, embarked at a point of the coast that lay out of the way (Ramsay, "St. Paul the Traveller" [1897], p. 70, 233, explains otherwise).

its foundation was Gentile Christian,[1] and mentions its founders;[2] he knows that at the very beginning it was extraordinarily flourishing (xi. 21: πολὺς ἀριθμός), that through the ministry of Barnabas, who came thither from Jerusalem,[3] it grew yet stronger (xi. 22–24), and that then for the space of a year it received instruction from St. Barnabas and St. Paul, whom the former had brought from Tarsus (xi. 25, 26).[4] He moreover knows (*loc. cit.*) that the name "Christians" arose in Antioch—of course invented by opponents; neither St. Paul nor the four Evangelists use it—; he knows an episode in the primitive history of the community—their offering on behalf of the brethren in Judæa;[5] and he has

[1] There exists a formal discrepancy between xi. 19 and xi. 20 (. . . Ἀντιοχείας, μηδενὶ λαλοῦντες τὸν λόγον εἰ μὴ Ἰουδαίοις and ἐλθόντες εἰς Ἀντιόχειαν ἐλάλουν καὶ πρὸς τοὺς Ἕλληνας), but the discrepancy is only brought about by stylistic awkwardness. We need not conclude therefrom that there must have been here two sources. Similar cases of pardonable awkwardness are also found elsewhere in the book.

[2] Chap. xi. 19: Some men of Cyprus and Cyrene of the number of those driven from Jerusalem. St. Barnabas the Cypriote did not belong to them; for it was not till later that he entered upon the mission in Antioch. On the other hand, the "old disciple" Mnason the Cypriote (xxi. 6), with whom St. Paul lodged at Jerusalem, may have belonged to them. St. Paul may even on this account have claimed his hospitality, because he had known him of old in Antioch.

[3] It is strange that Barnabas, who had been already mentioned at an earlier period, should here be again specially described (xi. 24). It may well be that the author wished in this way to explain and to emphasise the grandeur and the success of his work in Antioch.

[4] St. Luke thus distinguishes quite plainly three stages in the early history of the Church in Antioch.

[5] The importance which St. Luke seems to assign to this offering appears in an especially clear light if we remember what stress St. Paul laid upon the collections for Jerusalem. St. Paul continues what the Christians of Antioch had begun.

knowledge of the college of prophets and teachers in Antioch (xiii. 1): Barnabas, Simeon, surnamed Niger, Lucius of Cyrene, Mnason, once an intimate acquaintance of Herod the Tetrarch, and Paul. The great missionary journey of St. Barnabas and St. Paul he regards as an undertaking of the Church of Antioch (xiii. 1 *ff.* *οἱ ἐκπεμφθέντες*, xiv. 26 *f.*: *ἀνέπλευσαν εἰς Ἀντιόχειαν, ὅθεν ἦσαν παραδεδομένοι τῇ χάριτι τοῦ θεοῦ εἰς τὸ ἔργον ὃ ἐπλήρωσαν. παραγενόμενοι δὲ καὶ συναγάγοντες τὴν ἐκκλησίαν, ἀνήγγελλον ὅσα ἐποίησεν ὁ θεὸς μετ' αὐτῶν, καὶ ὅτι ἤνοιξεν τοῖς ἔθνεσιν θύραν πίστεως*). That the great controversy between the primitive community of Jerusalem and St. Paul was a controversy between Jerusalem and Antioch cannot be suspected from the Epistle to the Galatians; it is St. Luke who says this, and even expressly tells us that it was the Church of Antioch that had the high courage to take up the matter "officially," and that sent St. Paul and St. Barnabas with some others as delegates to Jerusalem (*οἱ ἀδελφοὶ ἔταξαν ἀναβαίνειν Παῦλον κ.τ.λ.—οἱ προπεμφθέντες ὑπὸ τῆς ἐκκλησίας*, xv. 1 *f.* 3). In the decree of the Council of Jerusalem the city of Antioch therefore is put first, then follow Syria and Cilicia (xv. 23). The city appears henceforth as so to say St. Paul's new home, whither again returns after his so-called second missionary journey (xviii. 18, 22). Only then does it vanish from the narrative.

The picture of this Church which one thus gains from the Acts of the Apostles is a very impressive, significant, and imposing one; and yet the Pauline epistles tell us nothing about it, with the exception of the painful scene of Gal. ii. 11 *f.* The representation given in the Acts fills a tremendous gap which has been left by the Pauline epistles. Indeed, we could not even suspect how great the gap is unless we possessed the accounts of St. Luke! Yet in these accounts there is nothing of that vivid distinctness which is to be found in most of the descriptions of the second half of the book; moreover, the actual amount of facts here recorded is not very great. The narrative depends not upon the personal experience and the eye-witness of the writer, but upon tradition.[1] We can control this tradition scarcely *at a single point;*[2] yet it contains nothing, so far as I can see, which is untenable, and much on the other hand which bears the stamp of trustworthiness. Abstract speculations concerning what may possibly be incorrect, or speculations which on *a priori* presuppositions would eliminate details of the tradition, are worthless.

The extraordinary prominence given to Antioch in the Acts may have been due to the actual importance of that Church,[3] but the ancient record that St.

[1] Even for this reason the "we" of codex D in xi. 28 is certainly not original; *vide Sitzungsber. der K. Preuss. Akad. d. Wissensch.*, 1899, April 6.

[2] If one restricts the old controversy, concerning the relationship of Gal. ii. to Acts xv., to Gal. ii. 1–2, and Acts xv. 1–4—and it is only with these verses that we are here concerned—we may declare that the two passages do not exclude one another. More than this cannot of course be said.

[3] Only after a comprehensive investigation of the sources of the first half of the book can it be ascertained how far the literary purpose of the author has contributed to give more prominence to Antioch than was given in his source. It is *a priori* possible that St. Luke has brought important questions into relationship with Antioch which really had no connection with that city.

Luke was a native of Antioch still remains most worthy of note in this connection. It of course does not therefore follow that he was ever a member of the Christian community of Antioch; indeed, the form in which this ancient record has come down to us is not even favourable to such a supposition.

Cyprus, Pamphylia, Pisidia, Lycaonia.

It is characteristic of the first mission of St. Paul and St. Barnabas in these regions that no dates are given. This in itself is a proof that the tradition from which St. Luke here draws was no longer exact. This conclusion is confirmed upon closer examination. St. Luke here only possessed the plan of the route and some anecdotes of the mission. More exact information concerning definite persons (eminent Christians, magistrates, hosts, &c.) are entirely wanting. "The Jews," "the Greeks," and some other generalities—of these he and his readers must make what they can.[1]

The description of the journey across Cyprus, whither the first missionaries had come from Jerusalem at a very early date and before the ministry of St. Paul, through the city Salamis—here St. Luke knows of the existence of several Jewish synagogues (xiii. 5)—and Paphos, is correctly given (xiii. 5, 6). That the proconsul resided in Paphos is also correct. Nothing is told us of St. Paul's success in Cyprus (with the exception of the gaining over of Sergius

[1] Ramsay, "St. Paul," p. 89 *ff.*, reads an incredible amount of information between the lines of chaps. xiii. and xiv., and entirely ignores the general want of precision throughout these chapters.

Paulus). The mission in Cyprus—taken up again some years later by St. Barnabas and St. Mark—is immediately followed (xiii. 14) by the mission in Antioch of Pisidia (the seaport Attalia is first mentioned in xiv. 25 on the return journey, when the mission in Perga is also recorded; Perga is only mentioned in xiii. 13 because St. Mark here separated himself from St. Paul).[1] The choice of a place of only moderate importance as the base of the mission, and generally the decision to start the mission to Asia Minor in Pisidia and Galatian Phrygia—a country that could be reached from the Pamphylian coast only by a long and dangerous journey—imply on the one hand the foregoing of a ministry to Hellenes, and on the other hand a decided purpose to minister to the Barbarians.[2] The large number of Jews in those regions does not explain this decision;[3] St. Paul could have found just as many large colonies of Jews on the coast. Wendt gives the correct explanation when he says: "It required at a later time special Divine intimations to induce St. Paul to approach genuine Hellenes as a missionary." The author shows in xiii. 49 how the success of the mission in the city extended to the whole surrounding country. The use of the word *χώρα* here is perhaps not accidental. An inscription has been found in Antioch which speaks of a *ἑκατοντάρχης ῥεγεωνάριος*.[4] But it

[1] Ramsay, "St. Paul," p. 89 *f.*, thinks otherwise.

[2] So we must judge—if the route was as St. Luke describes.

[3] This is the opinion of Blass; Ramsay gives a noteworthy explanation of the decision to go to Antioch in Pisidia (*loc. cit.* p. 92 *f.*).

[4] Ramsay, *loc. cit.* p. 103.

must nevertheless remain questionable whether St. Luke here was thinking of a "regio" of which Antioch, as a Roman colony, was the centre under the Roman Administration. The general significance of the word χώρα is at least equally possible here. The account of the mission in Iconium (xiv. 1–6) is quite formal in its style, and is moreover confused; but from the geographical point of view it is correct that the entry into a new province should be marked at Lystra,[1] and that in xiv. 19 the two cities of Antioch and Iconium, in spite of their considerable distance from one another, should be mentioned in close combination.

St. Paul betakes himself in flight (xiv. 6) to the cities of Lycaonia, Lystra (rightly put first),[2] and Derbe and εἰς τὴν περίχωρον.[3] Ramsay (*loc. cit.* p. 110 *ff.*) again lays great stress upon the circumstance that the χώρα is also mentioned in this passage. I cannot follow him here. The very expression περίχωρος, which is also used by St. Luke in his gospel

[1] It is probably true that at this time Iconium belonged, from an administrative point of view, to Lycaonia; but according to its nationality and its earlier history (Xen., *Anab.* i. 2, 19) it belonged to Pisidian Phrygia, and even in later times was still regarded as a Phrygian city (Acta Justini. 3; Firmil. in Cypr. Ep. lxxv. 7).

[2] In xvi. 1 Derbe rightly stands first, because St. Paul is coming from the south. It is straining at gnats to pay so much attention to the fact that St. Luke in xiv. 6 first mentions Lystra and Derbe together, then writes separately about Lystra and then about Derbe, and to conclude therefore that we have here different sources.

[3] The description of the route and of the trials which were endured receives good attestation from 2 Tim. iii. 10 (so also the account that Timothy came from Lystra): παρηκολούθησας . . . τοῖς διωγμοῖς, τοῖς παθήμασιν, οἷά μοι ἐγένετο ἐν Ἀντιοχείᾳ, ἐν Ἰκονίῳ, ἐν Λύστροις.

(iii. 3; iv. 14, 37; vii. 17; viii. 37), and by St. Mark (i. 28) before him, and by St. Matthew (iii. 3; xiv. 35) along with him, of itself makes it very improbable that he could here have had in his mind the special meaning which the word "regio" may have had for the country in question. If he had had this in his mind he would not have written ἡ περίχωρος, but χώρα or another word. Lystra could be reached from Iconium in a day,[1] Derbe from Lystra also in a day; yet the latter distance was greater. Both cities were seemingly unimportant.[2] St. Paul's flight thither

[1] Hence in xvi. 2 "the brethren in Lystra and Iconium" could also be mentioned together. Timothy, who belonged to Lystra, was also known to, and respected by, the neighbouring Church of Iconium. The combination of these two cities is not discrepant with the other combination (xiv. 19), where Antioch and Iconium occur together (*vide supra*). In xvi. 2 we have a combination suggested by the mere proximity of the two cities, in xiv. 19 one probably given by the united conspiracy of the Jews of the larger cities Antioch and Iconium against the ministry of the Apostle in the whole neighbourhood. It is strange that Derbe is not mentioned in xvi. 2: it follows that the churches of Iconium and Lystra were more closely connected than those of Derbe and Lystra, and this is explained by their greater proximity. The accuracy of the book at once strikes the reader as he considers the following combinations: (1) Lystra and Derbe are mentioned together as genuine Lycaonian cities, in distinction from the Phrygian cities Antioch and Iconium; (2) Lystra and Iconium are mentioned together in speaking of their churches, because the cities were very near to one another, and because a notable Christian of the one church was also known to the other; (3) Antioch and Iconium are mentioned together because the powerful bodies of Jews in those cities guarded the interests of Judaism in the whole province.

[2] In xiv. 6, 21, and xvi. 1 we read Λύστραν [in xiv. 21 τὴν Λ.], in xiv. 8 and xvi. 2, however, and in 2 Tim. iii. 11 Λύστροις. (The inscriptions only afford us the nominative Lustra, which decides nothing.) To conclude from this that we have here different sources is unjustifiable, and involves a strange conception of the

perhaps implied a change in his original plan; but we can never arrive at certainty on this point. The decisive turn had been taken in the journey from Pisidian Antioch to Iconium—*i.e.* towards the south-east, *i.e.* towards Tarsus (and Syrian Antioch)—St. Paul simply continues in this direction. That he did not follow this road to the end, but turned back upon his route, is strange and does not admit of further explanation. Did he shrink from making his way into the wild territory of Isauria? The people with whom the Apostle had to do in Lystra spoke the language of Lycaonia (xiv. 11); they did not therefore belong to the Greek or Latin [1] upper classes, but to the native and probably poorer classes. Derbe forms the turning-point of this journey of the Apostle. He returns by the same route (*vide supra*), and now the mission in Pamphylia (Perga) is first mentioned

procedure of the writer. We must perhaps assume that it is a case of irregular declension of a foreign proper noun, though there is here no special attestation, yet see Kühner-Blass, I. (1890), s. 492 *ff.*; Moulton, "A Grammar of New Testament Greek" (1906), p. 48; Ramsay (*loc. cit.* p. 129) who refers to Μύρα, acc. -αν and genit. -ων. The Isaurian cities with unusual names were treated as neuter plurals (*vide e.g.* the subscriptions to the decree of the Council of Nicæa); at the same time it might easily happen that a name like Lystra, which had a Greek sound, was declined in the accusative, seemingly like a noun of the first declension. Examples of such mixture are by no means wanting, indeed the addition of an irregular ν has actual attestation. In ix. 32, 35 the best codices treat Λύδδα as neuter plural (but C E H L P, &c., read Λύδδαν), yet in ix. 38 Λύδδας occurs as genitive singular. In ix. 35 we read in some authorities τον Σαρωνα, in others τον Σαρωναν; and in xxi. 1 εις τὴν Κῶ and εἰς τὴν Κῶν.

[1] Ramsay (*Expositor*, September, 1905) remarks that the most ancient graves in Lystra bear Latin inscriptions, while in Iconium Greek is the rule.

(xiv. 24 *f.*). On his second missionary journey the Apostle travelled by land through Syria and Cilicia, and came once again into these regions (xv. 41; xvi. 1 *f.*); but St. Luke gives us no further information of a geographical character.[1] The πόλεις (xvi. 4) may, however, have also included other cities than the four mentioned in chaps. xiii. and xiv.

Phrygia and Galatia (Mysia, Bithynia, Pontus).

Following the Acts of the Apostles, we usually speak of three missionary journeys of St. Paul; but the author did not so count them. He distinguishes the mission in Cyprus, Pisidia, Lycaonia, and Pamphylia (chaps. xiii.–xiv.) from a second great missionary undertaking which he describes in chaps. xv. 36–xxi. 17. Within this period there occurs a return to Antioch (xviii. 18–22), but the unity and continuity of the whole is not affected thereby. *In regard to this second missionary undertaking St. Luke was interested only in the mission on the coasts of the Ægean Sea.* In consequence the mission in Phrygia and Galatia is scarcely touched upon in his book. Nevertheless in xvi. 6, by means of the characteristic word διέρχεσθαι and in xviii. 23 by this same word combined with στηρίζειν πάντας τοὺς μαθητάς, it is clearly intimated that St. Paul had planted the Gospel in these regions; while

[1] In xvi. 1–3 Derbe and Lystra are yet again mentioned only for the purpose of telling how it was that Timothy, who belonged to the latter city, came into contact with St. Paul. St. Luke has thus a special interest in this companion of St. Paul, and very naturally so, seeing that he himself had worked together with him.

in regard to Mysia [1] (παρελθόντες, xvi. 8) and Bithynia (ἐπείραζον εἰς τὴν Βιθυνίαν πορευθῆναι, καὶ οὐκ εἴασεν αὐτοὺς τὸ πνεῦμα Ἰησοῦ) we are told why it was that in spite of St. Paul's own purpose to preach in those countries no mission was started there,[2] except in the Mysian port Troas (xvi. 9, 11; xx. 6 *ff*.). The passage xvi. 6–9 is one of the most remarkable in the whole book; for at the very moment when St. Paul makes up his mind to pass over to the genuinely Greek world, St. Luke here tells us of plans of the Apostle which he was not permitted to carry out. Seeing that we cannot regard all this as mere invention or supposition the passage accordingly shows intimate knowledge, on the author's part, of circumstances which occurred just before the we-sections begin. If, moreover, the passage as a whole is only intelligible in connection with the we-account, namely, as a prelude to it, so also in its details it testifies that the author of the we-account is identical with the author of the whole book. What is narrated in xvi. 6–9 presupposes information derived from St. Paul himself. He purposed to journey from Galatia westward to the coast, *i.e.* to Ephesus, Smyrna, &c.; but the "Spirit" restrained him; he then went northeastwards towards Mysia with the object of preaching in Bithynia, *i.e.* in the great cities, Nicomedia, Prusa, &c.; but the accomplishment of this plan also was

[1] Mysia was not a Roman province. St. Luke, who elsewhere as a rule mentions the provinces, here selects the old name in order to give distinct expression to the geographical situation.

[2] Nothing at all is said about Pontus; it only occurs in ii. 9; and we are casually told in xviii. 2, that Aquila was a Jew of Pontus.

forbidden "by the Spirit of Jesus." Finally, he was also led through Mysia without venturing to preach there, and at last arrived at Troas; yet even here he had not reached the appointed goal, but the Spirit directed him to Macedonia. The final direction of the Spirit embodied itself in the vision by night of the Man of Macedonia. Nothing in the book approaches the conviction with which at this place the leading of the Apostle by the Spirit is pictured. In this way St. Luke heralds, not the entry of a new source, but the coming of St. Paul to Macedonia and his own meeting with St. Paul. According to Ramsay St. Luke himself was the man of Macedonia—an attractive conjecture, which had also once suggested itself to me before I knew of Ramsay's hypothesis—but it cannot be proved, and there is also much to be said against it. In its favour stands the circumstance that the appearance of the "we" at this point would receive a good explanation, and would no longer startle us like a sudden pistol-shot. It would well suit the delicacy of St. Luke's literary feeling that he should have introduced himself in this way, hinting that St. Paul learned to know him in Troas, and that God had used him as a means to bring the Apostle to Macedonia. But the thread here is too fine, and, moreover, it cannot be proved that St. Luke was at home in Macedonia. As for the unfulfilled plans of the Apostle, his sudden passage from Galatia to Macedonia—without preaching in the countries on his way!—is so paradoxical that it can neither have been invented nor does it admit of a "rational" explanation. The epithet "rational" can only be applied to the Apostle's original purpose to preach either in the cities on the west coast of Asia or in those of Bithynia or Mysia. The prohibition, however, when given certainly had for its positive side the thought of passing on to Macedonia, and perhaps even of passing on to Rome, for we cannot understand why Macedonia and Achaia should have been preferred before Asia. The eye fixed on Rome would explain the decision; it therefore needed a new and special revelation to summon the Apostle to the mission in Macedonia and to hold him there. In any case the unique character of the narrative in xvi. 6–9 prepares any one with literary perception for the entrance of the "we" at this point. It is in form only that the entrance is abrupt; in reality the intended contrast and at the same time the close connection with the context are as clear as possible. Only compare:—

> They were forbidden by the Holy Ghost to preach the Word in Asia.
>
> They assayed to go into Bithynia, but the Spirit of Jesus suffered them not.
>
> They passed by Mysia [so willed the Spirit] and came to Troas.
>
> [The vision in Troas: the man of Macedonia.]
>
> Straightway *we* sought to go forth into Macedonia, concluding that God had called *us* to preach the Gospel to them.

Under the assumption of a we-source it would be necessary to make such a source begin as far back as xvi. 6; but it is not in this style that a man writes who is simply passing on to a new source; rather the eager joyous rush of the narrative at this point implies a writer who is personally interested in what he narrates, and now wishes to pass on to things *quorum pars magna fuit.*

In Phrygia and "the Galatian region"—here at least the word χώρα is really highly significant, *vide supra*—St. Paul had actually preached the Gospel on a former occasion. Seeing that according to xvi. 1, 4, 6, first Derbe and Lystra, then "the cities," then Phrygia, then the Γαλατικὴ χώρα are named in order, and that then we at last are informed that at this point St. Paul wished to turn his steps towards Asia, it therefore follows that he travelled from Lystra to Iconium and Pisidian Antioch, and that after he had worked in south-eastern Phrygia he left Pisidian Antioch, travelling northwards (probably north-eastwards, for a route straight northwards would have led him into uninhabited regions). Here he worked in a district where cities were few, among the Galatians, to whom he afterwards wrote an epistle, and from Galatia he purposed to pass by way of Sardis to Smyrna or Ephesus; but this was forbidden him. When he came a second time into the Galatian χώρα this region is mentioned before Phrygia (xviii. 23), it follows that St. Paul on this occasion journeyed from Cilicia straight to the north-west, and then turned from Galatia towards Northern Phrygia. Thence διελθὼν τὰ ἀνωτερικὰ μέρη (xix. 1) he arrived at Ephesus, *i.e.* he now carried out the plan which he was prevented from carrying out previously (chap. xvi.). The "ἀνωτερικὰ μέρη" *scil.* τῆς Ἀσίας, situated between Phrygia and the Ephesian coastland, are the mountainous district of Lydia bordering on north-western Phrygia (on the road which leads to Sardis from the interior).

All that St. Luke directly or indirectly tells us concerning the provinces, countries, and cities of Asia Minor, and concerning the routes of St. Paul's journeys, is unexceptionable from the geographical standpoint. There is no flaunting of geographical erudition, but what is necessary is always given in correct form. The by no means insignificant culture of the author, who keeps the map in his head, as well as the homogeneity of his work, are herein conspicuously displayed.

Asia, Macedonia, Achaia.

Wherever in this book "Asia" stands together with another province, or where it denotes Ephesus and the neighbourhood, Asia in the narrower sense of the word (Asia proconsul.) is intended, *vide* ii. 9 (*Πόντον καὶ τὴν Ἀσίαν*, it always has the article except in vi. 9), vi. 9 (*Κιλικίας καὶ Ἀσίας*), xvi. 6 (with Phrygia, the *Γαλατικὴ χώρα*, Mysia and Bithynia), xix. 22 (with Macedonia and Achaia; here it moreover stands for Ephesus and the neighbourhood), xx. 16, 18; xxi. 27; xxiv. 28 (here also it stands for Ephesus). The province must also be understood in xx. 4 (*Ἀσιανοὶ δὲ Τυχικὸς καὶ Τρ.*), and also probably in xix. 10 (because as a result of the long stay of the Apostle *πάντες οἱ κατοικοῦντες τὴν Ἀσίαν* were enabled to hear the Word of the Lord). Nevertheless it is not always quite certain, and in xix. 26, 27 (*οὐ μόνον Ἐφέσου ἀλλὰ σχεδὸν πάσης τῆς Ἀσίας*

—ὅλη ἡ Ἀσία καὶ ἡ οἰκουμένη) it may be doubted whether the province is meant or whether the word has the wider significance. Seeing, however, that the province is also to be understood in **xxvii. 2** (ἐπιβάντες πλοίῳ Ἀδραμυττηνῷ, μέλλοντι πλεῖν εἰς τοὺς κατὰ τὴν Ἀσίαν τόπους)—for the ship of Adramyttium (Mysia) was bound for its native shores, *i.e.* for the province of Asia—it follows that it is improbable that in any part of the book Asia means anything else than the Roman province of Asia.

The coast of Asia from Samothrace (**xvi. 11**) and Troas to Patara and Myrra in Lycia (**xxi. 1** and **xxvii. 5**) is specially well known to the author. Assos (**xx. 13** *f.*), Adramyttium (**xxvii. 2**), Mitylene in Lesbos (**xx. 14**), Chios (**xx. 15**), Samos (**xx. 15**), Trogilium (**xx. 15**, *vide infra*), Ephesus (vv. ll.), Miletus (**xx. 15, 17**), Cos (**xxi. 1**), Cnidus (**xxvii. 7**), and Rhodes (**xxi. 1**), are mentioned by name. Also the distance of the places from one another are familiar to him. As a result of the disastrous voyage which he made we are specially well-informed concerning Crete (**xxvii. 7, 12, 13, 21**): Salmone on the eastern promontory (**xxvii. 7**), Kaloi Limenes and Lasea (**xxvii. 8**)—neither of these places is mentioned in ancient authors; they are to be found on the southern promontory — Phœnice (**xxvii. 12**, mentioned by Ptolemy, and to be found on the western portion of the southern coast), and the island Cauda (Gaudos, **xxvii. 16**), are all noted.[1] Nothing is said anywhere

[1] In **xxvii. 17** the Syrtes and in **xxvii. 27** the Adriatic are mentioned. Mommsen was of opinion that in the latter passage the author must be charged with a serious geographical blunder. There is no justification for this charge.

in the book of a mission in Crete. The author shows fairly detailed knowledge of Ephesus (mentioned eight times between xviii. 19 and xx. 17; Ἐφέσιοι xix. 28, 34, 35; xxi. 29), though we cannot ascertain from the Acts whether he himself had visited that city. On the so-called second missionary journey St. Paul only paid the city a passing visit, yet his ministry found at first a favourable reception in the synagogue there (xviii. 19, 20). The real founders of the Ephesian Church were Priscilla and her husband (xviii. 18 *f.*) together with the so-called "disciples of John." During the third missionary journey St. Paul at first, for three months, made the synagogue the centre of his work (xix. 8), then for two years he worked directly among the Gentiles of the city. We are told that he taught daily ἐν τῇ σχολῇ Τυράννου (xix. 9). This sounds as if the school were known to the first readers of the Acts. The fact that the number of Jews in Ephesus was very large is clearly expressed in the book, and the local colouring in the narrative of the riot of the silversmiths is most appropriate, although it is plain that St. Luke was not present. His authorities here would have been Gaius and Aristarchus of Macedonia. It is quite evident that the narrator regards the mission in Ephesus as at the same time a mission to the whole of Asia. Not only did the numerous provincials visiting Ephesus hear the Word of God (xix. 10), but it is suggested in passages where St. Luke writes Asia while we should expect Ephesus (*vide supra*) that St. Paul made missionary journeys from Ephesus. It is distinctly stated (xix. 1) that he passed through the mountainous districts of the province (*vide supra*), and his farewell discourse to the Ephesian elders in Miletus is reported as if it were a farewell to the whole of Asia. Of the cities in the interior of the province Thyatira alone is once cursorily mentioned (xvi. 14).

The province of Macedonia, whose churches stood in the closest personal relationship to the Apostle, is often mentioned in chaps. xvi.–xx. (see also xxvii. 2). In xix. 21 Macedonia and Achaia stand together as in Rom. xv. 26 and 1 Thess. i. 7, 8. Philippi is the first Macedonian city—and at the same time the first European city—to which St. Paul brought the Gospel. It is also the only Christian community the history of whose foundation is related in the we-sections. It is therefore the more important that the planting of the Church in this city proceeds *mutatis mutandis* in the same way as that of the other churches (St. Paul begins with the Jews). The details of the narrative are, however, as might be expected, specially vivid and trustworthy (the rôle which St. Luke assigns to himself [he does not belong, as do Timothy and Erastus, to the διακονοῦντες τῷ Παύλῳ xix. 22], the προσευχὴ ἔξω τῆς πύλης παρὰ ποταμόν, Lydia the πορφυρόπωλις πόλεως Θυατείρων, the reception into her house, the girl with the dæmon, the στρατηγοί). Yet such traits are found only in the first half of the account, the second half (the imprisonment and the release of St. Paul) leaves much to be desired; *but just here the "we" is wanting.* St. Luke had therefore again left the Apostle; probably he had returned to Asia. If he were at that time at home in Philippi, perhaps temporarily, as Ramsay supposes—an hypothesis which is favoured by the fact that in **xx. 6** he joins the Apostle a second time at Philippi—he must at this time have left the town for unknown reasons; for he was not involved in the fate which overtook St. Paul and Silas in Philippi. It is unsafe to conclude that the remarkable description of Philippi (*ἥτις ἐστὶν πρώτη τῆς μερίδος Μακεδονίας πόλις κολωνία* **xvi. 12**) is due to special local patriotism on the part of St. Luke. The import of this note, the interpretation of which is moreover not clear,[1] is fairly obvious if one considers that Philippi was by no means a very important city and that its Jewish population was only small. To explain why St. Paul came first to this place (passing by Samothrace and Neapolis **xvi. 11**), all is said that could be said in favour of its importance. At the same time it still remains unexplained why St. Paul passed so hurriedly from Galatia (!) straight to Philippi; and it still remains an attractive hypothesis that it was St. Luke, who, having relations of some kind with Philippi, influenced the Apostle to go to that city.

In reference to Thessalonica (xvii. 1, 11, 13), the native city of Aristarchus and Secundus (xx. 4; **xxvii. 2**), which St. Paul reached by the great road

[1] It contains an error if it was intended to signify that Philippi was the capital of that district (*μέρις*) of Macedonia; for Amphipolis was the capital. Perhaps the words may be translated "the most considerable city that was a colony in the particular district of Macedonia." Blass's conjecture, *πρώτης* for *πρώτη τῆς*, is ingenious and elegant, yet scarcely right, seeing that *πρῶτος* in the sense of "prominent" is usual with St. Luke (*vide* St. Luke xix. 47; Acts xiii. 50; xvii. 4; xxv. 2; xxviii. 7, 17); and on the other hand, one does not expect so detailed a statement as "in the first district."

passing through Amphipolis and Apollonia (xvii. 1),[1] we only learn that there was a synagogue there (*loc. cit.*; if ἡ συναγωγή is to be read we must assume that it was the only synagogue in the district), that St. Paul was entertained there by one Jason, that he preached on three Sabbath days in the synagogue, and that the magistrates of the city were called "Politarchs." As for the rest of Macedonia mention is made of the mission in Berœa (xvii. 10, 13), where the Jews were more friendly disposed. From Berœa came Sopater the son of Pyrrhus (xx. 4), the companion of St. Paul. The addition of the name of the father—unusual in the Acts—would show that the man was of good birth. The name "Pyrrhus" is, besides, characteristic of the country.

Achaia is first mentioned where Gallio residing in Corinth is described as ἀνθύπατος τῆς Ἀχαΐας (xviii. 12). Elsewhere it is found again only twice: xviii. 27 (Apollos wishes to go from Ephesus into Achaia, *i.e.* to Corinth to work as an evangelist, but not exclusively in that city) and xix. 21 (St. Paul determines to pass through Macedonia and Achaia). In xx. 2 instead of Achaia we find "Hellas" (here only in the New Testament). The provincial council of the Achæans calls itself in an inscription of the time of Caligula (*vide* Guirand, *Les Assemblées Provinc. dans l'empire romaine*, Paris, 1887, p. 116) Πανέλληνες, πάντες οἱ Ἕλληνες, σύνοδος τῶν Ἑλλήνων. This varia-

[1] Διοδεύσαντες, τὴν Ἀμφίπολιν καὶ τὴν Ἀπολλωνίαν ἦλθον εἰς Θεσσαλονίκην. Not only the article before the first two cities, but likewise the verb διοδεύειν [only here in the Acts, but see St. Luke viii. 1] proves that St. Luke is thinking of the well-known road (*vide supra*).

tion between Achaia and Hellas is characteristic of the Hellenic author.

The description of the visit to Athens (xvii. 15, 16, 21, 22; xviii. 1) is not only of special nobility and beauty, but also, so far as we are able to judge, both appropriate and unexceptionable. The synagogue in that city, the Agora, the Areopagus,[1] the Epicureans and Stoics are mentioned. The characterisation of these people and the gentle sarcasm of his words concerning the Athenians (xvii. 21: Ἀθηναῖοι πάντες καὶ οἱ ἐπιδημοῦντες ξένοι—he knows also of these people—*εἰς οὐδὲν ἕτερον ηὐκαίρουν ἢ λέγειν τι ἢ ἀκούειν τι καινότερον*), the poetical quotation, and every detail, betray the cultured writer who paints his portraits on a background of the very best tradition. The use that is made of "the Unknown God," which need not necessarily be changed into "the unknown gods," is a masterpiece of art, and I do not see why we must ascribe this masterpiece to St. Luke and not to St. Paul himself. The discourse, spoken in such a place, may well have dwelt in the memory of those who heard it, and the author with perfect integrity has recorded the slight results of St. Paul's teaching.

During the so-called second missionary journey St. Paul worked for eighteen months in Corinth (xviii. 1, 8; xix. 1). However, as usual, only the beginning and close of the ministry is pictured in the book. St. Paul abode first with Aquila and Priscilla (xviii. 3), then with one Titius Justus in the neighbourhood of the syna-

[1] Here Curtius' explanation seems to me untenable.

gogue.[1] The port of Cenchreæ is mentioned in xviii. 18. On the third journey the Apostle once again spent three months in "Hellas," *i.e.* in Corinth and the province (xx. 2 *f.*).

[1] Interest in the houses in which St. Paul (or St. Peter) had stayed—sometimes with detailed descriptions—may be traced through the whole of the book. Here again we have a trait which shows the close connection between the we-sections and the other parts of the book.

St. Paul stays in Damascus ἐν οἰκίᾳ Ἰούδα in the street that is called "straight" (ix. 11).

St. Peter stays in Joppa παρά τινι Σιμῶνι βυρσεῖ, ᾧ ἐστιν οἰκία παρὰ θάλασσαν (ix. 43; x. 6).

St. Paul stays (μένειν) in Philippi with the purple-seller Lydia (**xvi. 13** *ff.*).

He stays in Thessalonica ἐν τῇ οἰκίᾳ Ἰάσονος (xvii. 5).

He stays (μένειν) in Corinth first with Priscilla and Aquila (xviii. 3).

He next stays in Corinth ἐν οἰκίᾳ τινὸς ὀνόματι Τιτίου Ἰούστου, οὗ ἡ οἰκία ἦν συνομοροῦσα τῇ συναγωγῇ (xviii. 7).

He stays (μένειν) in Cæsarea with the evangelist Philip τούτῳ δὲ ἦσαν θυγατέρες τέσσαρες παρθένοι προφητεύουσαι (**xxi. 9**).

He stays in Jerusalem with one Μνάσων Κύπριος, ἀρχαῖος μαθητής (**xxi. 16**).

He stays (μένειν) in Rome καθ' ἑαυτὸν σὺν τῷ φυλάσσοντι αὐτὸν στρατιώτῃ (**xxviii. 16**), or again, he stays (ἐμμένειν) there ἐν ἰδίῳ μισθώματι . . . ἀκωλύτως (**xxviii. 31**).

Cf. also the ὑπερῷον, οὗ ἦσαν καταμένοντες in Jerusalem (i. 13); the ὑπερῷον in Lydda (ix. 37, 39); the house of Mary the mother of St. Mark in Jerusalem (xii. 12); the house of the jailor in Philippi (xvi. 34); the ὑπερῷον in Troas, οὗ ἦμεν συνηγμένοι (**xx. 8**); the σχολὴ Τυράννου in Ephesus (xix. 9). How do the supporters of the we-source hypothesis stand in the face of a situation like this? Of these passages six stand in the we-sections, nine in the remaining parts of the book. It must be assumed, I suppose, that the author of the whole book was interested in "houses," and had the fortune to meet with the account of an eye-witness who was likewise interested in "houses"!!

Italy.

Italy and Rome lie on the horizon of the author of the Acts, and are terms which mark the limits of the scope of his work. St. Luke says in xviii. 2 of Aquila and his wife Priscilla that they had *προσφάτως* come from Italy, meaning thereby, as is shown by the conclusion of the verse, Rome. Likewise we read in the we-sections (**xxvii. 2**): "when it was determined that we should take ship for Italy" while Rome is intended. Also in a third passage (**xxvii. 6**) Italy perhaps stands for Rome; for it is here most natural to think of an Alexandrian corn-ship bound for Rome.

"Romans" are already mentioned in the list of nations (ii. 10); but as the goal of the journeys of St. Paul Rome appears first in xix. 21 (in Ephesus during the third journey). Then in xxiii. 11 we find the most significant words of Christ to the Apostle: *ὡς διεμαρτύρω τὰ περὶ ἐμοῦ εἰς Ἰερουσαλήμ, οὕτω σε δεῖ καὶ εἰς Ῥώμην μαρτυρῆσαι* (Jerusalem and Rome!). These words are again taken up in **xxvii. 24** (here the emperor stands in the place of Rome), and the arrival in Rome is at last recorded in **xxviii. 14, 16.**[1] We, however, learn but little of the Christians and the Jews in Rome. Of places belonging to Italy, Malta (**xxviii. 1** *ff.*), Syracuse (**xxviii. 12**), Rhegium (**xxviii. 13**), Puteoli (**xxviii. 13**), Appii Forum and

[1] Ῥωμαῖος has the meaning "Roman citizen" in xvi. 21, 27, 38; xxii. 25–27, 29; xxiii. 27. In xxv. 16 it occurs in a wider sense: *οὐκ ἔστιν ἔθος Ῥωμαίοις*, and here the Roman sense of justice is commended.

the Tres Tabernæ (xxviii. 15) are mentioned. The author presupposes in his readers a knowledge of the two last places, though they were not important.

Nor is the Acts wanting in references to Egypt and Cyrene. These are already mentioned in the list of nations (ii. 10) with the precise description: *Αἴγυπτος καὶ τὰ μέρη τῆς Λιβύης τῆς κατὰ Κυρήνην.* Egypt occurs elsewhere only in quotations from the Old Testament, and in xxi. 38 an Egyptian is mentioned who had stirred up a revolt, as is also told us by Josephus. In vi. 9 we hear of Alexandrian Jews who had settled in Jerusalem, and in xviii. 24 of an Alexandrian Jew, Apollos, who comes to Ephesus. As this man had already learned to know the Gospel —even though imperfectly—in his own country, it follows that the Acts contains an indirect notice of the beginnings of the mission in Alexandria.[1] Concerning the Jews of Cyrene in Jerusalem (vi. 9), St. Luke has not forgotten that some of these, in conjunction with Jews of Cyprus, were the first missionaries to the Gentiles (xi. 20), and he notes among the prophets and teachers of the Church in Antioch Lucius of Cyrene (xiii. 1). By an accident a reference even to Ethiopia is not wanting in this book (viii. 27): *ἰδοὺ ἀνὴρ Αἰθίοψ εὐνοῦχος δυνάστης Κανδάκης βασιλίσσης Αἰθιόπων.* Thus the glance of the author surveys the greater part of the known world (xi. 28; xvii. 6, 31; xix. 27; xxiv. 5) from the Parthians and Medes to Rome, and from the Ethiopians to Bithynia. In no instance does he lay himself open to an attack upon his accuracy, and in no place does his descrip-

[1] Alexandrian ships in xxvii. 6 and xxviii. 11.

tion fall into heterogeneous fragments. The geographical and chronological references and notices in the book show the circumspection, the care, the consistency, and the trustworthiness of the writer; and the parts where the "we" does not occur are also in this particular so firmly and closely riveted to the we-sections that the latter cannot be distinguished as a source from the rest of the book. The author of the we-sections is also the author of the complete work.

Appendix: Special Readings of the so-called β-recension.

Also in the passages of the book with which we are at present concerned the so-called β-recension offers a series of special readings.[1] I here neglect the variation between Ἱερουσαλήμ and Ἱεροσόλυμα.

1. viii. 1. Πλὴν τῶν ἀποστόλων has the seemingly superfluous addition: *οἳ ἔμειναν ἐν Ἱερουσαλήμ* (DLK).
2. viii. 4. In addition to the notice that those dispersed by the persecution preached the Word, we have also the seemingly superfluous addition: *κατὰ τὰς πόλεις καὶ κώμας* (*civitates et castella*) Ἰουδαίας (L). In the genuine text of the book *κώμη* is once found (viii. 25, *vide supra*).
3. viii. 5. In place of *εἰς τὴν πόλιν τῆς Σαμαρίας* a Latin authority gives the explanatory reading: *εἰς Σαμάρειαν τὴν πόλιν.*

[1] D denotes that the reading occurs only in Codex Bezæ, L stands for Latin, S for Syrian, and K for Coptic authorities.

4. ix. 32. Instead of the indefinite διὰ πάντων two Latin authorities read: διὰ πασῶν τῶν πόλεων καὶ χωρῶν (χώρα, *vide supra*).
5. xi. 2. Before ὅτε δὲ ἀνέβη Πέτρος εἰς Ἱερουσαλήμ DLS add: ὁ μὲν οὖν Πέτρος διὰ ἱκανοῦ χρόνον ἠθέλησεν πορευθῆναι εἰς Ἱεροσόλυμα· καὶ προσφωνήσας τοὺς ἀδελφοὺς [*scil.* in Cæsarea] καὶ ἐπιστηρίξας [αὐτοὺς] ἐξῆλθεν, πολύν τε λόγον ποιούμενος <ἐπορεύετο> διὰ τῶν χωρῶν διδάσκων αὐτούς. Concerning the secondary character of this interpolation see Weiss, *Texte u. Unters.*, Bd. 17, H. 1, s. 70 *f.* Here also χώρα is again used by the interpolator.
6. xii. 1. DSL here add: ⟨τῆς⟩ ἐν τῇ Ἰουδαίᾳ in order to connect the verse with xi. 30.
7. xii. 10. Here, in the description of the exit of St. Peter and the angel from the prison, D has the famous addition: κατέβησαν τοὺς ἑπτὰ βαθμοὺς καί, which may be original; yet this is not certain when we consider the tendency to embellishment in the β-recension.
8. xii. 25. Here a Latin authority inserts εἰς Ἀντιόχειαν in order to connect this verse with the following verse.
9. xiv. 6. D and the Codex Laudianus reinforce τὴν περίχωρον by adding ὅλην. Such reinforcing additions are frequent in D.
10. xiv. 25. DS insert εὐαγγελιζόμενοι αὐτούς, because they missed an express statement that a church had been founded also in Attalia. The interpolator probably knew of a church there.

11. xvi. 1. DSL interpolate *διελθὼν* [*διελθόντες*] *τὰ ἔθνη ταῦτα* because they had already made an interpolation in a previous verse (xv. 41). The secondary character here is shown by the constant repetition of *διέρχεσθαι* which already stands in xv. 41, stands again in xvi. 4 (D), then again in xvi. 6, and lastly also in xvi. 8 (D). This is not like St. Luke. The genuine text has the word only in xv. 41 and xvi. 6 (thus twice instead of five times). The use of *τὰ ἔθνη* here is also unusual.

12. xvi. 6. *One* Latin authority reads in place of *Γαλατικὴν χώραν* the plural "Galatiæ regiones"; this is unimportant. Yet Blass against *all* other authorities has received this reading into the text.

13. xvi. 8. Instead of the difficult but undoubtedly correct *παρελθόντες*, which has here a metaphorical significance, DL read *διελθόντες* (*τὴν Μυσίαν*).

14. xvii. 1. The insertion in D of *κατῆλθον εἰς* before *Ἀπολλωνίαν* (which must now lose its article) and of *κἀκεῖθεν* before *εἰς Θεσσαλονίκην* is probably intended to indicate that the Apostles also preached in Apollonia (*vide supra* on xiv. 25).

15. xvii. 15. Here is found in D the great interpolation: *παρῆλθεν δὲ τὴν Θεσσαλίαν· ἐκωλύθη γὰρ εἰς αὐτοὺς κηρύξαι τὸν λόγον.* The interpolator took offence at the circumstance that Thessalia was passed by, and endeavoured to explain it (after xvi. 7).

16. xviii. 25. Here D, in an explanatory interpolation (though it does not give any new information), reports that Apollos was instructed in Christianity ἐν τῇ πατρίδι (*i.e.* in Alexandria).[1]

17. xix. 28. The interpolation δραμόντες εἰς τὸ ἄμφοδον (DS also Mediolan.) naturally does not presuppose a special knowledge of the locality, but is intended only to inform us that the scene was now transferred to the street.

18. **xx. 15.** After παρεβάλομεν εἰς Σάμον D (also the codices HLP and very many cursives) SL read καὶ μείναντες ἐν Τρωγιλίᾳ [Τρωγυλλίῳ]. This seems to be the original reading; its omission also is intelligible; yet on this point absolute certainty cannot be attained *vide infra* on **xxi. 1** and **16.**

19. **xxi. 1.** Here DLK insert καὶ Μύρα after Πάταρα; probably an interpolation after **xxvii.** 5 *f.*

20. **xxi.** 16 *f.* DS read here: οὗτοι δὲ ἦγον ἡμᾶς πρὸς οὓς ξενισθῶμεν καὶ παραγενόμενοι εἴς τινα κώμην ἐγενόμεθα παρὰ Μνάσωνι Κυπρίῳ, μαθητῇ ἀρχαίῳ, κἀκεῖθεν ἐξιόντες ἤλθομεν εἰς Ἱεροσόλυμα. The host is thus represented as dwelling in a village between Cæsarea and Jerusalem, not in Jerusalem itself. This text appears at first sight very attractive; on closer

[1] I do not discuss the interpolations made by D and its satellites in xviii. 21, 27 *f.*; xix. 1, as they do not serve our present purpose with the exception of the reading "ταῖς ἐκκλησίαις" (Ἀχαΐας) for τοῖς πεπιστευκόσιν. Here we are informed that there were *several* churches in Achaia.

inspection, however, its meaning is not clear; moreover, we can see how it has arisen out of the genuine text (*vide* Weiss, *loc. cit.*, s. 101 *f.*). It is also somewhat incredible that St. Luke should have taken such interest in noting the person with whom St Paul with his large following of Gentile Christians found hospitality for one night on the way between Cæsarea and Jerusalem, while it would be not unimportant to mention the man who was courageous enough to offer shelter to St. Paul and his company during their stay in Jerusalem.

21. **xxvii. 5.** A Latin authority may perhaps have read διαπλεύσαντες τὸν Κιλίκιον κόλπον καὶ τὸ Παμφύλιον πέλαγος instead of τὸ πέλαγος τὸ κατὰ τὴν Κιλίκιαν καὶ Παμφυλίαν διαπλεύσαντες.

22. **xxviii. 16.** LS and Cod. Mediolan. read the words ἔξω τῆς παρεμβολῆς after μένειν καθ' ἑαυτόν (explanatory).

Many of these readings are not uninteresting; but only those in xii. 10 and **xx. 15** have a certain claim to originality. No certain conclusion can be drawn as to the birthplace of these interpolations. The interpolations in xiv. 25 (Attalia), and in xvii. 1 (Apollonia), the insertion of Myra in **xxi. 1** and of the village between Cæsarea and Jerusalem in **xxi. 16** *f.*, give us no information on this point. The interpolation of Thessalia in xvii. 15 is more important. It is natural to suppose that the interpolator had some interest in apologising for St. Paul's neglect of this province.

CHAPTER III

THE TREATMENT OF PERSONS

St. Luke, in his Acts of the Apostles, treats only *two* persons, *St. Peter and St. Paul*, as chief characters. The former is introduced in i. 15 as already known (from the gospel) and as the leader of the Apostles; but the author gives no further direct information as to his character and antecedents. His character is left to come out in his speeches and actions. St. Luke, in xii. 17, lets him drop out of the history of the Acts, though he afterwards mentions the part he played in the most critical scene of the book (xv. 7–11, 14). St. Paul is first introduced (vii. 58) as an unknown young man named Saul. Here again, as with St. Peter, no definite summary of St. Paul's character and antecedents is given, and the Apostle is left to describe himself in his own words and actions.[1] Emphasis is alone laid upon the fact that he, like St. Peter, spoke moved by the Holy Spirit, and a few details of his early history are referred to here and there (Tarsus, Roman citizenship, study under Gamaliel, &c.). From chap. xv. to the end of the

[1] The only exception is the passage in the letter of the Church of Jerusalem to Antioch, xv. 26, where we read of him and St. Barnabas that they were *ἄνθρωποι παραδεδωκότες τὰς ψυχὰς αὐτῶν ὑπὲρ τοῦ ὀνόματος τοῦ κυρίου ἡμῶν* 'I. *Χρ*. This, however, can scarcely be called an exception.

book he remains the hero, so that it is quite obvious that the two chief personalities of the book, as it were, relieve one another. In chap. xv., however, we find them together. There is this difference in the treatment of the two characters that St. Paul, in the great discourse of chap. xx. at Miletus, is made to look back upon his career and to give a searching description of his character and his work—in the style of the Epistles to the Thessalonians and Corinthians—; this is never the case with St. Peter. On the whole the book makes St. Paul stand out in ever so much clearer light than St. Peter—at the conclusion the reader possesses quite a distinct portrait of the former apostle,[1] while St. Peter as a *personality* is of a shadowy, indeed a somewhat conventional type.[2] Some have asserted, and with a certain plausibility have attempted to demonstrate, that St. Luke purposed a detailed parallelism in the history of the two apostles. This, however, does not admit of proof.[3]

[1] This is especially so because the three great speeches (in Pisidian Antioch, Athens, and Miletus) describe his active ministry according to its three principal phases—as missionary to the Jews, as missionary to the Gentiles, and as a leader of the Church.

[2] And yet the speeches contain some quite individual and characteristic traits (in reference to St. Peter's doctrine) which ought not to be overlooked.

[3] From the point of view of the space dedicated to St. Paul and of the whole structure of the book itself, one cannot definitely prove that St. Paul was not intended to be the sole hero of the Acts. We must, however, remember, that not only are several very important, indeed fundamentally important, discourses put into the mouth of St. Peter, but that the story of Cornelius, in which he plays the prominent part, also occupies a central position in the book, and that with this story chap. xv. is most closely connected (*vide* xv. 7, 14).

Some instances of parallelism presented themselves quite unsought for; nothing more than this can be said. The name of apostle is applied to St. Paul only twice in the book (xiv. 4, 14).[1] Weiss thinks that just on this account the word in both cases must have its more general and non-technical significance. But this cannot be proved, for the circumstance that in many passages the Twelve are called simply "the Apostles" (as if there were no others) is not a safe proof. In the book they are also called "the Eleven" or "the Twelve," and what could have induced St. Luke purposely to refuse to give St. Paul a name which he himself claimed with such complete conviction?[2]

Among persons of the second rank might be numbered the Apostles (the Twelve), who, although they were the witnesses of the Resurrection and formed a most important body—indeed at the beginning the leading and governing body—in the Primitive Community, are yet kept in the background. But if we would exclude these, then only *five* personages of secondary rank come under St. Luke's consideration, namely, *Stephen*, *Philip*, *Barnabas*, *James*, and *Apollos*. *Concerning the character and antecedents of four of these the Acts gives some direct and detailed information*

[1] In the same passages it is also given to St. Barnabas.

[2] The following conjecture is at least possibly true:—For St. Luke, and for the authority upon whom he depends for his knowledge of the relations of Jerusalem and Antioch, St. Paul was as much an apostle as the others (note that chaps. vi. and xiii., xiv. belong to a single body of tradition and that in chap. vi. the Apostles are called "the Twelve," while in chap. xiv. St. Paul and St. Barnabas are called apostles); but the source from which St. Luke borrowed his material for the description of the Church of Jerusalem avoided calling St. Paul an apostle.

(Stephen, vi. 5, 8, 10; vii. 55; xxii. 20; Philip, viii. 6 *f.*; Barnabas, iv. 36 *f.*; xi. 24; xv. 26; Apollos, xviii. 24 *ff.*). It is not insignificant that *these four are all Hellenists.* The greatest emphasis is laid upon the characterisation of St. Stephen, and—what is still more important—a long speech of his is recorded. Owing to this he approaches very nearly to St. Peter and St. Paul in the importance given to him in the economy of the book. We might describe him by the numeral 1[b], so important is he to the author, so great is his admiration for him. St. Barnabas comes next in importance, but no speeches of his own are recorded, though he speaks together with St. Paul (xiv. 14 *f.* 22[b]; xv. 3, 12). Likewise no reports are given of discourses of St. Philip, yet cursory reference is made in viii. 35 to a missionary sermon of his on a passage in Isaiah, and the renown of his miracles is celebrated in the strongest terms. These three persons of secondary rank have a very high, *and indeed the same,* significance in the plan of the work. They are to St. Luke of the highest importance for his representation of *the passage of the Gospel from the Jews to Gentiles.* There is no need to go more into detail on this point. In the second part of the book, however, there is no personage of secondary rank *within the general plan of the book* It is the more remarkable that *outside the general plan* there is *one* person, Apollos, who strongly excited the interest of St. Luke. The manner in which this personage is treated, *i.e.* characterised, in the book, makes him appear on a level with Stephen, Philip, and Barnabas. How came St. Luke to treat him with such distinction? The key to the answer seems to me to lie in xviii. 28. Here St. Luke emphatically states with what energy and success Apollos demonstrated the Messiahship of Jesus *publicly before the Jews* in Corinth (nothing is said of his preaching to Gentiles).[1] In this statement the account concerning Apollos culminates. Though the main subject of the book is the demonstration of the passage of the Gospel from the Jews to the Greeks, still the conquest of the Jews by this gifted apologist was so important to St. Luke that he has included the ministry of Apollos as an episode in his work. Thus the second half of the Acts acquired—as a companion figure to St. Paul—a personage of secondary rank, who in his teaching formed to a certain extent a parallel to St. Stephen. Seeing that St. Luke was personally acquainted with Silas and Timothy, and yet does not in his work give them special prominence as missionaries, it follows that Apollos must have appeared to him a much more important personality than either of them.[2] This deduction, moreover, agrees excellently with what we learn about Apollos from the First Epistle to the Corinthians. Here also he stands in the foreground beside St. Paul and St. Peter. Accordingly St. Luke's procedure in introducing Apollos

[1] Not only εὐτόνως but also δημοσίᾳ are strongly emphasised in the verse. This emphasis makes it improbable that St. Luke had in his eye only the discourses of Apollos in synagogues; he must have intended a ministry of wider publicity, wider than that of St. Paul to the Jews.

[2] May we not go a step further and conjecture that St. Luke counted Apollos a more successful converter of Jews than St. Paul himself, and therefore felt bound to mention him in his work.

to the scene of the Acts is brilliantly justified by St. Paul. St. James, the fifth personality of this series, occupies a peculiar position. It is presupposed that the four others are unknown, while it is assumed that he is known. The readers evidently knew—though this is nowhere stated—that he was the Lord's brother, and that he had become the head of the Primitive Community after the Twelve had quite given up the leadership, which had already been limited by the appointment of the "Seven." We receive no direct information concerning him, indeed in two of the three passages where his name occurs extraordinarily little is said about him (xii. 17; **xxi. 18** *ff.*). In the second passage we at once lose sight of him as an individual amid the body of presbyters at Jerusalem, and in the first passage one can only just recognise that he is the head of "the brethren" in Jerusalem.[1] But in the third passage (xv. 13 *f.*), for which xii. 17 is evidently intended to prepare, he plays a part of the highest, indeed of decisive, importance in the general plan of the book. As to St. Stephen, so also to him a speech is assigned, and it was this speech that settled the whole question under discussion.

We can, moreover, distinguish in the book personages of a third degree of importance, individuals whom St. Luke thought it worth while or necessary just to mention, without going into closer detail concerning them, either because they were of no import-

[1] This method of treatment of St. James in xii. 27 and **xxi. 18** *ff.* is of importance in connection with the question of the homogeneity of the book. Chap. **xxi. 18** belongs to the we-sections.

ance at all for the plan of his work, or because their importance seemed to him to be exhausted with the mere mention of their names, or because he had no further information about them. Among these we include the Apostles in so far as in i. 13 a list of their names is given; further, in the first part of the Acts, the Apostle John, the Apostle James—described in xii. as the brother of John, this can only be because it is presupposed that the latter was known to the readers —Joseph, Barsabbas, and Matthias (i. 23, 26), the Mother of our Lord (i. 14) and His brethren (*loc. cit.*); lastly, the Seven (vi. 5). Again in the second part of the book we also have as subordinate characters St. Mark (xiii. 5, 13; xv. 37 *f.*)—already mentioned in the first part (xii. 12,[1] 25), and thus forming a bond between the two parts—the prophets and teachers of Antioch (xiii. 1 *f.*), Silas (xv. 22, 27, 32, 40, and in chaps. xvi.–xix.), Judas Barsabbas (xv. 22, 27, 32), Timotheus (chaps. xvi.–xix.), Aquila and Priscilla (xviii. 1 *ff.*), Erastus (xix. 22), Gaius and Aristarchus (xix. 29; xx. 4; Aristarchus also in xxvii. 2), and the companions of St. Paul mentioned in xx. 4. Of these persons, who are only cursorily sketched or not sketched at all, St. Mark is the only one of whom we learn anything discreditable. We cannot see why St. Luke should have mentioned him at all if he only meant to tell his readers that when St. Mark had been chosen to accompany the two Apostles as their minister he had left them of his own accord, and that this behaviour of his was the cause of a

[1] In this passage he is, as it were, announced beforehand, just as it is with St. James in xii. 17.

quarrel between St. Paul and St. Barnabas, leading to their separation. As one recollects that St. Mark's gospel formed the chief authority for St. Luke in his gospel, all kinds of ideas concerning St. Luke's relations with him suggest themselves. The reader is evidently intended to notice that Timothy takes St. Mark's place with St. Paul (compare xv. 37–39 with xvi. 1 *ff.*), likewise that Silas takes the place of St. Barnabas (xv. 40). That Silas stood on a different footing with St. Paul from Timothy follows from xvi. 19 *ff.*; xvii. 4, 10; on the other hand, even according to the Acts, Timothy was not merely an attendant. Silas vanishes after xviii. 5; his place is supplied by Aquila and his wife Priscilla.

The lists of names of the Apostles, of the Seven, and of the prophets and teachers in Antioch, are all given from the same motive. The readers must know the names of the ancient leaders of the two—to St. Luke—most important churches, and this applies more particularly in the case of the Apostles. Of these, if we except St. Peter, the author shows special interest only in St. John. Seeing that he has simply inserted the name of St. John into the Petrine narratives after they had taken their final shape, it follows that he wished to give prominence to this apostle. We see his reason from xii. 2 (*vide supra*)—the readers knew this John, or at least knew of him.[1]

The brevity of the reference to the Herodian

[1] Why he is not mentioned in chap. xv. we cannot tell. St. Luke has not purposely left him out. The simplest supposition is that the tradition upon which he depends did not here make mention of St. John.

persecution is most strange. An apostle, St. James, suffered martyrdom, other Christians of Jerusalem became confessors, and yet the author, who describes the history of Stephen in such detail and with such enthusiasm, does not devote to this event a few sentences of recognition; indeed he tells us no details at all! This paradoxical fact can, in my opinion, only be explained on the supposition that the author here closely followed his source, and that he possessed no other information concerning the Herodian persecution (while Clement of Alexandria, over a century later, knew more). The source, however, did not contain a history of the Apostolic epoch, but only *stories about St. Peter*, and therefore mentioned this persecution only by way of an introduction. This circumstance is of high significance in view of the question concerning the nature of the source (written or oral).

Besides these three classes of actors, who are arranged in an order which displays an admirable sense of proportion and relative importance, there appear in the book about seventy other persons who are for the most part mentioned by name.[1] They are all of them introduced in subordination to those who have been already described as the actors, and it would serve no useful purpose to go through the list and to discuss them one by one.—A few points are, however, worthy of notice. In the first place, it is strange that some persons who play an important part in the plot of the narrative are not mentioned by name. Why is the lame man of iii. 2 *ff.* not

[1] We exclude references to characters of the Old Testament, to Pilate, &c.

named, nor the lame man at Lystra (xiv. 8 *ff.*)?[1] Why do we miss the names of the founders of the church in Antioch (xi. 20 *f.*)? why also the names of the confessors under Herod (xii. 1)? Why is it that no names are given to the Jewish Christians, hostile to St. Paul, who came down to Antioch (xv. 1)? nor to the companions of St. Paul and St. Barnabas (xv. 2)? nor to the Christian Pharisees in Jerusalem (xv. 5)? nor to the numerous teachers in Antioch who laboured together with St. Paul and St. Barnabas (xv. 35)? Why is it that we do not know the name of the damsel who was possessed by an evil spirit in Philippi (xvi. 6 *f.*)? nor the names of the prætors of that city (xvi. 20 *ff.*)? nor the name of the jailor (xvi. 23 *ff.*)? nor the names of the so-called "disciples of John" in Ephesus (xix. 1 *ff.*), nor of the Asiarchs and the Grammateus (xix. 31, 35) in the same city? nor the name of St. Paul's sister's son in Jerusalem (xxiii. 16)? The answer that St. Luke has not given their names because of their comparative insignificance will suffice for the majority of the instances;[2] but in some cases—as for instance the lame men in Jerusalem and Lystra, and the martyrs under Herod—we must suppose that he did not know

[1] Compare on the contrary the less important case of Æneas (ix. 33).

[2] This holds good also of the Strategi in Philippi and the Asiarchs in Ephesus. The author indeed mentions by name, when he can, persons in authority among the Jews and Gentiles who appear in his history (thus even Claudius Lysias, the centurion Julius, and Publius in Malta; Gamaliel is even characterised in v. 34 as τίμιος πάντι τῷ λαῷ; the proconsul Sergius Paulus is called ἀνὴρ συνετός [xiii. 7]), but the Strategi and Asiarchs did not come under consideration as individuals.

the names, otherwise he would certainly have given them.[1] On the other hand it is also strange that there are some very insignificant persons whom he has honoured by mentioning their names, in the first place a whole list of persons with whom St. Paul (or St. Peter) dwelt or lodged (*vide supra* p. 109)—this belongs to his scheme of narrative—then some other individuals, namely Blastus the chamberlain (xii. 20), Dionysius and Damaris at Athens (xvii. 34), Crispus at Corinth (xviii. 8), and Alexander at Ephesus (xix. 33). These are after all only a few instances. Except for the cases of "Blastus" and "Alexander," which stand quite by themselves—here the author has paid too much deference to his sources—we may well suppose that the persons in question, Dionysius, Damaris, and Crispus, played an important part in later days (for Crispus, see 1 Cor. i. 14; for Dionysius, see the notice concerning Dionysius of Corinth in Eus. Hist. Eccl. iv. 23), indeed that they were probably known to the first readers. They are thus named for the same reason that the Apostle John is named side by side with St. Peter, and that in xxi. 9 the information is given that St. Philip had four daughters who were prophetesses (concerning the importance of these daughters, see Papias and numerous other authorities, also Clem. Alex.).

The treatment of personalities is the same in character throughout the whole book. By this means also the book acquires an aspect of strict uniformity. Even the abrupt introduction of the "we" is paralleled

[1] This supposition is also probable in the case of the Grammateus at Ephesus.

by similar instances of abruptness in the introduction of persons as if they were already known; and the speaking in unison of St. James and the presbyters of Jerusalem in xxi. 20 has several parallels in the earlier parts of the book (St. Peter and St. John, iv. 19 *f.*, the whole congregation, iv. 24 *ff.*, the Apostles, i. 24 *f.*, and vi. 2 *f.*, St. Paul and St. Barnabas, xiii. 46 *f.*; xiv. 14 *ff.*—quite a long discourse!—xiv. 22, *cf.* xiv. 27; xv. 3, 4, 12). Only cursory reference is made to the teaching and discourses of subordinate characters (*e.g.* viii. 35 Philip; xv. 32 Judas and Silas; ix. 27 Barnabas; xviii. 26 Aquila and Priscilla, &c.). The speeches—and they are by no means few—that are attributed to Jewish and Gentile persons in authority have for the most part one and the same aim; *cf.* the words of the Sanhedrin (iv. 15 *ff.*), the speech of Gamaliel (v. 35 *ff.*), of Gallio (xviii. 14 *f.*), of the Ephesian Grammateus (xix. 35 *f.*), moreover xxiii. 9; xxiv. 22 *ff.*; xxv. 14 *ff.*; xxv. 24 *ff.*; xxvi. 31 *f.*, as well as the letter of Claudius Lysias (xxiii. 26 *ff.*). They are intended to bear witness to the innocence of the Christians in general and of St. Paul in particular.

In regard to the great speeches both the selection of ideas and the arrangement in the book are worthy of notice. The speech of St. Stephen (vii. 2 *ff.*), that of St. Peter to Cornelius (x. 28 *ff.*), those of St. Peter and St. James at the so-called Council (xv.), and indirectly the three apologies of St. Paul (xxii. 1 *ff.*; xxiv. 10 *ff.*; xxvi. 1 *ff.*), as well as the shorter fourth apology (xxviii. 17 *ff.*), all minister to the main theme of the book: that the preaching of the Gospel, in accordance with the Divine Will, is passing over from the Jews to the Gentiles. The book opens with the missionary discourses delivered by St. Peter before the Jews (ii. 14 *ff.*; iii. 12 *ff.*; iv. 7 *ff.*, 19 *f.*; v. 29 *f.*). Parallel to them stand the missionary discourse of St. Paul to the Jews (xiii. 16 *ff.*) and to the Gentiles (xvii. 22 *f.*), the latter having a sort of prelude in xiv. 15 *ff.* These are—with *one* exception which will be immediately dealt with—all the longer speeches that are to be found in the book. We see how completely they are in subordination to the main purpose of the book, which is to describe the history of the mission and of the passing over of the Gospel to the Gentiles. The more remarkable therefore is the contrast presented by St. Paul's speech at Miletus (xx. 18 *f.*). Its content is such as to set it somewhat outside the framework of the book. As is well known it stands between two we-sections, and it is for this very reason probable that we have here the report of words which St. Luke himself had heard, and that here—just as in his account of the perils of the voyage to Rome—he goes more into detail than is consistent with the plan of his work, because he allowed himself to be led away by the deep impression that the scene had made upon him. The speech at Miletus is therefore most probably authentic, in so far as a short report can be said to be authentic.[1] It has, however, been noticed long ago that in spirit and in phraseology no passage in the Acts is more closely allied to the Pauline epistles than this speech.

[1] Note also that in it subjects are discussed which are not touched upon elsewhere in the whole book.

It is also scarcely possible that the remaining speeches are the product of pure invention (if they were so the highest praise would be due to the author's creative and yet astonishingly correct imagination). How distinctly the speech of St. Stephen stands out from all the others! The subject itself of the speech is quite peculiar, and not according to the mind of St. Luke, who had great reverence for the *religio antiqua* of the Jews. In the parallel speeches of St. Peter (ii. 14 *ff.* and iii. 12 *ff.*) the eschatological implication of the outpouring of the Spirit is strongly emphasised, while St. Luke himself seems to regard this outpouring only as the foundation of the mission, and facts themselves had refuted the combination of the outpouring of the Spirit with the Final Judgment. Again our Lord appears as ἀνὴρ ἀποδεδειγμένος ἀπὸ τοῦ θεοῦ (ii. 22), whom God had first made Christ by the Resurrection from the dead (ii. 36), or again as παῖς θεοῦ (iii. 13, *cf.* iii. 26; iv. 27: ὁ ἁγίος παῖς σοῦ Ἰησοῦς, ὃν ἔχρισας, and iv. 30, but nowhere else in the book); the ἐπαγγελία τοῦ πνεύματος τοῦ ἁγίου which He had now poured forth, was first imparted to Him at His Ascension (ii. 33). The speech before Cornelius has similar Christological traits, and the reminiscence (x. 38): ὃς διῆλθεν εὐεργετῶν καὶ ἰώμενος . . . ὅτι ὁ θεὸς ἦν μετ' αὐτοῦ, is unique in the whole non-evangelic literature. Here again the eschatological point of view is strongly emphasised (x. 42), and the words: ἄφεσιν ἁμαρτιῶν λαβεῖν διὰ τοῦ ὀνόματος αὐτοῦ πάντα τὸν πιστεύοντα εἰς αὐτόν (x. 43) are certainly not borrowed from Paulinism, but contain primitive doctrine. Again with what delicate touches is the speech of St. James, in chap. xv., distinguished from that of St. Peter! Are we to assign all this to St. Luke the Hellenist without any source to guide him? And above all—how clearly the first two great programmatic speeches of St. Paul (chaps. xiii. and xvii.), the first addressed to the Jews, the second to the Gentiles, are distinguished from the speeches of St. Peter! Compare only xiii. 38, 39 with x. 43 (*vide supra*), and think whether in a short report the likeness and the difference between the teaching of the primitive apostles and that of St. Paul could have been more concisely and delicately expressed than in those words! As for the speech at Athens, with its prelude in xiv. 15 *ff.*, if only critics will again learn to see clearly and to feel rightly, none of them will fail to recognise that in this attempt to give a short summary of the probable nature of St. Paul's fundamental teaching in his sermons to Gentiles, the genius shown in the selection of ideas is just as great as the historical trustworthiness of the report.

It is most strange that St. Luke gives us no less than three great apostolic discourses of St. Paul in close succession (chaps. xxii., xxiv., xxvi.; compare, moreover, the speech in Rome, chap. xxviii.). Unless these separate discourses rested upon some traditional foundation that seemed to the author trustworthy and important, we can scarcely understand why *one* speech did not suffice for him. Probably he made use of several sources; for in *one* source these speeches would most probably have run together into one. If this, however, be true then it follows that where the speeches agree the one vouches for the other, and the critics will at last be compelled to give up one of those positions to which they cling with the most inveterate prejudice,—the assumption that St. Paul's doctrine is here brought into too close accordance with the doctrine of the Pharisees, and that he is here represented as adopting a line of defence which is unworthy of himself in that he renounces his own principles.

CHAPTER IV

MIRACLES AND SUPERNATURAL WORKS OF THE SPIRIT

Accounts of miracles and works of the Spirit play so great a part in the Acts of the Apostles that the mind of the author can be discerned from these narratives with special clearness. He himself is a physician endowed with peculiar "Spiritual" gifts of healing, and this fact profoundly affects his conception of Christianity. Moreover, these records are also of importance for the discovery of the sources of the book; they confirm its unity, but they also clearly show that distinct groups of subject-matter exist therein. I first proceed to give a summary of the material in question (see the tables on pp. 134 *et seq.*).

Merely a cursory glance at these tables discovers a sufficiently striking state of things. Let us, however, commence our closer investigation with a general survey:—

The we-sections, although they comprise only about one hundred verses (a tenth part of the book), contain one summary account of cases of healing, besides four accounts of single instances of the same sort (including one case of raising from the dead), two instances of interference by the Holy Spirit to prevent a course of action, the appearance of a man of Macedonia in a vision, the appearance of the angel

	Chaps. i.–xv.	Chaps. xvi.–xxviii., without the we-sections.	The we-sections.
I. Summary accounts of miracles and cases of healing (σημεῖα, τέρατα, δυνάμεις)	ii. 43 (The Apostles) (iv. 30) v. 12 (The Apostles) v. 14–16 (St. Peter, his shadow [1]) vi. 8 (5, 10) (St. Stephen) viii. 6 *f.* 13 (St. Philip) xiv. 3 (St. Paul and St. Barnabas) xv. 12 (St. Paul and St. Barnabas)	xix. 11 *f.* (St. Paul; the handkerchiefs)	xxviii. 9 (Cures wrought by St. Paul and St. Luke in Malta)
II. Miraculous cures (records of particular instances)	iii. 1 *ff.* (The lame man in Jerusalem) ix. 17 *f.* (Ananias cures St. Paul) ix. 33 (The lame man at Lydda) ix. 36 *ff.* (The raising of Tabitha from the dead at Joppa) xiv. 8 *ff.* (The lame man at Lystra) xiv. 19 *f.* (St. Paul receives no lasting injury from the stoning at Lystra)	xix. 15 *ff.* (The sons of Scæva expel a dæmon by invoking the name of "Jesus whom Paul preacheth")	xvi. 16 *ff.* (St. Paul cures a damsel possessed by a dæmon) xx. 9 *f.* (St. Paul raises up Eutychus) xxviii. 13 *ff.* (St. Paul receives no harm from the bite of a serpent) xxviii. 7 (St. Paul heals Publius in Malta)

III. Miracles of a singular character	i. 9 (The Ascension) ii. 4 *ff.* (The gift of tongues) iv. 31 (Miraculous earthquake as a sign from Heaven) v. 1 *ff.* (The death of Ananias and Sapphira) ix. 8 (St. Paul's blinding) [xii. 23] (Herod is smitten with a fatal disease) xiii. 11 (The blinding of Elymas)	[xvi. 26 *f.*] (The earthquake at Philippi)	
IV. Realistic[2] appearances of angels	i. 10 *f.* (The *angeli interpretes* at the Ascension) v. 19 (The angel of the Lord opens the prison and speaks to the Apostles) [viii. 26] (The angel of the Lord speaks to St. Philip; it can also be regarded as a vision)		

[1] In D and its satellites we here find also the interpolation: ἀπηλλάσσοντο γὰρ ἀπὸ πάσης ἀσθενείας, ἧς εἶχεν ἕκαστος.

[2] According to xii. 9 the author distinguishes sharply between a real appearance of an angel and an appearance in a vision that was brought about by the Spirit or by God. Hence we must omit here the appearance of the angel to Cornelius (expressly described in x. 3 as ἐν ὁράματι) and to St. Paul (**xxvii. 23**); the latter happened in the night, and therefore belongs to the class of visions sent by God. Neither may we include xii. 23; for the angel does not appear, and belongs only to the imagination of the author.

	Chaps. i.–xv.	Chaps. xvi–xxviii., without the we-sections.	The we-sections.
IV. Realistic appearances of angels—(*continued*)	xii. 7–11 (The angel of the Lord opens the prison for St. Peter and speaks to him)		
V. Filled with the Holy Ghost (full of the Holy Ghost)	ii. 4 (The Apostles) iv. 8 (St. Peter) iv. 31 (The Christians of Jerusalem) vi. 3 (Those who were chosen as the "Seven") vi. 5, 10 (St. Stephen) vii. 55 (St. Stephen) ix. 17 (St. Paul) xi. 24 (St. Barnabas) xiii. 9 (St. Paul) xiii. 52 (The disciples in Pisidian Antioch)		
VI. Giving and receiving the Holy Spirit, being baptized with Him (and anointed with Him); the coming, the falling of the Holy Spirit upon persons, &c.	i. 5 (The disciples will be baptized with the Holy Spirit) i. 8 (ἐπελθόντος upon the disciples) ii. 33 (τ. ἐπαγγελίαν τ. πν. τ. ἁγίου λαβών) ii. 38 (The gift of the Holy Spirit)	xix. 2 (The "disciples of John" had not received Him) xix. 6 (He comes upon them)	

	v. 32 (God gives the Holy Spirit to them that obey Him)		
	viii. 15 (Apostles are sent to Samaria to give Him)		
	viii. 17 (The Samaritans receive Him through the laying on of hands)		
	viii. 18 (The same)		
	viii. 19 (Simon Magus asks for the power of giving Him)		
	x. 38 (Christ was anointed with Him)		
	x. 44 (He falls upon Cornelius)		
	x. 45 (The gift of the Holy Spirit)		
	x. 47 (Cornelius and his house have received Him)		
	xi. 15 (He fell upon Cornelius)		
	xi. 16 (To be baptized with Him)		
	xv. 8 (God had also given Him to those who were Gentiles by birth)		

	Chaps. i.–xv.	Chaps. xvi.–xxviii., without the we-sections.	The we-sections.
VII. The Holy Spirit speaks, foretells, testifies, comforts, determines; Christians speak by the Holy Spirit	i. 2 (διὰ πν. ἁγ. ἐντειλ.) i. 16 (προεῖπε) ii. 4 (ἐδίδου ἀποφθέγγεσθαι) iv. 25 (διὰ πνεύμ. ἁγ. στόματος Δαυείδ) vi. 10 (τῷ πνεύμ., ᾧ ἐλάλει Στέφανος) viii. 29 (He speaks to St. Philip) ix. 31 (παράκλησις τ. ἁγ. πνεύμ.) x. 19 (He speaks to St. Peter) xi. 12 (The same) xi. 28 (Ἄγαβος ἐσήμαινε διὰ τ. πν.) xiii. 2 (He speaks to the prophets in Antioch) xv. 28 (ἔδοξε τ. πν. τ. ἁγίῳ κ. ἡμῖν)	xx. 23 (He testifies κατὰ πόλιν that afflictions await the Apostle) [xxviii. 25] (καλῶς τὸ πν. τὸ ἅγιον ἐλάλησεν)	xxi. 4 (The Tyrian Christians speaks by the Spirit to St. Paul) xxi. 11 (Agabus says: Thus saith the Holy Spirit)
VIII. The Holy Spirit appears as acting	viii. 39 (πνεῦμα κυρίου ἥρπασεν τ. Φίλιππον) xiii. 4 (He sends out missionaries)	xx. 28 (He appoints bishops)	xvi. 6 (He prevents a mission) xvi. 7 (He does not permit)

IX. Visions in the Spirit (ecstasy), in which the Spirit or the Lord speaks	vii. 55. (St. Stephen's vision; he sees the Lord) ix. 3 *ff.* (c. parall. St. Paul's vision on the way to Damascus) ix. 10 *f.* (The vision of Ananias) ix. 12 (St. Paul's vision in which he sees Ananias) **x.** 3 *f.* (The vision of Cornelius) **x.** 10 *f.* (St. Peter's vision) xxii. 17 *f.* (St. Paul's vision in Jerusalem)[1]	xviii. 9 (St. Paul's vision in Corinth; the Lord appears to him) xxiii. 11 (St. Paul's vision in Jerusalem; the Lord speaks to him)	xvi. 9 *f.* (St. Paul's vision in Troas: the man of Macedonia) xxvii. 23 (St. Paul's vision on the ship; the angel of the Lord appears to him)
X. *προφητεύειν*, *προφήτης* (see also under VII.)	xi. 27 (Prophets from Jerusalem) xiii. 1 (Prophets at Antioch)	[xix. 6] (The "disciples of John" when they had received the Spirit prophesy, *vide supra*)	xxi. 9 (The four daughters of St. Philip are *προφητεύουσαι*) [xxi. 11] (The prophet Agabus, *vide supra*)

[1] This vision must be set in this column because it occurred at an earlier period soon after the Conversion, and is only referred to here.

	Chaps. i.–xv.	Chaps. xvi–xxviii., without the we-sections.	The we-sections.
X. *προφητεύειν, προφήτης* (see also under VII.) —(*continued*)	xv. 32 (The prophets Judas and Silas)		xxvii. 24, 26, 31 (St. Paul foretells the future) xxvii. 34 (St. Paul[1] foretells the future).
XI. Varia	v. 3 (*ψεύσασθαί σε τὸ πν. τ. ἅγιον*) v. 9 (*πειράσαι τ. πν. κυρίου*) vii. 51 (*ἀντιπίπτειν τ. πν. τ. ἁγίῳ*)[2]		

[1] In Codex D, together with its satellites, or in these alone, are found the following interpolations which come under consideration here: under No. V. include the interpolation in xv. 32: *πλήρεις πνεύματος ἁγ.* of Judas and Silas—under No. VI. the interpolation in xi. 17: (*κωλῦσαι τὸν θεὸν*) *τοῦ μὴ δοῦναι αὐτοῖς πνεῦμα ἅγιον* and in xxvi. 1 (of St. Paul): *θαρρῶν καὶ ἐν τ. ἁγ. πνεύματι παράκλησιν λαβών*.—under No. VII. the interpolation in xv. 7: (*Πέτρος*) *ἐν πνεύματι ἁγ.* (*εἶπεν*), in xv. 29: *φερόμενοι ἐν τ. ἁγ. πνεύματι*, in xix. 1· *θέλοντος δὲ τοῦ Παύλου κατὰ τὴν ἰδίαν βούλησιν πορεύεσθαι εἰς Ἱεροσόλυμα, εἶπεν αὐτῷ τὸ πνεῦμα ὑποστρέφειν εἰς Ἀσίαν*, and in xx. 3: *εἶπεν τὸ πνεῦμα αὐτῷ* (*ὑποστρέφειν διὰ Μακεδονίας*).—Under VIII. the interpolation in xvii. 15: *Θεσσαλίαν, ἐκωλύθη γὰρ εἰς αὐτοὺς κηρῦξαι τὸν λόγον*.

[2] In xviii. 25; xix. 21 and xx. 22 it must remain doubtful whether the Holy Spirit or the human spirit is meant.

of the Lord in a vision, the Tyrians foretelling the future, Agabus foretelling the future, the daughters of St. Philip who were prophetesses, two instances in which St. Paul foretold the future—thus no less than fourteen instances of a "miraculous" character recorded in so small a space! In correspondence with this abundance we find in the first half of the book about seventy-seven similar instances of a miraculous character. Any one who wishes may ascertain by calculation that, taking into account the length of the first fifteen chapters, the proportion is much the same. Moreover, the categories of our list again repeat themselves. We again find summary accounts of cases of healing, accounts of separate miracles of healing, persons mentioned who speak in the Spirit, cases where the Spirit acts and speaks, visions (the appearance of an angel), prophets. On the other hand, the situation is quite different in the second half of the book, omitting the we-sections. Here in passages which picture St. Paul in Philippi (at the close of his visit), in Thessalonica, in Berœa, in Athens, in Ephesus, in Jerusalem, in Cæsarea, and in Rome, we find only ten instances of a miraculous character, and even these suffer serious reduction when we consider that the earthquake in Philippi was a natural occurrence treated as a special instance of Providential interference and so used in the narrative; that the two passages xx. 23 and 28 belong to a speech of St. Paul which in all probability must be assigned to the we-sections—seeing that it stands in their midst and that St. Luke was present on the occasion; and that xxviii. 25 is the customary introduction to a quotation from the Old Testament: τὸ πνεῦμα τὸ ἅγιον ἐλάλησεν διὰ Ἠσαΐου τοῦ προφήτου. We are therefore left with only six passages—namely, xviii. 9 *f.*; xix. 2, 6, 11 *f.*, 15 *ff.*; and xxiii. 11. Now, however, we at once see that xviii. 9 *f.* and xxiii. 11 are out of organic connection with the simple narratives in which they stand, and give the impression of having been thrust into the context like the lyric Christian passages in certain parts of the Apocalypse. Only consider:—

xviii. (8–11): Κρίσπος δὲ ὁ ἀρχισυνάγωγος ἐπίστευσεν τῷ κυρίῳ σὺν ὅλῳ τῷ οἴκῳ αὐτοῦ, καὶ πολλοὶ τῶν Κορινθίων ἀκούοντες ἐπίστευον καὶ ἐβαπτίζοντο.

> εἶπεν δὲ ὁ κύριος ἐν νυκτὶ δι' ὁράματος τῷ Παύλῳ· μὴ φοβοῦ, ἀλλὰ λάλει καὶ μὴ σιωπήσῃς, διότι ἐγώ εἰμι μετὰ σοῦ, καὶ οὐδεὶς ἐπιθήσεταί σοι τοῦ κακῶσαί σε, διότι λαός ἐστί μοι πολὺς ἐν τῇ πόλει ταύτῃ.

ἐκάθισεν δὲ ἐνιαυτὸν καὶ μῆνας ἓξ διδάσκων ἐν αὐτοῖς τὸν λόγον τοῦ θεοῦ.

Again xxiii. (10–12): Πολλῆς δὲ γενομένης στάσεως φοβηθεὶς ὁ χιλίαρχος μὴ διασπασθῇ ὁ Παῦλος ὑπ' αὐτῶν, ἐκέλευσεν τὸ στράτευμα καταβὰν ἁρπάσαι αὐτὸν ἐκ μέσου αὐτῶν ἄγειν τε εἰς τὴν παρεμβολήν.

> τῇ δὲ ἐπιούσῃ νυκτὶ ἐπιστὰς αὐτῷ ὁ κύριος εἶπεν· θάρσει· ὡς γὰρ διεμαρτύρω τὰ περὶ ἐμοῦ εἰς Ἱερουσαλήμ, οὕτω σε δεῖ καὶ εἰς Ῥώμην μαρτυρῆσαι.

γενομένης δὲ ἡμέρας ποιήσαντες συστροφὴν οἱ Ἰουδαῖοι ἀνεθεμάτισαν ἑαυτούς, λέγοντες, μήτε φαγεῖν μήτε πιεῖν ἕως οὗ ἀποκτείνωσι τὸν Παῦλον.

I do not mean it is here a question of later interpolation into an already complete text—it is by no means necessary to suppose a written exemplar—but the situation seems to be as follows: the author of the we-sections, *i.e.* of the whole work, has given the impress of his own peculiar temperament to accounts which were at his disposal. *In the whole subject-matter of the second half of the Acts*—with the exception of the we-sections[1]—*miraculous episodes do not occur as organic elements of the context except in the account of St. Paul's ministry in Ephesus* (xix. 2 *ff.*). Here we have the "disciples of John" who receive the Spirit and prophesy; here the exorcism of an evil spirit; and here the summary account of instances of miraculous healing by St. Paul.

The situation here presented is most interesting and admits of only *one* explanation. It is clear that St. Luke—whose own we-account shows him to have been a physician endowed with miraculous gifts of healing—possessed for the first half of his book a source or sources (oral or written) *which was congenial to his own peculiar temperament.* On the other hand it is also clear that for the second half of his book he did not possess such sources (with the exception of what is told us of Ephesus), but only had at his disposal simple records into which he has inserted nothing except two conventional accounts of visions which illustrate the development of the plot. It cannot be otherwise; for if he himself had introduced the supernatural element into chapters i.–xv., it is unin-

[1] And of the repeated narrative of St. Paul's conversion, which may be here neglected.

telligible why he should have refrained from doing the same thing in the second half, except, or almost only except, where he himself was an eye-witness. That the parts of his narrative where the colouring is most sober are not the we-sections, but the accounts of St. Paul's visits to Thessalonica, Berœa, Athens, Corinth, Jerusalem (the last visit), Cæsarea, and Rome, is a convincing proof that his narrative here is kept in close accordance with sources. Either the records given in these sources contained nothing of a supernatural character, or what they contained of this character seemed to him incredible; naturally, however, the latter alternative is altogether improbable when we take into account St. Luke's peculiar temperament. We reach no solution of the problem by supposing that the economy of the book prevented him from relating supernatural events in these passages; for his we-sections are full of the supernatural, and the account of the ministry in Ephesus shows that even for the second half of his work, in those passages where he was not an eye-witness, anything of a supernatural character was most welcome to him.

The circumstance that in chaps. i.–xv. the supernatural element is so abundant, indeed is wanting in no single chapter, is accordingly a proof that we have here a body of tradition, homogeneous in its treatment of the supernatural, which had been transmitted to the author in a form and with a colouring that were congenial to his temperament. That this form and colouring *belonged to the source itself*—the question whether it was oral or written may be left open—

follows not only from the fact that the supernatural element is almost entirely absent from the second half of the book (excluding the we-sections and chapter xix.), but still more clearly from the fact that while there is much in common between chapters i.–xv. and the we-sections in their attitude to the supernatural, there is much more of the supernatural in chapters i.–xv. than in the we-sections. For instance:

1. In the we-sections all that has been included under category III.—namely, what I have called miracles of a "singular" character—is entirely wanting. Stories like the Ascension, the Gift of Tongues, the death of Ananias and Sapphira, the blinding of St. Paul and of Elymas, the *mors persecutoris Herodis*, have no parallels in the we-sections (naturally also not in the rest of the second half of the book).

2. In the we-sections realistic appearances of angels (*vide sub* IV.), such as we find in i. 10 *f.*; v. 19; viii. 26; xii. 7–11, are wanting.

3. In the we-sections we are never expressly told that such and such persons are filled with the Holy Ghost. The more frequently we meet with such persons in chaps. i.–xv. (*vide sub* V.)—the Apostles in a body, those who were chosen as the "Seven," St. Peter, St. Stephen, St. Barnabas, St. Paul, the Christians of Jerusalem, and the Christians of Pisidian Antioch are so described—the more strange it must seem that nothing of the kind is said of any one in the second half of the book.

4. In the we-sections are to be found none of the passages, so frequent in chaps. i.–xv., which speak of

the coming, the giving, the receiving of the Spirit, or of the being baptized with Him (*vide sub* VI.).

5. In the we-sections there are no expressions parallel to those included under category XI.

The absence of these groups from the we-sections certainly brings out the distinctive character of chaps. i.–xv., but this distinction is no less clearly marked in the different treatment of parallel material here and in the we-sections. It is true that in the we-sections St. Luke appears as a man endowed with "Spiritual" gifts who seeks for and believes in the miraculous, yet in the parallel stories of chaps. i.–xv. the miraculous colouring is more thickly laid on. Compare the summary accounts of miracles, signs, and wondrous cures (*vide sub.* I.) in chaps. i.–xv. with the parallel passage **xxviii. 9**: καὶ οἱ λοιποὶ οἱ ἐν τῇ νήσῳ ἔχοντες ἀσθενείας προσήρχοντο καὶ ἐθεραπεύοντο, οἳ καὶ πολλαῖς τιμαῖς ἐτίμησαν ἡμᾶς. Here no more is said than a "Christian Scientist" could say, there the strongest expressions are used; we are intended to picture to ourselves the working of the strongest imaginable miraculous power. Or compare the accounts of raising from the dead here and there. In the one case we are told in plain words that Tabitha was dead and that her "corpse" was already prepared for the burial, and that St. Peter by prayer and an authoritative summons brought her to life again. In the we-sections, on the other hand, there is nothing told us in the account of the raising of Eutychus that is in itself extraordinary. Of course *St. Luke regarded*, and would have us regard, the occurrence as an instance of raising from the dead;

but he does not embellish the story from this point of view. It is the same with the story of the snake in Malta: here also nothing is said which is in itself extraordinary, though St. Luke would have the occurrence regarded as a miracle. Nor is it otherwise with the "Spiritual" element in the strict sense of the word. In chaps. i.–xv., in a quite realistic fashion, the Spirit is represented as speaking to St. Peter and St. Philip; in the we-sections the Christians of Tyre and Agabus speak in the Spirit, and the Spirit speaks in visions of the night. In chaps. i.–xv. we read that πνεῦμα κυρίου ἥρπασεν τὸν Φίλιππον (viii. 39) on the public highway; in the we-sections He hinders or prevents; but how this happens we are not told (we must suppose visions or something similar).

It is also very instructive to compare the account of the so-called first missionary journey of St. Paul (chaps. xiii.–xiv.) on the one hand with the accounts of the later journeys, and on the other hand with chaps. i.–xii., xv. Every one will at once see that it belongs to the latter and not to the former section of the book. In xiv. 3 we read of St. Paul and St. Barnabas: παρρησιαζόμενοι ἐπὶ τῷ κυρίῳ, διδόντι σημεῖα καὶ τέρατα γίνεσθαι διὰ τῶν χειρῶν αὐτῶν, just as in numerous passages in chaps. i.–xii. and in xv. 12, while no parallel passage is to be found in the second half of the book. The story of the healing of the lame man in Lystra (xiv. 8 *ff.*) has parallels only in iii. 1 *ff.* and in ix. 33 (in each case a lame man in Jerusalem and Lydda respectively). The story of the punishment of Elymas by blinding has an analogy only in ix. 8. Such expressions as πλησθεὶς πνεύματος ἁγ. (xiii. 9) and *οἱ μαθηταὶ ἐπληροῦντο πνεύματος ἁγ.* (xiii. 52)—concerning St. Paul and the Christians of Pisidian Antioch respectively—are used in the second part neither of St. Paul nor of any one of the communities he founded. Moreover, it is easily recognised that the whole narrative of chaps. xiii.–xiv. (with the exception perhaps of the scene at Lystra, where the people are about to sacrifice to the Apostles) is enveloped in the same atmosphere of generality and superficiality which is characteristic of most of the accounts in the first half of the book. It is not that the author's representation of St. Paul is altogether different from his representation of the leading figures of the Primitive Community—in chaps. xiii.–xiv. he shows that this is not so—but the difference in his treatment begins just at the point where St. Barnabas and St. Paul separate from one another because of St. Mark. All that is narrated before this time is essentially of *one* type, and all that is narrated afterwards is of a twofold type (namely, that of the we-sections and that of the remaining parts), though this does not affect the unity of style and vocabulary which obtains throughout the whole book.

Behind chaps. i.–xv. there accordingly stands an authority (or several authorities) who, as a "Christian Scientist" and a "man of the Spirit," was on the whole congenial to St. Luke, and whose word went very far with him, though he was considerably more credulous and uncritical in regard to the miraculous than St. Luke himself. St. Luke has not dared to narrate such stories where he himself was an eye-witness, but he trustfully accepts them when they are vouched for by this authority (or authorities).

Who was this authority, or who were these authorities? It may seem absurd even to propound this question, and certainly it cannot be satisfactorily answered on the basis of the material which is here collected; yet perhaps some indication may present itself that may help us to an answer. It is natural to suppose, and indeed has been already conjectured by several critics independently of one another, that the authorities for chap. xix., which is so very distinct in character from the rest of the narrative in the second half of the book (*vide supra*), were the Gaius and Aristarchus so abruptly mentioned in verse 29. Aristarchus, moreover—and Gaius also according to the conjecture of Blass—*together with St. Luke* meet St. Paul again a few months later, and Aristarchus also joins St. Paul and St. Luke on the voyage to Rome. The abrupt mention of his name and that of Gaius in xix. 29 receives its simplest explanation on the hypothesis that these very men were here St. Luke's authorities. May we not now attempt to discover among the persons who are mentioned in chaps. i.–xv. one or more who might also be claimed as authorities for what is here recorded? It must have been, as has been already remarked, a person of imposing authority, one whom St. Luke followed with confidence. The leading personalities in chaps. i.–xv. are St. Peter, St. Barnabas, St. Stephen, St. Philip, and St. Paul. Of these, according to his own testimony, he had learned to know *St. Philip* (also St. Paul). That he was also acquainted with St. Peter,

St. Barnabas, and St. Stephen is almost certain in the case of the first two persons, and quite certainly excluded in the case of the last. Moreover, of persons belonging to the Primitive Community he knew St. James, Silas, and St. Mark.[1] St. James, however, falls quite into the background in the book, and no one would dream of him as St. Luke's authority. If therefore this authority is to be sought among the persons mentioned in the book we can only think of *St. Philip*, *St Mark*, or Silas. That he is to be sought among these persons is, in my opinion, overwhelmingly probable; for if St. Luke had the opportunity of gaining information from these persons—what could possibly have prevented him from seizing it? Of the three persons just named Silas is expressly described as a prophet (xv. 32), St. Philip as a great worker of miracles (viii. 6 *f.* 13), both of them thus as imposing authorities, a thing which cannot be said of St. Mark. The latter does not play a very pleasing part in the book (xiii. 13; xv. 37 *ff.*). This, however, is as far as we can go at present.

We must, however, now glance at the character of the miracles narrated in the book. The question occurs whether these rest upon first-hand information, or whether they presuppose secondary or even tertiary tradition. If we neglect the instances of vision, of prophecy, and of other communications made by the Spirit, which are not miracles in the strict sense of the word, we are left in chaps. i.–xv. with six instances of miraculous cure, six (seven) "singular" miracles, and four realistic appearances of angels.

[1] He first learned to know St. Mark in Rome.

Dealing first with the miracles of healing, there is nothing in the three accounts of cures of lameness or in the one account of a cure of blindness that can be brought forward as evidence against the primary character of the tradition. In the first place, these cures of lameness as well as the cure of blindness (the cure of St. Paul who was suffering not strictly from blindness but from temporary loss of sight) could well have actually taken place—cures, and more especially cures of lameness, by suggestion are recorded at all times;[1] if, however, this is not allowed, it is nevertheless certain that from the very beginning belief in such miracles was current in the Primitive Community; nor are the stories told in such a fashion that primary tradition—*i.e.* tradition originating in the circle of those directly or almost directly concerned—must necessarily be excluded. Moreover, the circumstance that St. Paul, in spite of the stoning, still remained alive, and could return into the city, is not related as a miracle, *but is intended to be regarded* as an instance of special Divine protection (just as in the case of the snake-bite at Malta). Of the miracles of healing there is now left only the raising of Tabitha from the dead by St. Peter. It is idle to inquire what really happened on this occasion. It is,

[1] Notice also that each of the three accounts of the cure of lameness has its own distinctive character. The first (in Jerusalem) cannot possibly be broken away from the context, for it plainly gives the occasion for all that follows (indeed probably also for the outpouring of the Spirit—*vide infra*). The second (in Lydda) is an isolated anecdote leading on only to the vigorous extension of the Gospel in Lydda and Sharon. The third (in Lystra) is presupposed by the story of the apotheosis of St. Barnabas and St. Paul, a story that could not have been invented.

however, important that the daughters of St. Philip told Papias of a case of resurrection from the dead, and that even Irenæus writes (II. 31, 2): *ὁ κύριος ἤγειρεν [νεκροὺς] καὶ οἱ ἀπόστολοι διὰ προσευχῆς, καὶ ἐν ἀδελφότητι πολλάκις διὰ τὸ ἀναγκαῖον καὶ τῆς κατὰ τόπον ἐκκλησίας πάσης αἰτησαμένης μετὰ νηστείας καὶ λιτανείας πολλῆς ἐπέστρεψεν τὸ πνεῦμα τοῦ τετελευτηκότος καὶ ἐχαρίσθη ὁ ἄνθρωπος ταῖς εὐχαῖς τῶν ἁγίων.* I consider it to be quite probable that even during the lifetime of St. Peter stories were current concerning dead who had been raised again by that apostle, indeed that he himself may have believed that he had called a dead woman to life again. It is, moreover, favourable to the hypothesis of a primary tradition that the story, in spite of its crudity, is fixed in form and ministers to no special tendency. The event it records did not take place in Jerusalem, but in Joppa, a place which has no other significance in early Christian history, and its favourable results extend only to Joppa and the neighbourhood. None of the more notable Christians of Jerusalem accompanied St. Peter thither, and there is in the story no conscious imitation of a similar event in the Gospel: St. Peter prayed over the corpse, and then by his summons brought back to life this old woman, who had played a part of some importance in the little Christian community of Joppa. I do not see why decades of years should have been necessary for the creation of this legend; it could well have been told to St. Luke when he was staying with St. Philip at Cæsarea.

As for the miracles of "singular" character, we

need not discuss the two cases of sudden blinding (St. Paul and Elymas) and the punishment of Herod by death. The latter is simply a real event narrated from a religious point of view; St. Paul really lost his sight for a short time; and the story of the blinding of Elymas by St. Paul, which certainly did not occur in the way we are told, has probably some historical nucleus, though no one if he is wise will venture to state what it is, for it is possible to conjecture all kinds of things. It is enough to know that the Proconsul's magician lost his eyesight at the time that the influence of St. Paul won over his patron. We cannot well imagine that the story is pure invention; for why is it that nothing dreadful happens to Simon Magus, who is painted in much darker colours? This negative fact seems to me very important; for if St. Luke wished to invent miracles there was no more fitting place to insert one than here. And for this very reason I regard the recourse to similar traits of constant occurrence in novels of those times as quite uncalled for.

There remain therefore only the Ascension, the miracle of Pentecost, the Earthquake, and the story of Ananias and Sapphira. Here also we may at once eliminate the miracle of Pentecost. The countless learned essays on this subject are really not worth the paper on which they are written. There is only need of a little literary feeling and understanding in order to recognise that St. Luke the litterateur has here taken the liberty of dressing up the phenomenon of "speaking with tongues" in a grandiose style, although its real nature and its form of manifestation were naturally well known to him. There is absolutely no reason to assume the interpolation of secondary or tertiary tradition, or the combination of two sources, or such like hypotheses. Indeed, the very attempt to analyse and to test the inner unity of this passage is in itself an artistic crime. Neither is there anything extraordinary about the Earthquake of iv. 31. Besides, it is not a question here of an earthquake in the strict sense of the word: *δεηθέντων αὐτῶν ἐσαλεύθη ὁ τόπος, ἐν ᾧ ἦσαν συνηγμένοι, καὶ ἐπλήσθησαν ἅπαντες τοῦ ἁγίου πνεύματος.* The trembling of the ecstasy is transferred also to the place where they were assembled. Certainly the author intends a real miracle, but it is just as certain that the record that such a miracle occurred could have arisen at once and in the very locality of its supposed occurrence.

It is otherwise with the story of Ananias and Sapphira and of the Ascension; but they are of quite a different character.

The story of Ananias and Sapphira is certainly no "allegorical fable" (Pfleiderer), and by the fact that it presupposes not a general community of goods in the Church of Jerusalem, but a self-sacrifice which rested with the free-will of the individual, it shows that it belongs to very ancient tradition. Neither does it belong to the general plan of the Acts, *i.e.* it is not a necessary link in the chain of development of the narrative, but stands by itself. In its outward form it is entirely Lukan, though it contains singular elements in both vocabulary and subject-matter (*νοσφίζεσθαι, συστέλλειν, διάστημα, συνεφωνήθη ὑμῖν, ψεύ-*

σασθαι τὸ ἁγ. πνεῦμα, ψεύσασθαι τῷ θεῷ, οἱ νεώτεροι [οἱ νεανίσκοι]). Its point lies in the miraculous knowledge and power of St. Peter (in the second place, in the sanctity of the Church, in which every offence is avenged by God). Here again we cannot say what really happened, but it is not incredible that the sudden death of two members of the community, of doubtful character, should have been regarded in Jerusalem itself, and even by contemporaries, as a Divine act of punishment announced by St. Peter; and that the account of this event should have been worked up after the pattern of Jos. vii. and Levit. x. If, however, we recollect 1 Cor. v. 5, we may go a step farther and may very well suppose that St. Peter really pronounced a sentence of death against the guilty pair and that their death actually followed (*vide Macar. Magn.*, III. 21, 28). How this took place scarcely allows of conjecture. At all events this legend is not one of those that could only have been created by a later generation.

On the other hand, the account of the corporal Ascension is without doubt a narrative that could not have taken form in the circle of the "Eleven." I have collected together the material for the history of the tradition of the Ascension in Hahn's *Bibliothek der Symbole,* 3 Aufl. s. 382 *ff.* Apart from the Acts, it occurs in the New Testament only in the spurious conclusion of St. Mark, and in the interpolated passage in St. Luke xxiv. 51. St. Paul has no knowledge of it; but there is no need to show how natural it was that the primitive belief in the *descensus* and *ascensus* should take this form in dependence upon the story of Elijah (for the "cloud" *cf.* St. Mark ix. 7; xiii. 26; xiv. 62; Rev. xi. 12; xiv. 14 *ff.*). The most interesting points are the localisation on the Mount of Olives, and the term of forty days. The localisation need not necessarily have taken form in Jerusalem; yet it is overwhelmingly probable that this trait had its origin in that city, for such localisations are wont to be assigned in the place itself. Moreover, there can be no doubt that the Primitive Community very soon began to embellish the story of the last days of our Lord with local legends, according to their own taste, and with a view to their own glorification. *This accretion of legend was facilitated by the fact that after twelve years the Apostles left Jerusalem and only returned thither on short visits.* The Church there stood under the leadership of St. James, who did not belong to the Twelve. Perhaps it was only after his death that the legends arose that our Lord first appeared to him, that the women (or one woman) saw Him at the empty tomb, and that accordingly the appearances in Galilee were preceded by appearances in Jerusalem (the former were then persistently ignored). At the time when St. Luke was with St. Paul in Jerusalem these stories could scarcely have been current. The stories that were told at that time we learn from 1 Cor. xv. and the genuine St. Mark, and from St. Matthew. The dispersion of the Apostles after twelve years, and the dispersion of the Christians of Jerusalem during the Great War, gave the opportunity for such a luxuriant growth of semi-doctrinal legends concerning the appearances of the Crucified in Jerusalem. They took form in the second generation, perhaps not in Jerusalem, yet with the view to the glorification of that city, and then were further developed within the Church of Jerusalem when it had again gathered together in its old home.

But if St. Luke had once heard the more trustworthy story, how could he possibly have bartered his better knowledge for a later and inferior tradition? That he could do so is already shown in the two parts of his own work when we compare the conclusion of the first with the beginning of the second; for here he has exchanged a secondary for a tertiary tradition. Why may he not previously have given up a primary in exchange for a secondary tradition? In his gospel he indeed knows of an Ascension—in Acts i. 1 *ff.* he says in plain words that in his former work he had carried his narrative down to the point where our Lord was taken up into Heaven (see also St. Luke ix. 51)—but he only mentions the fact, he does not picture it as a visible ascension, he does not localise it on the Mount of Olives, and he does not fix its occurrence at the end of forty days, but on the day of the Resurrection. These are all points wherein this story is superior to the narrative of the Acts, though it is already legendary in character, and presupposes a development of tradition which must have occupied some considerable period of time. Now, however, St. Luke has met with what he thinks still better information, though it is really inferior: now the Ascension is visible like the ascension of Elijah, now it takes place on the Mount of Olives, and that after a period of forty days of continuous intercourse with the disciples. If it is thought incredible that St. Luke could have exchanged the tradition of St. Paul and St. Mark for that which appears in his gospel, then it ought also to be thought incredible that he should have given up the latter tradition in favour of that which appears in the Acts. And yet the latter exchange is a fact, unless we are to assume that the first twelve verses (certainly not intact) of the Acts have been, even to their innermost nucleus, edited and recast. There are, however, no grounds for such a radical hypothesis. Hence it follows that St. Luke has *twice* exchanged his better knowledge for that which is worse.

Yet, after all, is this so strange? Has not Christology its own history? and must we assume that its influence could not have been as strong as that of actual history? The problem here in question is simple compared with the problem of the gospel of St. Mark, *i.e.* compared with the problem presented by the fact that the legendary traditions concerning Christ actually took form within *the Primitive Community* during the first thirty years and under the very eyes of those who had witnessed the events themselves! Later legends and legends with a doctrinal tendency show themselves even more powerful than the memory of the actual history; and even the recollections of eye-witnesses are modified and transformed under the dominating influence of the thought "So it must have happened"! When some considerable time after the destruction of Jerusalem St. Luke wrote his gospel—perhaps in Asia—he reproduced the story of the last days of our Lord according to a recension which, though originating in Jerusalem, coincided in important points with the Johannine type. It was not until afterwards that he accepted the myth of the forty days and of the visible Ascension, and gave his vote for it in the Acts of the Apostles. This myth belongs to the by no means small number of those myths in which Israelitish and Hellenic ideas encounter one another. Those who suppose that the legend of the Ascension of our Lord took form on the soil of Gentile Christianity and in dependence upon the myths of the apotheosis of heroes and emperors are certainly mistaken, and yet it is no wonder that these legends when they reached the genuine Hellene were especially welcome, and therefore regarded as especially worthy of credence. Now for the first time, according to his view of things, the story of the Saviour of the World whose birth had been celebrated by the angelic choirs had received its appropriate finale! Therewith all earlier, more or less unsatisfying, "conclusions" were set aside.

It is true, therefore, that stories of miracles in the first fifteen chapters of the Acts include, in the story of the Ascension, a tertiary legend, indeed a myth, although St. Luke was originally better informed and also knew well what was written in the gospel of St. Mark; yet his reason for exchanging his better knowledge for the worse admits of very easy explanation. All the other stories of miracles occurring in these chapters, including the story of Ananias and Sapphira, can be ascribed to primary tradition, even though here and there a story has been worked up.[1] *It is a remarkable fact that* (apart from the Ascension) *only the miracles of the Lame Man, of the Death of Ananias and Sapphira, and of the Release of St. Peter from prison, are related in connection with Jerusalem itself.*[2] This self-restraint vouches well for the relative trustworthiness of the Jerusalem accounts; but we may also say, in regard to all the miracles narrated in the Acts, that measured by the miracles of the Acta Pauli or of the Acta Johannis and later apocryphal Acts of Apostles they appear scarcely miracles at all. The miracles of the we-sections are almost all miracles of the first degree; the miracles in chaps. i.–xv. are partly of the same degree, partly, however, miracles of the second degree. The miracles of the so-called apocryphal Acts are miracles of the second or third degree. By miracles of the third degree I

[1] I have not as yet dealt with the four realistic appearances of angels. The first (i. 10 *f.*) is insignificant; the two "men" at the Ascension as *angeli interpretes* are almost necessary embellishments of such narratives (*cf.* the appearance of angels at the sepulchre). The two narratives, v. 19 and xii. 7–11 (the angel unlocking the prison) are evidently doublets (on this *vide infra*). The more ancient form here is that St. Peter (not "the Apostles") was miraculously (*i.e.* by an angel) released from prison (chap. xii.). We may suppose that such a wonderful (*i.e.* entirely unexpected) release really occurred; the details of the story vouch for this. It was the general belief that every child of God, and especially St. Peter (xii. 15), had his own guardian angel. This at once afforded a means for explaining the manner of the deliverance, and even if we cannot suppose that St. Peter himself told the story as we read it in chap. xii., still it could have been so told by his friends, Laslty, the speaking of the angel to St. Philip (viii. 26) is as a "miracle" insignificant.

[2] The remaining miracles are connected with Damascus, Lydda, Joppa, Cyprus, and Lystra,

mean those absurd stories of wonders which have not the tiniest substratum of fact, but are demonstrably either false inventions from beginning to end or old stories of miracles or popular myths in a new setting. The critics of the Acts of the Apostles have not as a rule a sufficient acquaintance with this unwieldy collection of fabulous stories. If they knew them they would not make so much ado about the stories of miracles in the Acts.

The observation made above that only three stories of miracles are connected with Jerusalem suggests an inquiry into the whole question of the grouping of the narratives of the Acts. Starting in this way we may perhaps approach nearer to the solution of the enigma which the book presents. The next chapter is dedicated to this question.

CHAPTER V

THE SOURCES AND THEIR VALUE

IF St. Luke the Physician is the author of the Acts, the question of sources is simply and speedily settled for the whole second half of the book. So far as a considerable portion of this second half is concerned, he has written as an eye-witness, and for the rest he depends upon the report of eye-witnesses who were his fellow-workers. For what occurred during the second and third missionary journeys Timothy and Gaius and Aristarchus of Macedonia (xix. 29; xx. 4; xxvii. 2) come into the first line of consideration (*vide supra*, p. 149). As for the narrative of what occurred during the *final* visit to Jerusalem and Cæsarea we cannot point to any definite person who formed the author's authority here; but during the long voyage from Cæsarea to Rome which immediately followed these events, St. Luke was actually the companion of St. Paul. It is in itself improbable that the second half of the book (from xvi. 6 onwards) depends upon written sources, nor do we anywhere find indications of their existence.[1] It has, however, been already shown (pp. 141 *ff.*) that the records which stood at the author's service for this portion of the book are

[1] Whether the cases of discrepancy presuppose the use of sources is discussed later.

sharply distinguished by their sobriety from the sources for the first half of the book.[1]

As for the first half of the book, every attempt to make a scientific analysis of the sources on the basis of vocabulary and style has proved abortive. A most thorough and detailed investigation has taught me that everything here is so "Lukan" in character that by the method of linguistic investigation no sure results can be attained. The style of the first half is certainly distinguishable from that of the second half by certain obvious and tangible characteristics (*vide* "Luke the Physician," pp. 106 *ff.*); yet not only is the agreement much greater than the difference, but the problem which here exists is only part of the problem which dominates the whole question of the relationship between the gospel and the Acts. St. Luke is an artist in style, and always modifies his style in accordance with the content of his narrative and the geographical scene of action (*vide loc. cit.*, 103 *ff.*); from this established fact it follows that differences of style do not necessarily imply different sources. It is true that sources *may* lie in the background—in the gospel, for instance, by noting differences of style it might *perhaps* have been possible to arrive at a source like St. Mark and another like Q, even if we did not possess the gospels of St. Mark and St. Matthew (*vide* my "Sayings of Jesus," Williams and Norgate, 1908); but in no part of the Acts can the use of sources be proved on the basis of linguistic investigation.

[1] Local colouring is found in the second half only in the narrative of events in Ephesus and in the account of the voyage.

In the face of this negative result our inquiry into the first half of the book must approach the question from other starting-points—from the scenes and persons with which the narrative is concerned. All historical traditions are attached to persons or places; they are either local or personal or both together. St. Luke was necessarily dependent upon tradition. The scene, upon which the primitive history of the Church was enacted, was far removed from him, the Hellene, not only in time and space, but also in temperament and spirit. And yet it is on the other hand most important to recollect that he had been in Palestine—even though probably only on a flying visit—; that he had learned to know the Christian communities of Jerusalem, Cæsarea, and some churches on the eastern shores of the Mediterranean; that in company with St. Paul he had worked with Silas of Jerusalem, and in Rome with St. Mark, another native of Jerusalem; that he even came into personal contact with St. James, the Lord's brother; and that he had stayed in the house of St. Philip the Evangelist (*vide supra*, pp. 149 *f.*).[1] There is surely com-

[1] His acquaintance with, or fellowship in labour with, St. Paul's Hellenic fellow-workers, does not concern us here. The circumstance that Titus is not mentioned in the Acts would only present a difficulty if Titus were so constantly with St. Paul, and so intimately bound up with his ministry as was Timothy and, for a period of time, Silas. But in all probability he was as independent as St. Luke himself, and only temporarily placed himself at the disposal of the Apostle. He is, moreover, probably included in the words "καί τινας ἄλλους" of Acts xv. 2, and perhaps also in xv. 35 (μετὰ καὶ ἑτέρων πολλῶν). By mentioning the ἄλλοι St. Luke salves his own conscience as an accurate historian, and clearly enough informs us that he does not wish to suppress anything, though he

munication enough here to explain the character of the material for chaps. i.–xvi. 5 of the Acts and the means by which it was acquired; and it is obvious that we must start our critical investigation with the discussion of these means of communication. Whether these will suffice, *i.e.* whether we may not be compelled to search for other sources of information, is a wider question.

Considering first the scenes of action we find that they are as follows:—

Chaps. i.–viii. 1. Scene—Jerusalem.

Chap. viii. 1, 4. Scene—*αἱ χῶραι τῆς Ἰουδαίας καὶ Σαμαρίας.*

Chap. viii. 5–25. Scene—Samaria and Jerusalem.

Chap. viii. 26–40. Scene—The coast of Philistia (Azotus and Cæsarea; starting from Jerusalem: viii. 26).

Chap. ix. 1–30. Scene—Damascus and Jerusalem.

Chaps. ix. 32–xi. 18. Scene—The coast of Philistia (Lydda, Joppa, Cæsarea) and Jerusalem.

Chap. xi. 19–30; xii. 25. Scene—Antioch and Jerusalem.

Chap. xii. 1–24. Scene—Jerusalem (and Cæsarea).

Chaps. xiii. 1–xiv. 28. Scene—Antioch, and the places in south-eastern and central Asia Minor visited by the mission which started from Antioch.

thinks that he is justified in confining himself to the express mention of St. Paul and St. Barnabas as the chief characters. Besides, it is clear from Gal. ii. 1 (*μετὰ Βαρν. συμπαραλαβὼν καὶ Τίτον*) and Gal. ii. 9 (where Titus is wanting) that the others were really only secondary characters. St. Luke's procedure is therefore fully justified.

Chap. xv. 1–35. Scene—Antioch and Jerusalem; xv. 36–xvi. 5, a fresh visit to the churches of Syria, Cilicia, and south-eastern Asia Minor (forming the transition to what follows).

This survey seems to teach us that, with the exception of xiii. 1–xiv. 28, a section which begins and ends in Antioch, *we are throughout concerned with traditions connected with Jerusalem;* for even where the action of the narrative is carried on in other scenes, Jerusalem still remains the place whence it proceeds and to which it in many instances returns. We might accordingly formulate the very simple conclusion that the Acts in its first half, with the exception of chaps. xiii. and xiv., presents us with tradition purely connected with Jerusalem.

But the matter is not so simple as this. The "interpolated" passage, with its horizon so clearly Antiochean, of itself incites us to inquire whether Antiochean tradition may not be traced earlier in the book; and in chap. xv., also, we find that the narrative starts from Antioch (xv. 1 *f.*), and returns thither (xv. 30–35). Closer investigation shows that the Antiochean character of chap. xv. is as clear as that of chaps. xiii.–xiv.; for the arrangement of both passages is exactly parallel; the narrative begun in Antioch passes over to other scenes, and returns back to Antioch again. Accordingly xiii. 1–xv. 35 is Antiochean tradition, because the principal scene of action is Antioch. With this conclusion agree the exact statements concerning prophets and teachers in Antioch in xiii. 1, and the details given in xv. 1, 2, and xv. 30–35. It has been thought that a quite new division of the book begins with xiii. 1, because the section opens with the words: ἦσαν δὲ ἐν Ἀντιοχείᾳ κατὰ τὴν οὖσαν ἐκκλησίαν προφῆται καὶ διδάσκαλοι. But it was necessary to mention the name "Ἀντιόχεια" here (instead of omitting the name as in xii. 25 and writing "there"), because even in xii. 25 the name of the city is left to be supplied after ὑπέστρεψαν, and it would have meant too great reliance upon the memory of the reader if the name of the city had been again unexpressed. Again, the purpose of the words τὴν οὖσαν ἐκκλησίαν is not to inform us that there was a church in Antioch, but to distinguish the prophets who are here named as belonging to this city from those prophets belonging to Jerusalem who had come down to Antioch (xi. 27 *ff.*). Hence xiii. 1 *ff.* necessarily presupposes not only xii. 25 but also xi. 27–30. But now we at once notice that this section, although it introduces a journey of St. Barnabas and St. Paul to Judæa and Jerusalem, is nevertheless written from the standpoint of Antioch—even if we do not accept the reading of Codex D (συνεστραμμένων ἡμῶν) as original (this reading is correct in that it marks that the tradition here belongs not to Jerusalem but to Antioch)—for it is to Antioch that the prophets come from Jerusalem, and the Apostles depart from Antioch *and return thither again* (while nothing is said about the return of the prophets who came from Jerusalem). The setting of this passage is therefore found to be exactly similar to that given in xiii. 1 *f.* and xiv. 26 *f.*, and in xv. 1 *ff.* and xv. 30–35. Thus all from xi. 27–xv. 35 is Antiochean tradition, with the exception of xii. 1–24, a piece of

Jerusalem tradition which we can now see has been interpolated here.

But the passages written from the standpoint of Antioch do not first begin with xi. 27, rather as has been long recognised xi. 27 *ff.* presupposes xi. 19–26—a passage of even central importance—indeed, is bound up with it. In this passage the rapid development of the narrative is from the beginning directed towards Antioch, and in the shortest space presents a wonderful wealth of information (the preaching to the Gentiles; the foundation and the rapid growth of the Church; the sending of St. Barnabas from Jerusalem to Antioch; St. Barnabas' approval of the mission to the Gentiles, and the part he took in it; the bringing of St. Paul from Tarsus to Antioch by St. Barnabas; their united missionary work in the city during a whole year; the origin of the name "Christians" in Antioch). These facts in themselves, and, above all, the statement concerning the origin of the name "Christians," leave no room for doubt that we have here Antiochean tradition, even if xi. 19–26 were not bound up so closely as it is with what follows. It is not even forgotten that the first persons who dared to preach the Gospel directly to Gentiles—and that first in Antioch; for this is expressly emphasised—were exclusively Christians of Cyprus and Cyrene.

Their names are not mentioned, though afterwards the prophets and teachers of Antioch are introduced by name. This, however, cannot be because they met with slight success—for in xi. 21 we learn just the opposite—but only because they were not *authorised* prophets and teachers, or rather were not prophets and teachers by profession.

But these Christians of Cyprus and Cyrene who preached in Antioch, and founded in that city the mission to the Gentiles, are introduced in xi. 19 *f.* as members of an already well-known group—namely, those Christians who had fled from Jerusalem because of the episode of St. Stephen. They are introduced by the words: *οἱ μὲν οὖν διασπαρέντες ἀπὸ τῆς θλίψεως τῆς γενομένης ἐπὶ Στεφάνῳ.* The narrative thus goes back for some 146 verses, and connects directly with viii. 1, 4, as if nothing had intervened (note the catchword *διεσπάρησαν* in viii. 1 and *οἱ μὲν οὖν διασπαρέντες* in viii. 4). Thus viii. 1, 4 also belong to the Antiochean group of narratives.

Now comes the question, how much more of the preceding part of the book must we assign to this group? In order to answer this question it is obvious that we must begin with vi. 1 *ff.*; for all that precedes is of a different character, and is exclusively connected with Jerusalem. Besides, as we shall see more clearly later, vi. 1 *ff.* is sharply distinguished from chaps. i.–v. by the character and the precision of its narrative.

In vi. 1–6 we have the account of the election of the seven deacons in consequence of a controversy in the Church between the Hellenists and the Hebrews. Among the seven Stephen comes at once to the front (*ἀνὴρ πλήρης πίστεως καὶ πνεύματος ἁγίου*, again *πλήρης χάριτος καὶ δυνάμεως ἐποίει τέρατα καὶ σημεῖα μεγάλα ἐν τῷ λαῷ*, again *ἡ σοφία καὶ τὸ πνεῦμα ᾧ ἐλάλει*, compare the description of Barnabas in xi.

24: ἀνὴρ ἀγαθὸς καὶ πλήρης πνεύματος ἁγίου καὶ πίστεως), all the rest are simply named with the *sole* exception that the words "προσήλυτος Ἀντιοχεύς" are added to the name of Nicolas (vi. 5). Thus two traits—that the native of Antioch is the only one of the "Seven" whose place of origin is mentioned and that the Hellenists are introduced in controversy with Hebrews—a kind of preparation for the Ἕλληνες in xi. 20—make it in itself probable that vi. 1–6 belongs to xi. 19 *ff.* But there are yet closer bonds of connection between the two passages. For we must necessarily ask why this account of the choice of the seven deacons, which stands out in such contrast to the narratives of chaps. i.–v., has been given at all. Taking account of what follows we at once perceive that this election forms in one way or another the starting-point of no less than three lines of narrative: (1) St. Stephen's controversy with the Hellenistic Jews, and then all that follows up to the preaching of the Gospel in Antioch by those who had been scattered by the persecution concerning Stephen; (2) the missionary activity of St. Philip in Samaria, &c.; (3) St. Paul's zeal in persecution and his conversion on the way to Damascus. But it is only the first line which is really organically connected with the election of the "Seven"; for the two others this election is not an essentially necessary presupposition, nor are they especially concerned with the distinction between Hebrews and Hellenists. On the other hand, the connection is vital and complete throughout the following series of events:—

1. A dispute arises between Hebrews and Hellenists;

2. In order to remove the causes of the dispute seven Hellenists are chosen as deacons;

3. One of them, Stephen, contends with the rigidly orthodox Hellenists, and is accused of uttering blasphemy against "the holy place" and the Law and of proclaiming the destruction of the Temple and the abolition of the ἔθη of Moses;

4. A persecution arises, Stephen is put to death, and the Christians of Jerusalem (except the Apostles—thus not all the Christians of Jerusalem but most probably only the Hellenistic Christians) are compelled to leave Jerusalem;

5. At first they are dispersed throughout Judæa and Samaria, where they preach, but afterwards they wander farther, extending their mission to Phœnicia, Cyprus, and Antioch; and some of them, men of Cyprus and Cyrene, preach the Gospel to the Greeks in Antioch.

This is evidently *a single connected* narrative, the goal of which is from the first Antioch and the mission to the Gentiles, and which for this very reason begins with the controversy in Jerusalem itself between Hebrews and Hellenists. Its unity can, moreover, be proved from considerations of form; for in the story of St. Philip not only is there no special emphasis laid upon the circumstance that the Samaritans differed in religion from the Jews, but also this story is itself obviously and confessedly a digression. In fact, in viii. 4, St. Luke already makes a start to tell what he is about to tell us in xi. 19. He commences with the words: *οἱ μὲν οὖν διασπαρέντες διῆλθον, i.e. with the same words with which he commences in* xi. 19. But instead of continuing: (διῆλθον) ἕως Φοινίκης καὶ Κύπρου καὶ Ἀντιοχείας, he confines himself, without naming the countries, to the general phrase: (διῆλθον) εὐαγγελιζόμενοι τὸν λόγον, so that it was possible for him to pass over to the story of St. Philip, to connect therewith other digressions, and not to take up the thread again until xi. 19. Hence all that comes between viii. 4 and xi. 19 is digression, and accordingly vi. 1–8 and xi. 19–xv. 35 (with the exception of xii. 1–24) form one great homogeneous passage which stands in sharp contrast to the rest of the context: *It is an Antiochean tradition*, distinguished as such by the phrase Νικόλαος προσήλυτος Ἀντιοχεύς at the very beginning, characterised as such by the fact that the point is throughout directed towards Antioch, and proved to be such by the indissoluble connection of the earlier sections with the concluding sections, which are unquestionably Antiochean in character. In view of the verbal coincidence between viii. 4 and xi. 19 the question must occur whether a *written* source does not here lie in the background. The argument in favour of this conclusion is strong, but taken by itself it is not convincing; it is also possible that St. Luke may have repeated his own words.

But there is yet another consideration which makes it probable that St. Luke is here dependent on a written source. In vi. 13 the witnesses who charge St. Stephen with blasphemy against the Temple and the Law are described as *false* witnesses, and then there follows the long speech of St. Stephen; this speech, however, not only breaks off prematurely, but also shows evident traces of the hand of an editor, for while its depreciatory attitude towards the Temple is still clearly recognisable, its attitude towards the Law is quite obscure. It is not, therefore, too bold a conjecture to suppose that at the background here there lies a source in which the accusations concerning the Temple and the Law (*vide* "The Trial of Christ") were *not* described as false accusations, and in which the speech of St. Stephen had a sharper tone (in reference to the Law), and also contained at its close the declaration that Ἰησοῦς καταλύσει τὸν τόπον τοῦτον καὶ ἀλλάξει τὰ ἔθη ἃ παρέδωκεν Μωϋσῆς. It would be quite in correspondence with St. Luke's reverence for the Old Testament and for the pious ordinances of the ancient religion—which was all the greater because he did not know them from within—that he should have softened the tones here. Then, however, it is probable that for vi. 1–viii. 4, and xi. 19–xv. 35 (xii. 1–24 may be neglected in this connection) he possessed a written source. The unity of this source cannot, of course, be absolutely proved, but when we consider how the passages vi. 1–viii. 4 and xi. 19–30 carry on a connected and purposeful development of events whose goal is Antioch, and as we note the Antiochean setting of chaps. xiii. and xiv., as well as of xv. 1–35, this hypothesis seems at all events probable. We may also point out that in the first half of the Acts it is only in these Antiochean passages (and in chap. ix., a chapter which stands by itself) that the Christians are called οἱ μαθηταί, and that the Apostles (vi. 2) are called οἱ δώδεκα; and that such detailed accounts as those of vi. 5;

vi. 9; xi. 19, 20; and xiii. 1 are almost without analogy elsewhere in the first half of the book.

But is all the rest of the first half of the book, namely, chaps. i.–v.; viii. 5–xi. 18; xii. 1–24, really tradition connected with Jerusalem and also homogeneous? As a matter of fact the whole narrative of chaps. i.–v. is connected with Jerusalem, and we may say that all the rest has Jerusalem for its setting; but two considerations demand further examination. In the first place, the narrative concerning St. Paul in ix. 1–28 [1] (to which vii. 58[b] and viii. 1[a], 3 also belong) has Jerusalem indeed for its setting, but the fact that parallel accounts exist in xxii. 3–16 and xxvi. 9–18, of itself shows that we have here tradition of a distinctive character, and the possibility that St. Luke may have derived his information from St. Paul himself, compels us to treat this passage separately. It is also deficient in connection with the rest of the narratives. In the second place, the stories of St. Philip, though their scene of action lies outside Jerusalem, and also the records of the mission of St. Peter in Palestine, are certainly closely dependent upon Jerusalem; and yet there is another city to which they give special prominence, namely, Cæsarea. We read first at the conclusion of the stories of St. Philip: *Φίλιππος εὑρέθη εἰς Ἄζωτον, καὶ διερχόμενος εὐηγγελίζετο τὰς πόλεις πάσας ἕως τοῦ ἐλθεῖν αὐτὸν εἰς Καισαρίαν* (viii. 40). It is thus expressly noted that St. Philip took up his lasting abode in Cæsarea, and in this way we are prepared for xxi. 8, 9. Secondly, the conversion of

[1] The limits here are uncertain.

the centurion, an event only inferior in importance to that of chap. xi. 19 *ff.*, has its scene in Cæsarea; further the express, yet seamingly superfluous, information is given that the brethren who conducted St. Paul from Jerusalem to Tarsus came with him to Cæsarea (ix. 30); and lastly, there is the record of the punishment of Herod by death in Cæsarea (xii. 19 *ff.*)—a piece of supplementary information which lies quite outside the economy of the book. We must, therefore, describe the sections viii. 5–40; ix. 29–xi. 18; xii. 1–24 as Cæsarean tradition, or rather as tradition connected with both Jerusalem and Cæsarea. There is also a piece of personal tradition (the Conversion of St. Paul, ix. 1–28). It has, however, been shown in the previous chapter that all these traditions are strictly homogeneous in their attitude to the supernatural, and that this character cannot have been first impressed upon them by St. Luke; for otherwise it must have appeared in those parts of the second half of the book where the "we" does not occur; here, however, this character is almost entirely wanting.

The passages i.–v.; viii. 5–40; ix. 29–xi. 18; and xii. 1–24, do not give an impression of literary homogeneity such as would lead us to conclude that they are derived from a single source; but we cannot come to close quarters with this question until we have investigated the content of these passages with special reference to the chief personalities with which they are concerned.

The Antiochean traditions, as read in St. Luke, begin with St. Stephen, whom they extol—while St.

Paul does not mention him in any of his epistles—and then pass over from the "men of Cyprus and Cyrene" to St. Barnabas and St. Paul, gradually giving to the latter ever greater prominence (up to xiii. 7 St. Barnabas stands in the foreground—xiii. 9 St. Paul's change of name—xiii. 13 *οἱ περὶ Παῦλον*—in xiii. 43, 46, 50; xv. 2 [*bis*], 22, 35 St. Paul stands first—xiv. 20 *ἐξῆλθεν σὺν τῷ Βαρνάβᾳ*—but in xiv. 12; xiv. 14; xv. 12, 25, St. Barnabas still stands first). This gradually increasing accentuation of the importance of St. Paul, and the introduction of the name "Paul" for "Saul," are certainly due to St. Luke, and were foreign to the source, as may be seen even from xiv. 14 and xv. 12, 25. Hence we may not describe the Antiochean tradition as Pauline tradition, but must characterise it by the three names—Stephen—Barnabas—Saul. In it St. Barnabas is regarded as equal to, indeed as superior in importance to, St. Paul—as with St. Stephen we are told something of his character and antecedents (*vide supra*), nothing of the kind is told us of St. Paul; again, St. Barnabas is a prophet, St. Paul only a teacher. This again shows us that we are here concerned with a separate tradition which has been touched up by St. Luke.[1] According to this source St. Paul was not the originator of the mission to the Gentiles; on the contrary, the men of Cyprus and Cyrene were first in

[1] It is even possible that, in the source, St. Stephen and St. Barnabas were treated as the chief characters, and that Saul played only a secondary part. In favour of this hypothesis we have xv. 37: Βαρναβᾶς ἐβούλετο συμπαραλαβεῖν καὶ τὸν Ἰωάννην (*cf.* also παραλαβόντα in verse 39), if we may press the words. Yet it is no longer possible to speak here with certainty.

the field, and were followed by St. Barnabas, and only in the third place by St. Paul. In its references to Jerusalem this source is interested in the attitude of the *Church as a whole*; otherwise only in St. Peter and in St. James (chap. xv.), who is regarded as of equal importance with St. Peter. Here (in contrast with Gal. ii. 9) all remembrance of the attitude of St. John has vanished; on the other hand, the memory of the two men who were at that time sent from Jerusalem to Antioch has been preserved; they were the prophets Judas Barsabbas and Silas. The relations between Jerusalem and Antioch are, on the whole, carefully depicted. First Barnabas came from Jerusalem to Antioch as an ambassador (xi. 22), then a whole deputation of prophets (xi. 27), then teachers (xv. 1), then Judas and Silas. We are to note that these were all prophets or teachers; evidently it was considered that such men were alone suitable to conduct negotiations, and to establish relations in the correct way. By the mention of the thrice repeated despatch of prophets from Jerusalem to Antioch, and by the journeys of St. Paul and St. Barnabas from Antioch to Jerusalem, this body of tradition is again held together and characterised as homogeneous. Through the whole of these sections there also runs a connected theme: the foundation of the mission to the Gentiles in the foundation of the Church of Antioch, the extension of this mission from Antioch and its firm establishment by St. Barnabas and St. Paul up to its full recognition by the mother church of Jerusalem, which had from the beginning benevolently fostered good relations with Antioch, while on the part of Antioch there was no want of filial deference to Jerusalem.

The traditions connected with Jerusalem, and with both Jerusalem and Cæsarea, have in chaps. i.–v. St. Peter as their centre (in iv. 36 St. Barnabas is thrust into the context by St. Luke, very carelessly and inartistically so far as form is concerned, but in order to prepare for his later ministry; also St. John here and later in the work is depicted in quite a shadowy fashion). In viii. 5–40 St. Philip and St. Peter form the central points; in ix. 29–xi. 18 and xii. 1–24 St. Peter again stands by himself. We must accordingly describe these traditions as Petrine, with the proviso that two passages connected with St. Philip are found among them (viii. 5–13; viii. 26–40). The first is closely bound up with the Petrine sections by the Petrine passage viii. 14–25; but the second is quite independent, neither does the first lose anything of its real independence because of its conjunction with the Petrine sections. St. Philip here plays a primary part. Accordingly these traditions fall into two divisions very unequal in extent, the larger of which is grouped exclusively round St. Peter, the smaller round St. Philip. This distinction does not, however, coincide with the distinction between tradition purely connected with Jerusalem and that connected with Jerusalem and Cæsarea; in fact, the latter body of tradition is connected not only with St. Philip but also with St. Peter.

The Jerusalem-Cæsarean tradition (viii. 5–40; ix. 29–xi. 18), concerned both with St. Peter and St. Philip, may be regarded as an unity, for the style of narrative is the same, and the sections are bound together by similar traits. Moreover, the passage xii. 1–24 must be assigned to the same collection; for it is connected both with Jerusalem and Cæsarea and gives the necessary completion to the narrative of viii. 5–40 and ix. 29–xi. 18. As for chaps. i.–v., this passage of fundamental importance for the Acts is certainly not homogeneous, rather we can trace in it at least two strains of tradition. This fact has been long recognised with more or less clearness, though its details have been worked out in various ways. By means of a criticism totally wanting in method, and with an exaggeration which is simply colossal, the conclusion has actually been drawn that throughout the whole of the Acts, or at least throughout the greater half of that book, there run two parallel sources, veritable twin writings! We now proceed to state all that can be safely concluded on the basis of methodical investigation.

Every one who carefully reads chaps. ii.–v. and attempts to realise the connection and succession of events recorded in those chapters must necessarily recognise that the whole second chapter and chap. v. 17–42 are elements which disturb and obstruct the flow of the narrative—are, in fact, doublets which are in more than one respect liable to exception. If we at first simply omit them we arrive at the following scheme of narrative:—

1. St. Peter and St. John go to the Temple; the cure of the impotent man (iii. 1–10), clearly recorded as the first astounding miracle, one which determines the whole following course of events.

2. St. Peter's great missionary sermon in Solomon's Porch on the occasion of the miracle that had been wrought (iii. 11–26).

3. The extraordinary effect of the miracle and the sermon (5000 souls are said to have been converted [1]); St. Peter and St. John are at evening cast into prison by the Jewish authorities [the Sadducees are specially mentioned] (iv. 1–4).

4. The hearing in the morning; St. Peter's missionary discourse before the Council (the cure of the impotent man is still the fact upon which the argument rests); the command not to preach the Gospel; the protest of St. Peter and St. John against the same ("Judge ye yourselves whether it is right in the sight of God to hearken to you more than unto God"); the dismissal of the Apostles because of fear of the people (iv. 5–22).

5. The return of the Apostles to their brethren; [2] the great thanksgiving of the assembly ending with the prayer: *δὸς τοῖς δούλοις σου μετὰ παρρησίας πάσης λαλεῖν τὸν λόγον σου, ἐν τῷ τὴν χεῖρα ἐκτείνειν σε εἰς ἴασιν καί σημεῖα καὶ τέρατα γίνεσθαι διὰ τοῦ ὀνόματος τοῦ ἁγίου παιδός σου Ἰησοῦ* (iv. 23–30).

6. Directly afterwards—thus still before mid-day—the outpouring of the Holy Spirit accompanied by a kind of earthquake; the immediate result: *ἐλάλουν τὸν λόγον τοῦ θεοῦ μετὰ παρρησίας*,—further result: they were all of one mind, neither said any that ought of the things which he possessed was his

[1] Have we not here one cipher too many? *Vide* 1 Cor. xv. 6: *ἐπάνω πεντακόσιοι ἀδελφοί.*

[2] Thus still before mid-day.

own, and—δυνάμει μεγάλῃ ἀπεδίδουν τὸ μαρτύριον οἱ ἀπόστολοι τοῦ κυρίου Ἰησοῦ τῆς ἀναστάσεως (iv. 31–33).

7. Because of this grand spirit of self-sacrifice no one lacked anything; the appalling episode of Ananias and Sapphira; the great fear of the whole Church[1] because of the apostolic power of St. Peter (iv. 34–v. 11).

8. Many signs and wonders are now wrought by the Apostles' hands among the people (λαός—in contrast with ἐκκλησία); they were all together in Solomon's Porch; the people hold them in high honour and reverence; their number increases; St. Peter performs many miracles of healing; even from *the towns outside Jerusalem* many sick folk and those possessed with dæmons were brought to him (v. 12–16).

Here we have a narrative marked by consistency and logical connection in the succession of events.[2] If we now turn to chaps. ii. and v. 17–42, we read as follows:—

1. The outpouring of the Holy Spirit in visible form in the morning [where? in what connection or for what reason? Is it because the day of Pentecost was being fulfilled?]; immediate result: λαλεῖν ἑτέραις γλώσσαις, so as to be understood by all (ii. 1–13).

[1] Here the word ἐκκλησία makes its first appearance quite abruptly.

[2] It is noteworthy that in these passages our Lord is four times called ὁ παῖς θεοῦ. It is *possible* to eliminate from this connection the story of Ananias and Sapphira; whether it ought to be eliminated is a question which, in my opinion, cannot be decided. As an especially appalling instance of apostolic power it is quite in place in the context.

2. A great missionary sermon of St. Peter on the occasion of the outpouring of the Spirit which had been manifested in the fiery tongues and in the miracle by which those who heard understood what was said (ii. 14–36). St. Peter in his sermon presupposes that this outpouring was accompanied by "τέρατα," of which nothing is said in the narrative.

3. The extraordinary success (about 3000 conversions) of the miracle and the sermon (ii. 37–41); further result: they continue in the doctrine of the Apostles and in the fellowship, in the breaking of bread and in the prayers; fear came upon every soul; the Apostles work great miracles; all that believed were always together and had all things common; they were daily together in the Temple, and also in their own homes they held their sacred feasts in gladness and singleness of heart, having favour with all the people (ii. 42–47).

4. The Apostles are thrown into prison by the Jewish authorities [the Sadducees are specially mentioned], but are set at liberty by an angel who directs them to go into the Temple and to preach there to all the people; this they do (v. 17–21[a]).

5. The Jewish authorities, who wish to condemn them, in vain seek for them in the prison; being, however, informed that the Apostles were teaching in the Temple, they command that they should be brought before them ("not with violence; for they feared the people") and forbid them[1] to preach the Gospel.

[1] Here St. Luke expressly introduces the prohibition as a reminiscence of an earlier one—thus as a second prohibition—because he had already narrated it once before.

The protest of St. Peter ("We must obey God rather than men"). The purpose of the Council to condemn the Apostles to death is changed by a speech of Gamaliel. The scourging and release of the Apostles (v. 21^a–41).

6. The Apostles continue their teaching in the Temple and at home (v. 42).

It is, in my opinion, so clear that we have here a second narrative of the same events, that one can only wonder that the knowledge that this is so has not long ago become common property. The correspondence becomes still more striking if we add to the first account (A) the story from the Jerusalem-Cæsarean section (*vide supra*) of the miraculous deliverance of St. Peter from prison by an angel during the night (chap. xii.; here also without the knowledge of the guards); and this we ought to do (as Weiss also thinks). The first recension (A) is, however, far superior to the second recension (B). We may with confidence leave it to the reader to test that this is so both on the whole and in detail (the editorial touches of St. Luke in both recensions do not often affect the subject-matter, and can be easily discerned;[1] St. Luke did not perceive that he was reproducing two traditions concerning the same occurrences, so that the connection of events in the narrative which he has compiled is altogether poor, illogical, and incredible). In B there is no clear motive given either for

[1] St. Luke's character as an historian quite excludes the hypothesis that the recension B is a free invention of his; there is, however, no doubt that here as elsewhere he has added his own touches.

the outpouring of the Spirit,[1] or for the presence of the multitude, or for the fear of the people, or for the fear of the authorities because of the people, or for the imprisonment of the Apostles. In A everything has hands and feet: the cure of the impotent man —this astonishing miracle that it had been granted to St. Peter to perform—explains everything:—the courage with which St. Peter openly and loudly proclaimed Jesus in Solomon's Porch before the people who were present, and were rushing together to him; the many conversions; the imprisonment of St. Peter (and St. John ?); his open testimony before the Jewish authorities on the following day; his dismissal through fear of the people. And now after the return of the Apostle the enthusiasm of the first believers (the 5000, *i.e.* probably the 500) arose into an ecstasy *which opened the way to the reception of the Spirit, i.e. what then happened was the actual, the historical, Pentecost.*[2] And though there is no speaking with tongues —this at least is not mentioned—what happened then had the result upon which everything depended: ἐλάλουν τὸν λόγον τοῦ θεοῦ μετὰ παρρησίας and: δυνάμει μεγάλῃ ἀπεδίδουν τὸ μαρτύριον οἱ ἀπόστολοι τοῦ κυρίου Ἰησοῦ τῆς ἀναστάσεως.

After the appearance of the Risen Christ to St. Peter and to the Twelve (1 Cor. xv. 5) the cure of the lame man was the next great stirring event; after the two speeches in which St. Peter bore public testi-

[1] Are the words: καὶ ἐν τῷ συνπληροῦσθαι τὴν ἡμέραν τῆς πεντακοστῆς (ii. 1) intended to supply the motive which is here wanting? The correction in D seems to have such an intention.

[2] And probably also the appearance of our Lord before the brethren, more than 500 in number, of which St. Paul speaks.

mony before the people and the Council and after his own imprisonment and deliverance this miracle resulted in the "Outpouring of the Spirit" (and the birth of the Church into active life). That this "Outpouring" should have shaken itself free from its connection with this miracle and should have made its appearance as an independent event is very intelligible, and indeed the whole description in B, in every trait and every detail of the transformation, is best explained as the next stage after A in the process of legendary development. Here again the proof may with perfect confidence be left to the reader. It is most noteworthy that in B St. Peter, in his discourse, mentions τέρατα, which were bound up with the "Outpouring," though nothing had been said of these in the foregoing narrative. In A, on the other hand, we find the earthquake![1]

According to A on the night preceding the outpouring of the Spirit St. Peter was cast into prison, and on the next morning released by the religious authorities; according to B the Apostles were cast into prison after the "Outpouring," but were released

[1] By combination of the two accounts A and B concerning the "Outpouring," taking A as our foundation, we arrive at the following historical picture: After the cure of the lame man, the public witness of St. Peter (before the people and the Council) and his suffering as a confessor, we learn that the resulting ecstasy of the little company of believers was assisted and confirmed by an earthquake. This created public amazement; St. Peter then delivered a discourse, explaining this "outpouring" as being also the initial stage of the "Day of Judgment." By this the listeners were cut to the heart; and under this influence many joined the new community. The great majority of them were Hellenists; while the natives of Jerusalem held themselves aloof.

during the first night by an angel. This release by an angel (in reference to St. Peter) is in chap. xii. rightly set at a much later time, and is recounted with details which show that we have here the more ancient stage in the development of the legend, wherein are still preserved some genuinely historical traits.

Seeing, therefore, that chaps. ii. and v. 17–42 bear the same relationship to chap. xii. as to chaps. iii. 1–v. 16 it is natural to suppose that chap. xii. belongs to iii. 1–v. 16. Chap. xii., however, is one of the passages containing tradition connected with Jerusalem and Cæsarea. These passages (*vide supra*) begin with the mission of St. Philip in Samaria, with which the mission in the cities on the coast is connected. But we notice that the section iii. 1–v. 16 concludes with an outlook towards the πέριξ πόλεις Ἱερουσαλήμ. The missions we have mentioned would therefore follow in very good connection with this section. The source must naturally have contained a short introductory description of St. Philip and of his appearance on the scene of action; but the introduction which we now read in the Acts—the election of the Seven, among whom St. Philip is only named, nothing more being said about him—is quite out of connection here and belongs (*vide supra*) to the Antiochean source which knows St. Philip only as a deacon, and in which St. Stephen alone appears as an evangelist. Here, however, St. Philip appears as a missionary. There is no doubt, therefore, that an hiatus lies between the mention of St. Philip in vi. 5 and the narratives concerning him in viii. 5 *ff.* This hiatus is explained most simply by the results of our analysis of the sources: the account in vi. 5 belongs to the Antiochean record, while the accounts in viii. 5 *ff.* belong to the tradition connected with both Jerusalem and Cæsarea.[1] It is accordingly probable that the sections iii. 1–v. 16 and viii. 5–40; ix. 29–xi. 18 and xii. 1–24 belong together, that they form to a certain extent a homogeneous whole, and that they may be described on the one hand as tradition connected with both Jerusalem and Cæsarea, and on the other hand as tradition relating both to St. Peter and St. Philip. Surveying them we find before us a collection of traditions which is tolerably homogeneous, and which though far from being so connected and logically consistent as the Antiochean source, nevertheless displays certain common characteristics and a distinct connection in the events it records. This compilation concludes with the Herodian Persecution, the death of St. James, the

[1] So far as viii. 5 *ff.* is concerned it must remain quite an open question whether the Philip here is the Apostle or the Evangelist. The question is first settled in xxi. 8. The very attractive hypothesis of the identity of the two Philips, for which support might easily be derived from later tradition, indeed seemingly also from the gospel of St. John, breaks down at this passage belonging to the we-sections. The theory that there never was a Philip among the Twelve, but that the name of the Evangelist found its way into the list of the Apostles, so that he was numbered as one of the Twelve, presupposes a mistrust of this list which I cannot share, and which seems to me quite unjustifiable. The name "Philip" was very common, and the confusion of the two Philips in the second century was not only suggested by the name and the missionary activity of the Evangelist, but also by the highly probable fact that the Evangelist had been a personal disciple of our Lord; for we may well assume that all the "Seven" were once personal disciples of our Lord.

miraculous release of St. Peter, who now leaves Jerusalem (xii. 17: ἐξελθὼν ἐπορεύθη εἰς ἕτερον τόπον), and the death of the persecutor Herod in *Cæsarea.* This source thus comprises the first twelve years of the history of the Church of Jerusalem and the fundamentally important missions of St. Peter and St. Philip.

Herewith the analysis of sources as regards the first half of the Acts is carried as far as, in my opinion, it can be carried;[1] let me once again cursorily summarise its results:—

Chap. ii. Recension B of the history of the outpouring of the Holy Spirit and its consequences.

Chaps. iii. 1–v. 16. Recension A of the more intelligible history of the outpouring of the Holy Spirit and its consequences (the Jerusalem-Cæsarean or, in other words, Petro-Philippine source).

Chap. v. 17–42. Continuation of B.

Chaps. vi. 1–viii. 4. The Jerusalem-Antiochean source (with at the end an interpolated reference to St. Paul).

Chap. viii. 5–40. Continuation of A.

Chap. ix. 1–30 (?). A passage concerning the

[1] I have left chap. i. on one side. The former of its two divisions, including the introduction and the account of the Ascension, is probably the latest tradition in the Acts, and has been inserted by St. Luke on the authority of a legend of very advanced development. Whether the second part, recounting the completion of the apostolic college, belongs as an introduction to chap. ii., or to the traditions of iii. 1 *ff.*, or is a quite independent piece of tradition, is a question which, in my opinion, cannot be settled.

conversion of St. Paul interpolated from a separate source.

Chaps. ix. 31–xi. 18. Continuation of A.

Chap. xi. 19–30. Continuation of the Jerusalem-Antiochean source.

Chap. xii. 1–23. Continuation of A.

Chaps. xii. 25–xv. 35. Continuation of the Jerusalem-Antiochean source.[1]

This analysis of sources first makes it possible to enter upon a thoroughly scientific criticism of the traditions of the first half of the Acts, in so far as such criticism is at all possible; for almost the only information which here presents itself for comparison is afforded by the epistles of St. Paul, though after all this is not so scanty as is sometimes supposed (*vide infra*). It is, however, more important for us to keep in view the fact that these traditions were actually compiled by St. Luke, the companion of St. Paul, and in face of this fact not to throw to the winds the general axioms of historical criticism.

Taking first the body of tradition which we have called A, we have already pointed out the logical sequence and the trustworthiness of the narrative in the passage iii. 1–v. 16 so far as the leading features are concerned. Also on pages 154 *f.* attention has been drawn to the fact that even the story of Ananias and Sapphira in its main outline need not be a fable of late invention. Of course what is given us even here is

[1] No notice is here taken of the few passages which have been touched up by St. Luke, or which have been transferred from one body of tradition to another in order to bind these together; we at once are lost in uncertainty if we try to explain every detail.

never tradition absolutely primitive and unaffected by legend, it is rather historical tradition handed down by enthusiasts. This is also shown in the description of St. Philip as the great wonder-worker (viii. 6, 7), and in the supernatural colouring given to the accounts of his and St. Peter's actions throughout the mission. But, on the other hand, we ought not to forget the historical excellences of these sections. It has been the greatest mistake of modern criticism that it has suspected all sorts of things in the story of the relations between St. Peter, St. Philip, and Simon Magus, and has read its boldest surmises into this story, while it has overlooked the relative simplicity of the tale as here told, and the complete absence in the narrative of any hint of the importance which Simon Magus and the Simonians are supposed to have gained later in the history of the Church. Again, certain as it is that the story of Cornelius is thickly overlaid with the colouring of supernatural legend, this story nevertheless contains in its principal features, and in several secondary traits, history that could not have been invented; and in that it represents St. Peter as, at first, drawing no further practical conclusion from the baptism of Cornelius, it keeps within the sphere of the probable and—we must therefore conclude—of the historical.[1] Lastly, in the concluding section, the manner of the release of St. Peter presents a difficulty—and yet the "angel" could have been invented on

[1] St. Luke plainly enough gives us to understand that St. Peter did not understand the *general intention* of the Divine vision vouchsafed to him, as related in the story of Cornelius; and that it was necessary for the mission to be set on foot by others before he could be brought to the right way of thinking.

the very next day (even the first listeners could have invented it, *vide* xii. 15; ὁ ἄγγελός ἐστιν αὐτοῦ); apart from this many secondary traits, having all the characteristics of authenticity, give to the greater part of the story an appearance of probability and trustworthiness.[1]

Here, however, we receive a hint as to the origin of these traditions. If we note that the horizon of this source includes both Jerusalem and Cæsarea, and that *St. Philip*—and no other, so far as we are told in the book—*belonged to the churches of both Jerusalem and Cæsarea*, and that St. Luke has not only expressly recorded St. Philip's migration to Cæsarea (ix. 40), but has also told us that he himself met him there and stayed with him (xxi. 8 *f.*) for a fairly long time (perhaps a week); if we further consider that though many Christians preached the Gospel in the πέριξ πόλεις Ἱερουσαλήμ, yet the Acts only records the mission of St. Philip together with that of St. Peter;

[1] The fact that, according to chap. xii., St. Peter (and the Apostles) definitely vanish from the scene is an additional proof that with chap. xii. this source comes to an end, and that we now pass over to another source (namely, the Antiochean). He who writes: "Peter departed to another place," shows that he intends to let this person drop out of his narrative. The fact that St. Peter again appears abruptly—and that in Jerusalem—in chap. xv. seems necessarily to point to the use of another source, and to a certain carelessness on the part of the editor. This, however, makes it probable that at least one written source lay before St. Luke. Wellhausen remarks (*Nachrichten d. k. Gesellsch. d. W. z. Göttingen*, 1907, s. 9, *n.* 1): "We may conjecture that εἰς ἕτερον τόπον is a correction of St. Luke perhaps for Antioch; for the name of this city could not be left standing if xv. 1-34 was to follow." The conjecture is very daring; for why could not St. Luke have mentioned the return of St. Peter to Jerusalem before chap. xv.?

if, moreover, we take into account those peculiar traits in the character of St. Philip which remind us of the "Christian Scientist" (traits which were inherited by his daughters), and compare therewith the supernatural colouring of this source, and if we lastly consider that St. Luke himself was a Christian Scientist, and that therefore this man of the Primitive Community must have appeared to him specially worthy of reverential trust—if we take all these facts into consideration it is surely not too bold an hypothesis to suppose that the body of tradition we have called A was derived from St. Philip, or from him and his daughters.[1] Together with them we may and indeed must also think of St. Mark and Silas; for they were both natives of Jerusalem, and St. Luke for a time lived and perhaps worked with both of them. It is also strongly in favour of St. Mark that St. Luke has taken his work as the basis of his own gospel; and, in fact, the story of the miraculous release of St. Peter from prison (chap. xii.) in its

[1] The mention of the daughters in xxi. 9 is very remarkable. Papias expressly tells us (Eus., *Hist. Eccl.* III. 39, 9) *that they transmitted traditions connected with the Gospel history—among others a story of one who was raised from the dead.* "A" also contains an instance of raising from the dead (ix. 36 *ff.*); such fanciful tales are, however, very rare in the most ancient tradition; St. Paul says nothing about them. St. Luke may well have again met with these daughters in Asia, and have then first heard of these accounts (*vide* "Luke the Physician," pp. 153 *ff.*). Besides, it must be remembered that St. Luke must have seen St. Philip himself a second time, namely, in the days before his voyage with St. Paul from Cæsarea to Rome. We do not know how long during that visit he was in touch with St. Philip, the most notable member of the Church in Cæsarea; it may have been days, but it may also have been months.

details (the house of St. Mark's mother, the assembly there, Rhoda the maid-servant) looks quite like an account derived from St. Mark, and probably is so, or rather information derived from St. Mark has found its way into the story. "A" is not so strictly homogeneous as to prevent us from supposing that a second or even a third source has been used in it. But apart from this passage, nothing can be found in A which can be ascribed to St. Mark with greater probability than to St. Philip; indeed there is absolutely no other detail of the source which points at all to St. Mark. The same also holds good of Silas. Naturally St. Luke also received from him information concerning Jerusalem, but A in its essential character is bound up not only with Jerusalem, but also with Samaria and Cæsarea. We are accordingly left only with St. Philip.[1] But it may now be objected if this source depends upon St. Philip, and if, moreover, he and his Samaritan mission may have originally stood in some kind of opposition to St. Peter and his mission in Jerusalem and Judæa, is it not strange that in one and the same source St. Philip and St. Peter appear in such peaceful proximity? We may answer that the story of the mission of St. Philip, at all events, does not belong to the Jerusalem-Antiochean source, and that at a later time even St. Philip himself would have felt that any trace of opposition between himself and St. Peter had been smoothed

[1] I have already shown in "Luke the Physician," pp. 153 *ff.*, and I will not here enlarge upon the point, that the investigation of the sources of the gospel of St. Luke points to a special source connected with Jerusalem which has a certain relationship with A of the Acts.

away. Only we must not suppose that the Samaritan mission met *at once* with the approbation of St. Peter and the Apostles (viii. 14 *ff.*); some considerable time may well have elapsed in the meantime. This, moreover, seems to be implied by the text itself; the Apostles only approve after *ἡ Σαμαρία δέδεκται τὸν λόγον τοῦ θεοῦ*. But even if this interpretation of the passage is not accepted, we must recollect that little dependence can be placed upon the chronology of the first half of the Acts. It is certain that St. Peter at a relatively early date preached the Gospel in the districts on the coast, and in after times we know that this was reckoned to him for righteousness by those of more liberal opinions; why not also by St. Philip?

As for B—the unfavourable opinion which has been above passed upon this recension may be hardened into the critical verdict that, apart from some few details, as compared with A it is worthless: where it is trustworthy in its record the order of events is confused, it combines things that have no real connection with one another, it omits what is important, it is devoid of all sense of historical development. It gives a much later and more impressive representation of events, and for this very reason it met with acceptance. It is, however, correct in recording that the outpouring of the Holy Spirit was manifested in the "speaking with tongues." Whether the exaggeration of this speaking with tongues into a speaking in foreign tongues or into a miracle of hearing—though the transformation is of course not complete—is due to the source itself, or first to

St. Luke, is a question which cannot be definitely settled. The former alternative is to me the more probable. At all events the outlook upon the Gentile world—again, of course, not logically and courageously developed—must have been present in the source; for therein lies the point of the whole narrative; though at the same time we must make the reservation that St. Luke himself has drawn up the list of nations according to his own discretion. It is, on the other hand, very remarkable that in this account the results of the "Outpouring" extend not to the natives of Jerusalem but to the Jews of the Dispersion. In this point we note its relationship with the Antiochean source. Unfortunately there is no evidence that would help us to discover the person upon whose authority this account rests. It probably first appeared after the Gospel had been preached in the Empire. It, however, certainly proceeded from Jerusalem or Palestine; and we may also suitably connect with it the account of the Ascension (i. 1–14); for we may safely assume in St. Luke so much critical sagacity as would prevent him from accepting such stories concerning Jerusalem on foreign testimony when he had so many opportunities of communication with Palestinian Christians. In regard to the account of the Ascension, it has been already shown above (pp. 155 *ff.*) that the legend originated in Palestine, though not perhaps until after the destruction of Jerusalem.

Passing now to the Antiochean source, we may assign to it a high historical value; but here distinctions must be made. As far as chap. xiii. 4 inclusive it lays itself open to depreciatory criticism in a few details which can be easily recognised as editorial touches. From this source alone we learn of the important dispute between the "Hebrews" and the "Hellenists" in the Church of Jerusalem,[1] of the election of the "Seven"—a second group of apostles—which arose from this dispute; and above all, we learn that St. Stephen and his following taught in Jerusalem a peculiar "Paulinism before Paul," that the Twelve by no means thoroughly acquiesced in this doctrine—for they were not affected by the persecution concerning Stephen—and that this teaching led up to a mission to the Gentiles before the ministry of St. Paul.[2] If St. Stephen taught that Jesus would not only destroy the Temple but would also abrogate the *ἔθη ἃ παρέδωκεν ἡμῖν* Μωϋσῆς, it is at once intelligible that some of his followers should have preached the Gospel directly to the Gentiles in Antioch. The source perhaps contained more than St. Luke took from it, as has been already pointed out in the case of the story of St. Stephen, and is also suggested by other passages. For example, the narrative of xi. 19–30 quite gives the impression of an extract from a fuller account.[3] There is difficulty, as is well

[1] The mention of the Hellenists in ix. 29 probably belongs to the editorial touches of St. Luke, and is an imitation of vi. 9.

[2] Wellhausen also (*loc. cit.*, s. 9 *f.*, 11 *f.*) allows this. As he rightly remarks, St. Matt. x. 5 protests against this mission.

[3] So also Wellhausen (*loc. cit.*, s. 7 *ff.*). But seeing that he without just reason throws doubt upon the homogeneity of the source here, and thinks himself justified in a criticism so incisive as to lead him to assert that St. Barnabas in all likelihood himself belonged to the fugitive Hellenists, that the representation of him as "the inspector from Jerusalem" is due to tendency, that the Hellenists on principle would have confined their mission simply to

known, in the narrative of the journey of St. Paul and St. Barnabas with an offering for Jerusalem (xi. 30^{b}; xii. 25). I allow that the narrative does not appear to be *absolutely* excluded by Gal. ii. 1 (*διὰ δεκατεσσάρων ἐτῶν πάλιν ἀνέβην*).[1] If, however, this

the Jews, and that St. Peter is represented as the apostle to the Gentiles—I find it impossible to follow him. Again I cannot accept his other objections that "the people of Jerusalem suffer from a famine that had been merely prophesied," and that the same cause moves the people of Antioch to help them, further that the delegates from Jerusalem were not prophets but other folk. All these objections are disposed of partly by reference to the brevity of the narrative, partly by the fact that they do not rest upon sufficient evidence.

[1] The two journeys to Jerusalem recounted in Gal. i.–ii. are characterised as follows: *ἀνῆλθον ἱστορῆσαι Κηφᾶν—πάλιν ἀνέβην καὶ ἀνεθέμην αὐτοῖς* (the Christians of Jerusalem) *τὸ εὐαγγέλιον ὃ κηρύσσω ἐν τοῖς ἔθνεσιν*. We may say that he does not count the journeys he actually took, but only those journeys that had anything to do with his relations with St. Peter and the rest or with his gospel. So we *may* decide, *if hard pressed*, nor do I wish to maintain more than this. The identification of the journey of Gal. ii. with that of Acts xi. 30^{b}, commended by Ramsay and by others before him, that is, the reduction of the two journeys of St. Paul and St. Barnabas recorded in the Acts to *one* which took place before the first missionary journey, I regard as an hypothesis attractive but difficult to establish. Wellhausen has lately (*loc. cit.*, s. 7 *f.*) again given it his sanction, but the way in which he thinks himself bound to criticise the stories of the Acts and to throw them into new combinations makes it scarcely possible to come to close quarters with him. It seems to be in favour of the identification of the journeys (that is, of the transference of xv. 1 *ff.* to the time of xi. 30) that xv. 1 *ff.* (Gal. i. 21) is concerned only with the Gentile Christians of Syria and Cilicia, while one would expect that the Gentile Christians in Lycaonia (the district passed through in the so-called first missionary journey) would have been also mentioned. But the question here in the first instance concerns an *acute* "*στάσις καὶ ζήτησις οὐκ ὀλίγη*" which had broken out in *Antioch* (and therefore also affected the regions of Syria and Cilicia connected with

detail is unhistorical it only follows that the Antiochean source has erred for once; and yet even in this case it is left open to us to suppose that the whole account of this journey does not belong to the Antiochean source, but has been inserted by St. Luke on mistaken information. It can be omitted without difficulty.

The account of the so-called first missionary journey belonging to this source is not so vivid in its style nor so trustworthy (*vide supra*, pp. 92 *ff.*) as the greater part of the narrative in the second half of the Acts. Here also St. Luke has evidently taken certain liberties. I conjecture that the source only gave the route (without dates, which are almost entirely absent), and that St. Luke *taliter qualiter* fashioned this into a "history" in which the great interpolated discourse at Antioch takes up more than a third part of the space. He here gradually allows St. Barnabas to fall into the background behind St. Paul—in opposition to the attitude of the source (*vide supra*). If this source originated in Antioch one understands why

that metropolis), and had been stirred up by unauthorised meddlers from Jerusalem, not a general spontaneous effort to regulate the whole relations between Jewish and Gentile Christians. It stands to reason that the decision arrived at was afterwards of importance for Gentile Christians in general (xxi. 25). Instead of pulling St. Luke to pieces, one ought rather to recognise that here he does not move in generalities, but has given a fairly detailed representation. To bring the collection for the famine-stricken Christians of Jerusalem (xi. 29 *f.*; xii. 24) into connection with the compact made in Gal. ii. 10 belongs to that class of combinations which compromises historical criticism. The attractiveness of the hypothesis lies in the fact that St. Peter is still in Jerusalem, while according to chap. xii. he seems to have definitely left that city.

in this section it only shows interest in leading features.

It seems to me most important for the criticism of chap. xv. 1–35 that the Antiochean origin of this passage should be kept in view. If the tradition here is Antiochean—and from the words of verse 2: γενομένης δὲ στάσεως καὶ ζητήσεως οὐκ ὀλίγης τῷ Παύλῳ καὶ Βαρνάβᾳ πρὸς αὐτούς as well as from τινὰς ἄλλους of verse 2, and μετὰ καὶ ἑτέρων πολλῶν of verse 35, it follows that the source knew more than St. Luke tells us, and that it could only know this because it was *Antiochean*—everything at once explains itself. There was no need to record what St. Paul and St. Barnabas had said at Jerusalem. The whole interest would be concentrated upon the attitude adopted by the whole Church of Jerusalem, under the leadership of St. Peter and St. James, towards those teachers of the Law, who without authority (xv. 24: οἷς οὐ διεστειλάμεθα), had come down to Antioch (xv. 1), and who belonged to the party of Christian Pharisees in Jerusalem (xv. 5). Neither does the passage on the whole give any other information, and to try to coax more out of it is quite inadmissible. It simply marks the result, while defining the attitude of St. Peter and St. James more clearly by a free reproduction of their speeches. It is at the same time clearly shown that the standpoint of the former was somewhat different from that of St. James. According to St. Luke both recall the Divine leading given in the history of the centurion of Cæsarea—those men of Cyprus and Cyrene who first preached to the Gentiles in Antioch could not therefore, in St. Luke's opinion, claim such Divine leading—;

but St. Peter then dwells upon the manifest inability of even the Jews and Jewish Christians to bear the yoke of the Law, and passes on to speak of the grace of the Lord Jesus which brings redemption to those who believe; while St. James dwells upon the fact that the Law is everywhere proclaimed in the synagogues (and is accordingly assured of its position of due respect within the ancient nation [1]).[2]

We shall return to the Apostolic Decree in Chapter VI. It may therefore be set aside for the present. And yet it is not possible to give a final decision as to the date of the Antiochean source before this Decree has been discussed. Neglecting it, however, for the moment, we find in the source nothing that demands a late date of composition, while the excellent accounts

[1] The "synagogues" of xv. 21 can only mean purely Jewish synagogues, not those in which Jews and Jewish Christians were found together.

[2] So these words of somewhat doubtful significance are to be understood. The other explanations (*vide* Wendt on this passage) almost all include the Jewish Christians here, and regard the words as a declaration of conditions to be imposed. They, however, read into the text a significance which is quite foreign to it, and which if it were intended must have been expressly stated. The opinions delivered by St. Peter and St. James really complete one another; the former calls attention to the absolute impossibility of keeping the Law, and points out that in consequence everything depends upon faith in the grace of the Lord Jesus; St. James declares that the Law still retains its inviolable character for the Jews, and that thus its rights were preserved. St. James does not intend by his words to commend the positive side of the so-called Apostolic Decree, but, like St. Peter, merely its negative side (μὴ παρενοχλεῖν). What St. Peter says and what St. James says could also have been said by St. Paul, for even according to his teaching the Jews were still bound to keep the Law; but it is important for the standpoint of St. James that this is just the point which he emphasises.

concerning Jerusalem and St. Stephen, and the special veneration shown to St. Barnabas, lead us to conclude that we have here a writing of high antiquity. With due precautions we may perhaps go one step further. We have described the source as "Antiochean." But we may, indeed we must, also call it "Jerusalem-Antiochean"; for, as has been shown, the bond of connection between Jerusalem and Antioch is in it most carefully noted and recorded, and it includes accounts concerning the primitive history of the Church of Jerusalem which are quite unique, important, and trustworthy, and even more detailed than those concerning Antioch. It demands, therefore, as its authority one to whom the connection between the two Churches was a matter of special importance, to whose heart Jerusalem and Antioch were equally dear, one who knew the early history of the Church of Jerusalem, and was moreover a convinced believer in, and himself endowed with, the supernatural gifts of the Spirit. Now we know that Silas came as an ambassador from Jerusalem to Antioch, *and stayed for a considerable time in the latter city*, and that he then, starting from Antioch, accompanied St. Paul in the so-called second missionary journey during which he fell in with St. Luke, and for a time worked together with him. Nothing can be more probable than that St. Luke owes these records concerning both Jerusalem and Antioch to this prophet of Jerusalem who had lived in Antioch, and who had gladly entered upon the mission to the Gentiles; nothing at least can be said against such a supposition. This does not yet amount to a proof; but we may well venture the conjecture that the authority of Silas is to be claimed for these accounts concerning Jerusalem and Antioch.

We have now completed the analysis of the sources of the Acts of the Apostles in their main outlines. There still, however, remains the important question whether the three sources of the first half of the Acts were written sources either as a whole or in part, or whether they simply depend upon oral tradition. This question can only be dealt with in connection with a discussion of the "discrepancies" of the Acts. To these the next chapter is dedicated.

CHAPTER VI

INSTANCES OF INACCURACY AND OF DISCREPANCY—WRITTEN OR ORAL SOURCES ?—CONCLUDING REMARKS CONCERNING THE VALUE OF THE SOURCES AND OF ST. LUKE AS AN AUTHOR.

WHAT we include under the term "instances of inaccuracy and of discrepancy" in the Acts of the Apostles will be learned from the following collection of examples. We group them according to the separate bodies of tradition into which we have already analysed the book, more especially in the preceding chapter.

1. The We-sections.

We must here note that the ἡμεῖς has not in every passage the same connotation. It is not always quite certain what persons are included in the word.

xvi. 10. The "we" is, without any explanation, abruptly introduced in ἐζητήσαμεν.

xvi. 10. εἰς Μακεδονίαν . . . εὐαγγελίσασθαι αὐτούς.

xvi. 12, 18. The relation of ἡμέρας τινάς to πολλὰς ἡμέρας remains undefined.

xvi. 13, 16. It is not certain whether one or two different visits to the προσευχή are intended.

xx. 7. The αὐτοῖς after ἡμῶν is inexact, seeing

that it refers to the Christians in Troas, while they are also included in the ἡμεῖς.

xx. 12. ἤγαγον δὲ τὸν παῖδα ζῶντα ought to have occurred earlier in the narrative, and in the following words: καὶ παρεκλήθησαν οὐ μετρίως there is a change of subject.

xxi. 4. St. Paul does not attend to the prophetic revelation.

xxi. 8 *ff.* In Cæsarea St. Philip is so important to the writer that he forgets the church in that city; it is first mentioned afterwards in verses 12 and 16.

xxi. 10. Agabus is introduced as if he here appeared in the book for the first time; yet see xi. 28.

xxi. 11. The prophecy afterwards meets with only a general not a detailed fulfilment.

xxi. 16, 17. The reception in Mnason's house in Jerusalem is recorded before the arrival in Jerusalem (this has given rise to the correction in β). Prolepsis.

xxvii. 2. Aristarchus is described as Μακεδὼν Θεσσαλονικεύς, although he had been already described in xix. 20 as a Macedonian, and in xx. 4 as a native of Thessalonica—it seems thus to have been forgotten that he had been mentioned before.

xxvii. 10. Here the construction with ὅτι abruptly changes into the Acc. c. Inf.

xxvii. 12. Ἀνευθέτου δὲ τοῦ λιμένος connects with verse 8, although verses 9–11 intervene (Wellhausen explains verses 9–11 as an interpolation).

xxvii. 12. After the mention of the ἑκατοντάρχης, the κυβερνήτης and the ναυκλῆρος, it is strange that οἱ πλείονες should occur. Who were they?

xxvii. 21. Here the μέν is not followed by δέ.

xxvii. 21–26 (from τότε onwards); xxvii. 31; xxvii. 33–38 (from παρεκάλει onwards) are explained by Wellhausen as interpolations.

xxviii. 1, 2. It is somewhat inexact that the clause: ἐπέγνωμεν ὅτι Μελίτη ἡ νῆσος καλεῖται should come before the meeting with the inhabitants is mentioned. Prolepsis.

xxviii. 10. Again an instance of prolepsis. The friendly offices of the Maltese at the time of embarkation are mentioned too soon, seeing that this embarkation did not take place until after three months.

xxviii. 14. Another instance of prolepsis. The arrival in Rome is mentioned too soon; it is not in place until verse 16.

2. The second half of the book (omitting the We-sections).

xvi. 4. τὰς πόλεις . . . παρεδίδοσαν αὐτοῖς.

xvi. 22. Why does not St. Paul *now* appeal to his Roman citizenship?

xvi. 23, 24. ἔβαλον εἰς φυλακήν . . . ἔβαλεν αὐτοὺς εἰς τὴν ἐσωτέραν φυλακήν the repetition here is awkward.

xvi. 27. The jailor is about to kill himself, although no one could accuse him of anything, and although he could not yet have known whether the prisoners had escaped or not.

xvi. 28. It is difficult to see how St. Paul could have marked the purpose of the jailor, or how he could have known that all the prisoners were still there.

xvi. 29. *αἰτήσας*, a strange change of subject.

xvi. 30. No motive is given for the jailor's reverence for his two prisoners, and no motive at all for his appealing cry to them, seeing that he could not have known that the miracle had been wrought on their behalf.

xvi. 32. The abrupt appearance of the jailor's family is unexplained.

xvi. 33. It seems strange that the baptism should have taken place at once in the prison.

xvi. 35. No motive is given for the action of the *στρατηγοί*. They issue a sudden command for the release, though no hint is given that they were influenced by anything that had happened during the night. The whole passage, verses 24–34 (inclusive), looks like an interpolation.

xvi. 37. *πρὸς αὐτούς*—though the lictors did not themselves go in to the prisoners but sent a message by the jailor.

xvii. 3. Passage into *oratio directa*.

xvii. 5. Prolepsis. The house of Jason is mentioned, though it is not until verse 7 that we learn that Jason had received the missionaries into his house.

xvii. 9. *λαβόντες ἀπέλυσαν*—change of subject.

xvii. 15. *ὡς τάχιστα*—but St. Luke does not tell us that the command was not carried out.

xvii. 18. *οἱ δέ* is grammatically without antecedent.

xviii. 5. The connection of *συνείχετο τῷ λογῷ* with *κατῆλθον ὅ τε Σίλας καὶ ὁ Τιμόθεος* is strange, because the author does not fully explain.

xviii. 6. *πορεύσομαι* is strange when followed by verses 7 *f*.

xviii. 8. This verse concerning Crispus breaks into the context both in thought and in form, and therefore seems out of place here.

xviii. 11. ἐν αὐτοῖς is not quite correct.

xviii. 17. It is not clear who the πάντες were (Jews? or Greeks?), nor whether the Sosthenes so abruptly introduced, and beaten without any given reason, was a Christian or a Jew.

xviii. 18. It is not at once clear whether it was St. Paul or Aquila who had taken the vow.

xviii. 22. It is not quite clear whether ἀναβάς implies the going up from the harbour into the city of Cæsarea or the going up to Jerusalem.

xviii. 22, 23. Here the brevity of the narrative is strange.

xviii. 24–28 looks like an episode that has been interpolated.

xix. 1. We should expect ἀνελθεῖν, not ἐλθεῖν (Wellhausen).

xix. 3. The expression βαπτίζεσθαι εἰς τὸ Ἰωάννου βάπτισμα is a solecism which is only formally excusable because of the preceding εἰς τί.

xix. 16. It is not till now that we learn that the seven exorcists did not all participate here, and that the occurrence took place in a house (the house is described as if it had been already mentioned, so also the dæmoniac himself). Yet it is possible that ἀμφότεροι may be carelessly used for "several." The whole episode is recorded as if it were only needful to recall a well-known occurrence; the notoriety of the event is indeed afterwards referred to in verse 17 and rendered comprehensible in verses 18 *f.*

xix. 29. The Macedonians Gaius and Aristarchus are introduced quite abruptly.

xix. 32 takes up the thread of verse 29, though verses 30 and 31 intervene.

xix. 33. Alexander is abruptly introduced without comment. We are left in darkness as to his personality and his intentions; even the construction of *ἐκ δὲ τοῦ ὄχλου συνεβίβασαν τὸν Ἀλέξανδρον* is not at all clear; moreover, the purpose of the sudden intervention of the Jews is not obvious.

xix. 34. *ἐπιγνόντες . . . κράζοντες.* Anacoluthon.

xix. 37. It is doubtful who the *ἄνδρες οὗτοι* are. Are they St. Paul and his companions? Probably Gaius and Aristarchus. What then is the intention of the whole intervening episode with Alexander? Moreover, verse 38 has better connection with 36 than with 37 (Wellhausen).

xx. 16. It is not said whether St. Paul actually arrived at Jerusalem for Pentecost.

xx. 19. What St. Paul recalls here is not covered by the narrative in chap. xix.

xx. 23. Here also the summary statement gives quite new information.

xx. 32. Here *τῷ δυναμένῳ* either refers to *τῷ κυρίῳ* instead of the nearer *τῷ λόγῳ* or the whole phrase is incorrect as an epithet.

xxi. 20. *ἀκούσαντες εἶπαν,* here we expect St. James to speak, but the words are put into the mouths of St. James and the presbyters speaking together!

xxi. 27. The seven days are spoken of as if it had been said before that seven days were still wanting for the accomplishment of the vow.

xxi. 27. *ἐπέβαλαν ἐπ᾽ αὐτὸν τὰς χεῖρας.* Prolepsis.

xxi. 34. *μὴ δυναμένου αὐτοῦ γνῶναι ἐκέλευσεν,* grammatically incorrect.

xxi. 36. *τὸ πλῆθος τοῦ λαοῦ κράζοντες,* incorrect.

xxii. 6. *περὶ μεσημβρίαν,* wanting in the account of chap. ix.

xxii. 9. A case of discrepancy with ix. 7 (though it may at a pinch be smoothed away).

xxiii. 5. The words of St. Paul: *οὐκ ᾔδειν ὅτι ἐστὶν ἀρχιερεύς* are unintelligible.

xxiii. 1–11. The details of this story taken by themselves and in conjunction with xxiii. 15 are somewhat strange. Here, just as in the first half of the book, St. Luke seems to have followed parallel accounts which, because they differed from one another, he did not recognise as parallel accounts.

xxiii. 12. The general term *οἱ Ἰουδαῖοι* is still more strange here than in xxii. 30.

xxiii. 16. St. Paul's sister's son is introduced as a well-known character.

xxiii. 22. *ὁ μὲν οὖν* without a following *δέ*.

xxiii. 22. Transition into *oratio directa.*

xxiii. 24. Transition into *oratio indirecta.*

xxiii. 25. *γράψας* passing over verse 24 connects directly with *εἶπεν* in verse 23.

xxiii. 26. Now at the end we are first told the name of the military tribune.

xxiii. 27. *μαθὼν ὅτι Ῥωμαῖός ἐστιν* is either an instance of gross carelessness on the part of St. Luke, or is written purposely: the tribune gives a representation of events which was false, but favourable to himself.

xxiii. 30b is not covered by the previous narrative.

xxiii. 33. *οἵτινες*—a strange change of subject.

xxiv. 5. *εὑρόντες*—anacoluthon; it is followed by no principal verb.

xxiv. 17 is not covered by the earlier narrative.

xxiv. 18. The syntax of the clause: *τινὲς δὲ ἀπὸ τῆς Ἀσίας Ἰουδαῖοι* is incorrect.

xxiv. 22. It is very strange that here a more accurate knowledge of the Christian movement is ascribed to Felix (*ἀκριβέστερον εἰδὼς τὰ περὶ τῆς ὁδοῦ*). Was it derived from his wife Drusilla? Or does *εἰδώς* here mean "noting," and is *ἀκριβέστερον* to be understood as superlative?

xxiv. 22b. This promise is strangely never fulfilled.

xxiv. 23. *καὶ μηδένα κωλύειν*—strange change of subject.

xxiv. 24–27. St. Paul's situation as here described is less favourable than we should have judged from the preceding verses (22, 23), but there is no real discrepancy here.

xxv. 4. *ὁ μὲν οὖν* without a following *δέ*.

xxv. 16. Festus does not give a correct report of the wish of the Jewish authorities.

xxv. 21. *τ. δὲ Παύλου ἐπικαλεσαμένου τηρηθῆναι αὐτόν*—grammatically incorrect.

xxv. 24. *τὸ πλῆθος ἐνέτυχον*—incorrect.

xxvi. 4. No *δέ* follows the *μέν*.

xxvi. 14. Discrepancy with ix. 7 (*εἱστήκεισαν*).

xxvi. 16. In distinction from the previous accounts St. Paul is here at once appointed a missionary to the Gentiles.

xxvi. 20. That St. Paul preached in Jerusalem and in all Judæa is not recorded elsewhere in the Acts.

xxviii. 17. *δέσμιος ἐξ Ἱεροσολύμων παρεδόθην εἰς τὰς χεῖρας τ. Ῥωμαίων* is very inaccurate, for he was already in the power of the Romans when he was bound in fetters; verse 19 [b] is also inexact.

xxviii. 22. *μέν* without *δέ*.

xxviii. 25 *ff*. The quotation from Isaiah does not suit well the information given in verse 24.

3. Chapter i. and the source B (ii. ; v. 17–42).

i. 1. No *τὸν δὲ δεύτερον* follows *τὸν μὲν πρῶτον λόγον*.

i. 2. The style here is confused.

i. 4. The construction by means of a relative sentence passes over into a principal sentence.

i. 4–6. It is not clear where the summary ends and the narrative of particular events begins (probably already at verse 4).

i. 4[c]. The *oratio obliqua* passes into *oratio directa*.

i. 6. It is not said where the disciples had come together; we do not learn this until verse 12. Neither is it clear whether the meeting of verse 6 is identical with that of verse 4.

i. 15. In verse 14 mention is made only of the brethren of Jesus side by side with the Apostles and the women. It is strange that now quite abruptly a whole company of brethren is presupposed—120 persons.

i. 18. *μὲν οὖν* without a following *δέ*.

i. 17–20. Here it has been supposed that there is confusion between the apostolic office of Judas and the plot of land which he had purchased (Weiss): the *ἔπαυλις* of verse 20 is supposed to refer to the plot of land.

i. 22. The words *ἀρξάμενος* to *ἡμῶν* are subject to exception both in form and meaning (Wellhausen); Weiss extends this criticism also to verse 21 (from *ἐν πάντι* onwards).

i. 24. It is strange that all the brethren together say what follows.

i. 26. *μετὰ τῶν ἕνδεκα ἀποστόλων* is strange seeing that elsewhere in the book not much stress is laid upon the number "twelve" of the Apostles.

ii. 1. It is not clear whether the day of Pentecost itself is meant or only its approach.

ii. 1. *ὁμοῦ* with *τὸ αὐτό* is superfluous; we are left in doubt where they were met together.

ii. 4 *ff.* It is doubtful whether a miracle of speech or hearing is intended, or (verses 12, 13) simply ecstatic speech ("speaking with tongues").

ii. 4. *πάντες*—in ii. 1 *πάντες* means all the Christians, so it must also here; but already in ii. 7 only the "Twelve" seem to be comprehended under *πάντες*, and this seems to be confirmed by verses 14 and 15 (*οὗτοι* = *οἱ ἕνδεκα*).

ii. 5 *f.* According to what is here said only the Jews of the Dispersion living in Jerusalem seem to have gathered together; where then are the natives of Jerusalem (yet see verse 14), and how came it that this outpouring of the Spirit was noised abroad in the city?

ii. 8. With τῇ ἰδίᾳ διαλέκτῳ the word signifying "the speakers" is wanting.

ii. 9. οἱ κατοικοῦντες τὴν Μεσοποταμίαν is in form discrepant with εἰς Ἱερουσαλὴμ κατοικοῦντες Ἰουδαῖοι.

ii. 9. Ἰουδαίαν is impossible.

ii. 11. Κρῆτες καὶ Ἄραβες comes very strangely after Ἰουδαῖοί τε καὶ προσήλυτοι.

ii. 12 *f.* πάντες—ἕτεροι—careless.

ii. 14. This introduction of the sermon obliterates the first impression that the effect of the outpouring of the Spirit was confined to the Jews of the Dispersion, *i.e.* to the Hellenists.

ii. 19 *f.* Yet no such τέρατα had accompanied the outpouring of the Spirit. On the other hand, in the parallel account in iv. 31, it is related that an earthquake accompanied the outpouring.

v. 21. The tautologous phrase: τὸ συνέδριον καὶ πᾶσαν τὴν γερουσίαν τῶν υἱῶν Ἰσραήλ is strange.

v. 22 init. and v. 25 init. are so alike that verses 22–24 seem like an interpolation—an hypothesis to which Weiss gives additional support by noticing the double mention of the στρατηγός in verses 24 and 26.

v. 28. Weiss thinks that the two reproaches cannot stand side by side, and he ascribes the second to the editor.

v. 36. The historical mistake in reference to Theudas (also the μετὰ τοῦτον in verse 37).

4. The Source A (iii. 1–v. 16; viii. 5-40; ix. 31–xi. 18; xii. 1-23).

iii. 1 *ff.* The Healing of the lame man is narrated as the first miracle (see especially verses 10 and 16); but, according to ii. 43, many miracles had already happened. The whole of ii. 42–47 is proleptic when compared with iii. 1 *ff.*

iii. 1 *ff.* St. John appears as a mere figurehead in the whole narrative.

iii. 1. ὁ λαός . . . ἔκθαμβοι.

iv. 1. λαλούντων αὐτῶν—but St. Peter alone had been speaking.

iv. 1–3. Prolepsis; for iv. 4 connects with iii. 26, and iv. 5 with iv. 3 (αὔριον corresponds to ἑσπέρα and αὐτῶν to ὁ λαός in verse 2).

iv. 6. Anacoluthon; Annas and the others appear in the nominative in apposition to τοὺς ἄρχοντας κ.τ.λ.

iv. 7. Weiss concludes from τοῦτο, from οὗτος in verse 9, from the presence of the people in verse 10, from the very strange ἐπεγίνωσκον κ.τ.λ. in verse 13[c], from the similarly difficult verse 14, and from verse 22, that the scene was originally set in the Temple-court, and that it was the editor who first transferred it to the Sanhedrin.

iv. 10[c]. Here οὗτος stands for the man who was cured; in 11[a] οὗτος represents Christ; this is very strange.

iv. 12. ὑμᾶς—a strange transition to the second person.

iv. 16. The release of the Apostles is represented as due to the fact that the miracle was notorious, and could not be denied; in verse 21, however, it is represented as due to fear of the people. Therefore Weiss regards iv. 15–20 as an interpolation by the editor.

iv. 19. Here St. Peter and St. John speak together.

iv. 22. It is strange that we should only now learn the age of the lame man; seeing that ἀπολυθέντες of verse 23 connects with ἀπέλυσαν of verse 21, it would seem that verse 22 is interpolated.

iv. 24. οἱ δέ refers back to οἱ ἴδιοι in verse 23, passing over the ἀρχιερεῖς καὶ πρεσβύτεροι.

iv. 24 *ff*. The whole company speak together.

iv. 27. The expression: λαοὶ Ἰσραήλ is strange.

iv. 29. αὐτῶν does not refer to Herod and Pilate, but to the βασιλεῖς κ. ἄρχοντες of verse 26; thus verses 27 and 28 look like an interpolation.

iv. 30. καὶ σημεῖα καὶ τέρατα γίνεσθαι does not fit in well with what has been said before, and looks like an interpolation.

iv. 33 connects closely with verse 31, so that 32 looks like an interpolation (introduction to the story of Ananias), or, since verses 34 and 35 belong to verse 32, like the too early commencement of a new story.

iv. 36–37 does not agree with verses 32, 34 *f*., seeing that in the earlier passage the renunciation of possessions is represented as universal, while in iv. 36–37 it seems to be regarded as exceptional, and a particular case is recorded as worthy of special praise (the same idea lies behind v. 1 *ff*.).

v. 6. It is presupposed that the readers know who the νεώτεροι were (*cf*. νεανίσκοι, verse 10).

v. 11. The word ἐκκλησία appears here for the first time (in place of οἱ ἀδελφοί).

v. 12. After ii. 43 this summary, written as if the information were given for the first time, is very strange.

v. 15 is closely bound up with verse 13, hence verse 14 looks like an interpolation that is out of place here.

v. 15. After the αὐτοῖς of verse 13 it is strange that St. Peter alone is spoken of here.

viii. 5. πόλις τῆς Σαμαρείας . . . αὐτοῖς.

viii. 7. A gross and yet very natural case of anacoluthon: πολλοὶ τῶν ἐχόντων πνεύματα ἀκάθαρτα . . . ἐξήρχοντο.

viii. 14. Σαμαρεία . . . πρὸς αὐτούς.

viii. 16. βαπτίζειν εἰς τὸ ὄνομα τοῦ κυρίου Ἰησοῦ, but in ii. 38 βαπτίζειν ἐπὶ τῷ ὀνόματι Ἰησοῦ Χριστοῦ.

viii. 17. Strange change of subject (ἐλάμβανον).

viii. 26. ἄγγελος κυρίου, but in verse 29 it is the Spirit that speaks; in viii. 39 the Spirit is called πνεῦμα κυρίου.

viii. 35. εὐαγγελίζεσθαι αὐτῷ τὸν Ἰησοῦν, but in viii. 25, 40: εὐαγγελίζεσθαι τὰς κώμας (πόλεις).

ix. 31. The Church in Galilee appears here abruptly.

x. 10. αὐτῶν stands without reference.

x. 15. πάλιν ἐκ δευτέρου—pleonastic.

x. 19. Weiss thinks that διενθυμουμένου makes the διηπόρει of x. 17 superfluous, but it only carries on the idea of the earlier word quite naturally.

x. 23. Weiss sees here an awkward interruption in the flow of the narrative, but the verse is necessary as a preparation for verse 45.

x. 25–27. The cases of discrepancy which are believed to have been discovered here disappear with closer attention to the interpretation of the text (*vide* Weiss)

x. 36. The connection with verse 35 is remarkably loose.

x. 39ᵃ is a doublet of verse 41 and disturbs the connection between verses 38ᵇ and 39ᵇ.

x. 42. τῷ λαῷ conflicts with i. 8, since it excludes the commission to preach the Gospel to the Gentiles.

x. 43ᵇ. The infinite clause determines μαρτυροῦσιν in a way for which one is not prepared, and which narrows the significance of the verb.

x. 45. ἐκ περιτομῆς is superfluous, but its addition is quite intelligible. Seeing that this verse refers back to verse 23ᵇ which, according to Weiss, belongs to the editor, Weiss decides that x. 45 is not original, and conjectures that Jewish Christians belonging to Cæsarea were originally intended here.

xi. 12. διακρίναντα, *cf.* x. 20 διακρινόμενος—the difference, if there is any at all, is considered by Weiss to be great enough to make it necessary to suppose an editor, to whom he would attribute the small formal differences both before and after this verse (between the narrative of chapter x. and St. Peter's report of the events). It is strange that the name of Cornelius is not once mentioned in St. Peter's report.

xi. 12. We do not learn until now that the brethren (*vide* x. 23, 45) were six in number, and that they accompanied St. Peter to Jerusalem.

xi. 14ᵇ is more than a free reproduction of the narrative.

xi. 15. Weiss finds a discrepancy between ἐν τῷ ἄρξασθαί με λαλεῖν and ἔτι λαλοῦντος τοῦ Πέτρου (x. 44); I cannot allow that this is so.

xi. 15. Weiss writes: "ἐπ' αὐτούς refers to the ἄνδρες ἀκροβυστίαν ἔχοντες in verse 3, however impossible this may be grammatically"; but it really refers to verse 14 (σὺ καὶ πᾶς ὁ οἶκός σου), so that all is in order.

xi. 17. Weiss here discovers a case of discrepancy with x. 47, but I cannot see it.

xi. 18. Weiss raises the point that μετάνοια is never mentioned in chapter x.; it was not, however, necessary to mention it. In spite of this, in giving a summary of the events of chapter x., it was not out of place to speak of ἡ μετάνοια εἰς ζωήν.

xii. 3. ἦσαν δὲ ἡμέραι τ. ἀζύμων. A parenthesis; but ὃν καὶ πιάσας (verse 4) coming after συλλαβεῖν (verse 3) is tautologous; it therefore appears that an editor has been at work here.

xii. 6. ὅτε δὲ ἤμελλεν προαγαγεῖν after βουλόμενος ἀναγαγεῖν αὐτόν (verse 4) is tautologous, and τῇ νυκτὶ ἐκείνῃ of verse 6[b] does not fit in well with 6[a]. It seems therefore that 6[a] originally followed verse 4, and that the night in question was the first which St. Peter spent in prison (Weiss), while the editor treated it as the last night before the intended execution.

xii. 17. Weiss thinks that the command to tell the brethren is discrepant with the purport of verses 5 and 12[b].

xii. 17. εἰς ἕτερον τόπον—very strange; the narrator must surely have known the place.

5. The Jerusalem-Antiochean Source (vi. 1-viii. 4; xi. 19-30; xii. 25 [xiii. 1]-xv. 35).

vi. 1. Abrupt introduction of the Hellenists and the Hebrews (*οἱ μαθηταί* also appears here for the first time).

vi. 1. *πληθυνόντων τῶν μαθητῶν*, a very modest way of speaking after the great numbers recorded in chapters ii.–v.

vi. 1. *τῇ διακονίᾳ τῇ καθημερινῇ*—this regular ministration to the needs of the poor is something quite different from the community of goods spoken of in chapters ii.–v.

vi. 2. *οἱ δώδεκα* only here (yet see ii. 14).

vi. 2. The assemblage of the whole *πλῆθος* (verse 5) seems still to imply only a moderate number. Evidently the Apostles up to this time had also ministered to the needs of the poor.

vi. 5. If viii. 5 *ff.* comes from the same source, it cannot but seem strange that more is not said here about St. Philip.

vi. 6^{b}. A very awkward change of subject.

vi. 7. The verse does not fit very well into the context.

vi. 8. This second characterisation of St. Stephen (*vide* verse 5) is strange, especially seeing that no *τέρατα κ. σημεῖα* are afterwards recorded in connection with him.

vi. 9. It is doubtful how we are to distinguish, or rather to arrange, the Hellenists here introduced to our notice.

vi. 12[b]. Weiss here supposes a change of subject, but this is not quite certain.

vi. 12. εἰς τὸ συνέδριον (*vide* verse 15)—but verses 13 and 14 (ὁ τόπος οὗτος), and vii. 54 *ff.*, suggest rather a public place (the Temple-court) and the action of a riotous crowd. This is still further suggested by the circumstance that, except in the conventional verse 1 of chapter viii., there is no indication of a judicial trial, and that the speech of St. Stephen does not in the least begin as if it were a direct answer to charges preferred in a court of law.

vi. 13 *f.* is essentially a doublet to verse 11.

vii. 4. μετώκισεν—a change of subject, which vanishes if we delete 4[a] as an interpolation.

vii. 7. Transition into the *oratio directa.*

vii. 8. ἐγέννησεν—change of subject.

vii. 10. κατέστησεν—change of subject.

vii. 8–16 (incl.) is ascribed by Weiss to the editor. He appeals to the superfluous and unsuitable character of the details given here (compare, however, verse 17), as well as to the harsh changes of subject and to what seems at least to be a discrepancy between verses 5 and 16.

vii. 19. The construction of ἐκάκωσεν with τοῦ ποιεῖν is almost intolerably harsh; from here onward to verse 23 (incl.) Weiss sees the hand of the editor; but his reasons are weak; neither is it obvious how, according to Weiss, Moses is in this case introduced. He also sees the editor in verses 26, 36, and 37, but again his reasons are weak.

vii. 21. ἐκτεθέντος αὐτοῦ ἀνείλατο αὐτόν—incorrect construction.

vii. 51 *f.* The conclusion, with its indignant reproaches, follows very abruptly; we must suppose that examples justifying these reproaches have been omitted, and that something was said about our Lord and His attitude towards the Temple. The Vision of chap. vii. 56 also seems to demand this.

vii. 57–viii. 3. These seven verses have much in them that is strange: (1) The information given about Saul is scattered in three places (vii. 58; viii. 1, 3); (2) the ἐλιθοβόλουν of verse 58 is without an object, and is repeated in verse 59; so that 58[b] and the first two words of verse 59 look like an interpolation, especially as the *μάρτυρες* of vi. 13 suddenly appear again in a very disconcerting fashion, and now serve as the executioners of St. Stephen; (3) 59[a] and 60 look like a genuine doublet, of which the second member is probably the interpolation; (4) the second passage concerning Saul (viii. 1[a]) is also probably interpolated, since viii. 1[b] connects excellently with vii. 60 or 59; (5) *πάντες . . . πλὴν τῶν ἀποστόλων* (viii. 1[c]) cannot be correct, and must belong to the editor; for the Hellenists (the followers of St. Stephen) were the only persons affected, and the Apostles on the other hand were not without a following. Lastly, this notice is inconsistent with verse 2; for the *ἄνδρες εὐλαβεῖς* must surely have been Christians. The *πάντες διεσπάρησαν κ.τ.λ.* is thus intended to prepare for viii. 5. Chap. viii. 3 is perhaps original; *κατὰ τοὺς οἴκους* shows yet again that viii. 1[c] is an interpolation.

viii. 4. The source extends to *διῆλθον* (incl.), *vide* xi. 19.

xi. 20, compared with xi. 19, is somewhat awkwardly expressed; nothing more, however, is to be said.

xi. 26^b. χρηματίσαι—change of subject; also the clause depends not upon ἐγένετο αὐτοῖς, but only upon ἐγένετο; neither does xi. 27 (ἐν ταύταις τ. ἡμέραις) refer to 26^b, but to 26^a; hence 26^b is possibly interpolated.

xi. 30. Presbyters in Jerusalem are here first mentioned without any introduction.

xiii. 2, 3. The subject of the verbs in the passage from ἀφορίσατε to ἀπέλυσαν is not quite certain.

xiii. 5. εἶχον δὲ καὶ Ἰωάννην ὑπηρέτην comes somewhat late.

xiii. 8. It is noteworthy that a second name is here given to the man.

xiii. 13. The abrupt introduction of "οἱ περὶ Παῦλον" (instead of Βαρν. κ. Π.) loses its strangeness if great stress is laid on the phrase, and 13^a is taken closely together with 13^b as cause and effect (Weiss): "Under the leading of *St. Paul* they came to Perga; St. Mark left them (in consequence) and returned to Jerusalem." And yet this exegesis is perhaps a little too ingenious!

xiv. 1. εἰς τ. συναγωγὴν τ. Ἰουδαίων—pleonastic.

xiv. 7. κἀκεῖ εὐαγγελιζόμενοι ἦσαν, namely in Lystra, *Derbe and the neighbouring districts*—hence the story of the occurrence in Lystra acquires the appearance of an appended anecdote, but there is nothing really strange in its having been appended in this way (*vide supra*, p. 94).

xiv. 8. ἐκάθητο—we must assume from verse 13

that the lame man was sitting outside the city (at the gate of the city?).

xiv. 14 *f.* St. Paul and St. Barnabas speak together.

xiv. 22[b]. Transition to the *oratio directa;* they again speak together.

xv. 2. τινὰς ἄλλους—strange that they are not named.

xv. 4 *fin.* coincides with xiv. 27[b].

xv. 5. αὐτούς does not refer at all to the previous αὐτῶν; we are compelled, therefore, to supply "the Gentiles" from the context; this is certainly awkward and yet tolerable. The remarks of Weiss on verses 5 *f.* seem to me too ingenious. Neither can I allow any weight to the objection he makes against ἀφ' ἡμερῶν ἀρχαίων (verse 7). Note that St. Peter speaks like one who at the time did not belong to the community in Jerusalem.

xv. 12. πλῆθος . . . ἤκουον.

xv. 12. It is true that nothing had previously been said of the πλῆθος, but verse 6 does not exclude it (against Weiss), the less so since it is mentioned in verse 4 (this holds good even if, as is probable, verse 6 describes a different assembly from verse 4 [*cf.* verse 4 and verse 12]). Over and above this, in verse 22 the ἐκκλησία is mentioned together with the Apostles and prophets, and in verse 23 οἱ ἀδελφοί.

xv. 12, 13. I cannot see sufficient reason for the objections which Weiss makes here.

xv. 14. It is strange that St. Peter is here called "Symeon."

xv. 23. γράψαντες—anacoluthon.

xv. 23. Brethren, *i.e.* Churches, in Syria and Cilicia have not been mentioned up to this point, also the *ὑμᾶς* is covered only by xv. 1 (Antioch).

xv. 31. *ἀναγνόντες*—change of subject. The participle also refers to *πλῆθος*.

xv. 32 connects so closely with verse 30 that verse 31 looks like an interpolation (*vide supra*); however, *καὶ αὐτοί . . . παρεκάλεσαν* is against such a supposition (the apposition begins *after* not *before καὶ αὐτοί*, and is confined to the two words: *προφῆται ὄντες*).

xv. 35. *μετὰ καὶ ἑτέρων πολλῶν*—the narrator thus knows more than he says, or does he only look back to xiii. 1? This verse would not, however, cover the word *πολλοί*.

xv. 36. *πόλιν πᾶσαν, ἐν αἷς*.

xv. 40. It is most strange that here, in opposition to verse 33, it is presupposed that Silas was in Antioch.

6. Chap. ix. 1–30.

ix. 1. *ἔτι* connects with viii. 3.

ix. 2. We are not prepared by viii. 1 for Christians in Damascus.

ix. 11. We learn only now (see verse 8) that St. Paul had taken lodging with a man named Judas in the street that was called "straight." Here also for the first time we learn that St. Paul was a native of Tarsus. I cannot see, with Weiss, that Saul is here introduced as a person quite unknown to Ananias (so that a discrepancy with verse 13 would result).

ix. 17. It is strange that Ananias knows about the appearance of Christ to St. Paul.

ix. 26. It is now forgotten that it had been said in viii. 1 that all the Christians except the Apostles had fled from Jerusalem.

ix. 26. *μὴ πιστεύοντες . . . ἐφοβοῦντο*—strange, seeing that he had now been in active work as a Christian missionary for a considerable time (*vide* ix. 23).

From this survey we may confidently conclude that the majority of the instances of inaccuracy and discrepancy in the Acts, seeing that they occur so frequently, ought not to be regarded as indications that sources are here used. They belong as much to the style of St. Luke as other phenomena of constant appearance in his work, and accordingly contribute to strengthen the character of literary unity in the book. For this very reason we have here included instances where the question of sources does not at all come into consideration. Let us group together some examples of various character as follows:—

In A we read (iii. 11) *ὁ λαὸς . . . ἔκθαμβοι*, (viii. 5) *κατελθὼν εἰς τὴν πόλιν ἐκήρυσσεν αὐτοῖς*, (viii. 14) *ἡ Σαμαρία . . . πρὸς αὐτούς*, but we also read in the Antiochean source (xv. 12) *ἐσίγησεν τὸ πλῆθος καὶ ἤκουον*, (xv. 30 *f.*) *τὸ πλῆθος . . . ἐχάρησαν*, (xv. 36) *κατὰ πόλιν πᾶσαν, ἐν αἷς*, and in those sections of the second part which certainly were not drawn from any written source, (xvi. 4) *διεπορεύοντο τὰς πόλεις παρεδίδοσαν αὐτοῖς*, (xxi. 36) *τὸ πλῆθος τοῦ λαοῦ κράζοντες*, (xxv. 24) *τὸ πλῆθος ἐνέτυχόν μοι*, see also

xix. 33, 34, lastly in the we-sections (xvi. 10) εἰς Μακεδονίαν . . . εὐαγγελίσασθαι αὐτούς.

In B (i. 24) a prayer is recorded, and it is left indefinite which of the company said it.

In A (iv. 1) we read λαλούντων αὐτῶν, when St. Peter alone had spoken; (iv. 19) St. Peter and St. John are represented as speaking the words which follow, while it is clear that only one can have spoken them; lastly (iv. 24), the whole community is represented as saying the long prayer that follows. Moreover, in the Antiochean source (xiv. 14 *f.* and xiv. 22^{b}), on two occasions words are placed in the mouths of St. Barnabas and St. Paul speaking together, and in the passages of the second part, which are certainly drawn from no written source, we read (xxi. 20) that St. James and the presbyters of Jerusalem speak together the passage that follows that verse.

Instances of abrupt change of grammatical subject, such as might lead us to conjecture the presence of new sources that have been clumsily inserted into the narrative, are found in all parts of the book. In the we-sections (xx. 12) the two words ἤγαγον and παρεκλήθησαν standing almost side by side have different subjects. In the passages of the second part, which are certainly not drawn from any written source, abrupt change of subject is found in xvi. 28, 29; xvii. 8, 9; xxiii. 32, 33; again in A in iv. 12; iv. 24; v. 15 (where we should expect the Apostles in place of St. Peter); viii. 17; lastly, in the Antiochean source in vi. 6; vi. 12 [uncertain]; vii. 4, 8, 10; xi. 26^{b}; xv. 31.

It is altogether characteristic of St. Luke's style

of narrative that details of a story are here and there inserted later or again earlier than their proper place (compare also St. Luke's gospel). It is specially worthy of note that examples are to be found in the we-sections. We are thereby warned, when we meet with similar examples in other parts of the book, not to fly at once to the hypothesis of interpolation and the like (as critics have very often done). In the we-sections (xx. 12) *ἤγαγον δὲ τὸν παῖδα ζῶντα* comes too late, we hear (xxi. 12, 16) somewhat too late of the Church in Cæsarea, on the contrary Mnason (xxi. 16) is mentioned somewhat too early, xxviii. 1 is not quite in its correct place before xxviii. 2, *ἀνάγεσθαι* in xxviii. 10 and *εἰς τὴν Ῥώμην* in xxviii. 14 come a little too soon. Nor is it otherwise in the passages of the second part of the book, which certainly are not drawn from a written source. We learn a little too late of St. Paul's Roman citizenship (xvi. 37), that Jason entertained the Apostles (xvii. 7), that only two of the seven brethren who were exorcists took part in the exorcism (xix. 16)—if the passage is to be so understood—of the plots of the Jews in Asia (xx. 19) and of the prophecies that had been delivered concerning the coming troubles (xx. 23). The conclusion of xxi. 27 (*vide* xxi. 30) seems to come too soon. The name Claudius Lysias (xxiii. 26) and the preaching of St. Paul in Judæa (xxvi. 20) come later than they ought. So also in B (i. 12) we are told somewhat late that the scene was the Mount of Olives. In A the age of the Lame Man (iv. 22), and again the notice that there were six brethren (xi. 12) are given rather late in the narrative. In the Antiochean source we learn that St. Mark was a companion of St. Paul (xiii. 5) later than we should have expected; again in xiv. 6 *ff*. Derbe καὶ ἡ περίχωρος are mentioned rather too soon, and the scene of action of xiv. 8 *ff*. is only hinted at rather late in the story (xiv. 13). Lastly, it is not until ix. 11 that we learn that St. Paul put up at the house of a man named Judas in Damascus.

Cases of anacoluthon and of change of construction have also led to the supposition of written sources, but scarcely ever is such an explanation justifiable, for they are of frequent occurrence, and are indeed met with in very many authors. In the we-sections (xxvii. 10) the construction with ὅτι passes over into the Acc. c. Inf.; in the passages of the second part of the book, which are certainly not drawn from a written source, we find cases of transition into *oratio directa* in xvii. 3; xxiii. 22; xxiii. 24 (transition into *oratio indirecta*), and an instance of harsh anacoluthon in xxiv. 5. In B (i. 4) the relative construction changes into a principal sentence, and (i. 4^{c}) the *oratio obliqua* into *oratio directa.* In A we find in (iv. 6) an instance of harsh anacoluthon, so also in viii. 7. In the Antiochean source we find transition into *oratio directa* in vii. 7, also in xiv. 22^{b}, and in xv. 23 an instance of anacoluthon (γράψαντες).[1] In very many passages we find that by omitting one or several verses a better connection is gained. But this is not surprising

[1] The Gen. Abs. is incorrect both in vii. 21 (Antiochean source) and in xxi. 34.—Μέν without δέ (or δέ in isolation) is found, if I am right, only in the second part of the book and in the we-sections (*vide* xxvii. 21 and xvii. 18; xxiii. 22; xxv. 4; xxvi. 4; xxviii. 22), but this is unimportant.

in the case of an author who has the somewhat careless habit of referring to things that he should have told us beforehand (*vide supra*). These are notably the passages which critics have seized upon in order to put in practice their well-known methods of amputation. It is possible that in some cases interpolation may be safely assumed, yet seeing that the phenomenon in question is of such frequent occurrence, strong reasons must exist to justify this critical operation. In the we-sections we gain better connection if we omit xxvii. 9–11. In the remaining passages of the second part of the book the same is the case if we omit xvi. 24–34; xviii. 8; xviii. 9, 10, 24–28; xix. 30, 31, 37. In B, i. 22 disturbs the connection; again, v. 22–24 is easily dispensed with. In A, iv. 1–3 is awkward before iv. 4; one is tempted either to omit the latter verse or to transform the former passage; also we could well dispense with iv. 15–20, with iv. 22, 27–28, with the words καὶ σημεῖα καὶ τέρατα γίνεσθαι (iv. 30), with iv. 32, and with v. 14 and x. 39[a]. Lastly, in the Antiochean source the connection seems to be improved if we omit vii. 4 and other details of the speech; again, the passage vii. 57–viii. 3 looks like an awkward shuffling together of two sources with repetitions (here at all events it is difficult to avoid the hypothesis that sources are really present); xi. 26[b] gives the impression of unskilful attachment, and xv. 31 of an awkward interpolation. And yet in almost all these cases the reasons are not quite convincing, and there still remains the simpler hypothesis of a certain literary carelessness on the part of St. Luke.

On the latter hypothesis we may most probably explain those cases where St. Luke introduces persons with a certain unconcern, or in other places seems to forget that he has already introduced them. Instances of the latter kind occur in the we-sections in xxi. 10 and xxvii. 2. In the remaining passages of the second part of the book we notice the abrupt appearance of the household of the jailor (xvi. 32), of Jason (xvii. 5), of Sosthenes (xviii. 17), of Gaius and Aristarchus (xix. 29), of Alexander (xix. 33), and of St. Paul's sister's son (xxiii. 16). In A (ix. 31) the Church in Galilee, of which nothing has been said hitherto, appears all at once; likewise (xii. 17) St. James, the Lord's brother. In the Antiochean source (vi. 1) mention is abruptly made of Hellenists and Hebrews in the Primitive Community, of presbyters in Jerusalem (xi. 30), of the brethren in Syria and Cilicia (xv. 23); from xiii. 1 we might suppose that as little had been previously said about Barnabas and Saul as about the other men mentioned in the verse. From ix. 2 we suddenly discover that there were Christians in Damascus.

Instances of redundancy, of awkward repetition, of silence upon important points, and of extraordinary brevity, can be adduced from different parts of the book. Still greater is the number of instances of ambiguity, of accounts and expressions whose significance is not quite clear, of trifling cases of literary inaccuracy. They can be easily found in the lists given above. Nor are there wanting instances of discrepancy. Such (though insignificant) are to be found in the three descriptions of the conversion of St. Paul [they do not point to different sources], in the letter of Claudius Lysias (xxiii. 26 *ff.*) compared with the previous narrative, in Festus' report (xxv. 14 *ff.*), and finally in the last speech of St. Paul (in Rome, xxviii. 17 *f.*). Such are, moreover, to be found in B (ii. 9 compared with ii. 5); in A (iv. 36 *f.* compared with iv. 32; and x. 42 compared with i. 8); and lastly in the Antiochean source (xv. 40 compared with xv. 33; concerning this instance of glaring discrepancy *vide infra*).

Under these circumstances we are compelled to conclude that *an analysis into written sources based upon phenomena such as have been mentioned, or of a similar kind, rests on insecure evidence, and is as a rule unjustified.* Taking into account the literary temperament of St. Luke we are justified in proceeding to such analysis only when the concurrence of many such phenomena compels us to adopt this procedure. In such cases, however, the question always arises whether we have to do with written sources that have been unskilfully pieced together, or with *later interpolations* inserted either by the author himself or by succeeding editors.

I. The we-sections have about them the character of a diary, and it is therefore probable, if not certain, that St. Luke employed in them notes which he possessed. In these sections, however, there is no certain indication of later interpolation. We may naturally conjecture that xxi. 9 (τούτῳ δὲ ἦσαν θυγατέρες τέσσαρες παρθένοι προφητεύουσαι) is such an interpolation, but we cannot here reach more than a vague possibility. Wellhausen has, however, with absolute confidence pronounced that xxvii. 9–11, 21–

26, 31, 33–38 are interpolated. If this is really so, then the whole account of the voyage contains no reference to St. Paul and becomes an anonymous sea-story, which St. Luke with great audacity has turned into a story concerning St. Paul. Wellhausen has not shrunk from drawing this conclusion, although the sections in question are entirely Lukan in style, and although the very questionable procedure thus ascribed to St. Luke demands the strongest proof before it can be accepted as probable. The indications which have led the critic to omit these passages as interpolations made by a third person, may have justice done to them without recourse to such an hypothesis of dynamite. We may well suppose that for the description of the facts the author followed either his own memory or—as is more probable—the brief notes of his own diary. His accounts of St. Paul's behaviour, and of what the Apostle *said* on that occasion, would naturally be deduced from his memory of the whole situation thus recalled to him, with colouring from his own imagination, and would necessarily have been inserted by him at suitable points in the narrative which he composed from his notes.

II. In reference to the second half of the book (excluding the we-sections), I may say that the most minute investigation has strengthened me afresh in the conviction that on the whole, and in almost every particular instance, it is most highly probable that written sources were not used.[1] It is possible to

[1] The tradition here is certainly not *homogeneous;* in the last quarter it is quite possible that doublets exist.

regard xvi. 24–34; xviii. 8; xviii. 9, 10; xviii. 24–28, and perhaps other passages here and there, as later interpolations, and xviii. 5–17, 19–23, and perhaps other passages, as abbreviations of a more extensive written source. But in xviii. 5–17 the former supposition excludes the latter, and then the assumption of later interpolation is by far the more probable, although I cannot speak even in favour of this hypothesis. The section xviii. 24–28, though it certainly falls somewhat outside the scope of the whole work, is yet to the point if one assumes that St. Luke did not wish to pass over so important a missionary as Apollos; and even the best writer could not have treated the ministry of this man otherwise than as an episode, nor could he have inserted it into the context at a more appropriate place. The passage xix. 19–23 is purposely brief and sketchy, for St. Luke did not wish to say nothing about St. Paul's return to Syria, and yet it did not fit in well with the continuous onward movement of his plot. As for the passage xvi. 24–34, I would here admit the probability of later interpolation if the verses were not so entirely Lukan in style, and if after their removal a good and consistent story were left behind. But it is scarcely credible that St. Luke only narrated the imprisonment in Philippi in order to show how proud St. Paul was of his Roman citizenship.

Chapter xix. (the story of Demetrius) has been subjected by Wellhausen to criticism similar to that with which he has treated chapter xxvii. (the account of the voyage). Wellhausen here remarks: "The original source here simply described a rising in Ephesus against the Jews. The author was neither Jew nor Christian, but an impartial and superior observer, a trifle malicious but quite *sine ira et studio*. St. Luke has taken up the ready-made narrative and altered it to suit his purpose, and yet with so little thoroughness that it still shows itself everywhere." This is the impression given by the passage after the omission of verses 26 (the mention of St. Paul), 29^b, 30, 31, and 37. Against such a theory we may set: (1) The general consideration of the improbability that a writer who, as even Wellhausen agrees, had access to all kinds of trustworthy information about St. Paul's long stay in Ephesus, should have been at such a loss for material for his narrative as to seize upon the description of a chance rising against the Jews in Ephesus, and in a most audacious way to paint St. Paul's portrait into it; and (2) the special consideration that we can scarcely believe that if the writer had inserted the Apostle into the narrative he would have handled him so discreetly—*i.e., would have allowed him not to be affected by the persecution!* Who can possibly believe that any one making up a story would act thus! Lastly—verse 37 does not fall out of the context (it connects quite well with προπετές of verse 36), and therefore does not break the bond between verses 36 and 38, rather this bond remains intact even if one reads 37. It is true that the entry of Alexander upon the scene remains obscure—perhaps he was known to the first readers, perhaps we must simply assume an ambiguity arising from an effort to be brief, as in the case of Sosthenes (xviii.

17), and in not a few other cases.[1] On the whole this section, which is in no way necessarily dependent on a written source, bears the stamp of historical trustworthiness just because it does not eulogise St. Paul —indeed, leaves him open to possible accusations of want of courage. If, however, it is believed that here and there in the second half of the book we cannot dispense with the hypothesis of written sources, it need not at all follow that the authorship of St. Luke is excluded.

When attempting to answer the question whether a temporary companion of St. Paul could have written the second half of the book, we ought to keep all trivial details out of sight. The few historical mistakes in matters of detail, with which it is possible to charge the author, are not at all to the point; for St. Luke has the right to make a mistake, especially when he was not an eye-witness and was dependent upon the reports of others. This, however, does not prevent people from confidently asserting that xxi. 20 *ff.*, and the manner in which St. Paul is represented as defending himself before the Jewish (and Gentile) tribunal in the last chapters of the book, either exclude a companion of St. Paul as author, or destroy all hope that we shall ever arrive at an intelligible conception of the actual course of events.[2] Here one representation

[1] It has been already recognised by Storr that this straining after brevity, leading here and there to ambiguity, is to be noticed in the gospel as well as in the Acts.

[2] *Vide e.g.* Julicher, *Neue Linien*, s. 60: "If one of the most intimate companions of St. Paul tells us without the slightest hesitation how St. Paul for the sake of peace wished by an elaborate act of hypocrisy to convince the Jews that he still walked in the strict

of the character of St. Paul stands opposed to another, *i.e.* to the conception which we ourselves have formed concerning St. Paul. Of course I do not mean that St. Paul was capable of an act of hypocrisy, or that St. Luke was capable of supposing that he was; for such an hypothesis is absolutely devoid of evidence. According to my conception of the attitude of St. Paul towards his nation and the Law, as I derive it from his own letters, he, as a Jew by birth, would not only be capable at any moment of performing ceremonial and other Jewish functions with a good conscience, but where Jewish opposition to the interests of the mission did not come into play he would even perform such functions of his own free will and from ingrained feelings of reverence. St. Paul not only "became" a Jew to the Jews—*i.e.* he not only accommodated himself to them in matters of religious practice, even in those wherein he had outgrown them —but he *was* and he *remained* a Jew. Nothing in his letters prevents us from supposing that on his visits to the Holy City he, like his Jewish Christian brethren in Jerusalem, took part in the ceremonial worship of the Temple. It must be allowed that the epistles to the Romans and the Galatians *might seem* to suggest that this was no longer possible for him, but they *need not* be so interpreted; and if we here receive

observance of the Law, and if this representation, given by a *friend* who must have possessed true information concerning St. Paul's attitude to the Law, deserves to be taken as evidence, then all hopes that we shall ever arrive at an intelligible conception of the actual history of the Primitive Church are reduced to zero, and we are no longer safe in opposing any negation of things which have even the best attestation."

additional information concerning the character and practice of the Apostle—no matter whether it is to his credit or not[1]—we have only to examine most carefully whether this additional information is to the point. In my opinion, it stands the test. Moreover, in judging of St. Paul and his controversy with the Jewish Christians, people are always overlooking the fact the liberty of all Christians was not the subject of debate but the freedom of the Gentile Christians from the yoke of the Law. There was no question at all as to the practice of Jewish Christians in reference to the Law, so far as their own persons were concerned. As for the point of the defence made before the Jewish tribunal, St. Luke may well have added an accent or an emphasis which might here so readily suggest itself to him. But the main question, that St. Paul in his apology laid the greatest stress upon his teaching in defence of the Resurrection of the dead and of the Hope of Israel (xxiii. 6 *f.*; xxiv. 14 *f.*; xxvi. 6 *f.*; xxviii. 17, 20; see, however, on the other hand, xxvi. 23), and that he also emphasised points wherein he agreed with the Pharisees as opposed to the Sadducees, may very well be historical. Perhaps St. Luke might with advantage to St. Paul have shown a little finer ethical feeling in his reproduction of these speeches, but in my opinion it is only a question of nuance. Accordingly there is no justification for the assertion

[1] He loses somewhat in determination and in that consistency of character wherein the eye is always sharply fixed upon a single object, but he gains in freedom and in absolute devotion to the interests of the mission.

that because of these passages no companion of St. Paul could have written the Acts. Those who advance such an assertion make upon both author and Apostle demands which are too rigorous, too heroic, and too abstract.

Seeing that there is no proof that the second half of the book depends upon written sources, we may not forthwith build up the hypothesis of written sources for the first half upon the basis of faults similar to those which are found in the second half.

III. Passing to chapter i. and the "source" B (chap. ii.; v. 17–42), we find that the instances of discrepancy and unevenness are so numerous in the first verses of the first chapter that we cannot well reject the hypothesis that they have been subjected to later correction. We can, however, no longer ascertain the extent of this correction, nor the wording of the original text.

In the passage concerning the election of Matthias (i. 15–26) Weiss distinguishes a written source and editorial touches due to St. Luke. He bases his conclusions upon the different significance given to the word ἡ ἔπαυλις (the Apostleship and the plot of ground of Judas), as well as upon the grammatical and practical difficulties that are to be found in the verses 21[b, c], 22. The latter verses may be a later interpolation—though we are by no means forced to this conclusion; but the fact that ἔπαυλις is used in a double significance gives no ground for assuming a written source. Double interpretations of a word are out of place according to our ideas of exegesis, but they were not so according to ancient ideas (especially where a sacred text was concerned); rather it was thought that exegesis approached nearer to the truth, and was the more edifying, the more things—often quite heterogeneous—it read into the text and the more it combined together things quite distinct from one another.

Chapter ii. suffers much from obscurity. It is not at all clear whether the event narrated took place on the day of Pentecost or shortly beforehand, nor is it clear where the scene of action is placed; there is obscurity as to the character of the miracle; it is doubtful whether the Spirit fell only upon the Apostles or upon all the Christians; it is not clear what became of the natives of Jerusalem (only Jews of the Dispersion dwelling in Jerusalem are spoken of; yet see verse 14); it is not explained how the phenomenon could have been brought to the notice of several thousand persons; it is not clear how St. Peter could speak of great cosmic miracles, which certainly did not occur, nor are they mentioned afterwards in the narrative—many other things also are obscure. But to attempt to clear away these obscurities by assuming a written source, containing none of these faults, which has been spoiled by the correction of an editor—the editor is always a simpleton—is a strange way out of the difficulty. It is ever so much more natural to suppose that we have here a worked-up narrative of a character that of itself forbids close examination into the clearness and definiteness of its details, because throughout one single point is kept in view. The unprejudiced reader does not notice these instances of obscurity—on the other hand, the essential point of the narrative stands out quite clearly—nor were they probably noticed by St. Luke himself.[1] How much of this "working up" is due to St. Luke, how much to the source itself, cannot be determined. It was only natural that this first occasion of "speaking with tongues" should be distinguished from the later occasions in its miraculously attractive power. The same considerations hold good for the section v. 17–42. We are tempted to regard the unnecessary verses 22–24 as an interpolation; but St. Luke could easily have been somewhat diffuse in his narrative; at all events the verses do not disturb the context. Neither can I see why Weiss should object to see the two reproaches of verse 28 standing side by side.[2] Here also it is enough to say that the ordinary style of narrative loves to heap up motives, and is not concerned about their consistency with one another. Accordingly B may pass as a source, but not as a written source. It is, however, worthy of note that this source is related to the Jerusalem-Antiochean source, in so far as it seems to have sprung from Hellenistic circles. In ii. 5 *οἱ ἐν*

[1] It is characteristic of by no means few of his narratives that he has not quite thoroughly thought out his situations, as so easily happens when one recounts an event of which one has not been an eye-witness. From the instances of unevenness and of slight discrepancy that must thus arise, to conclude the existence of a written source free from such faults, which has been spoiled by abbreviation and interpolation, is not the first course that presents itself, but rather the last resource. Many critics, however, prefer it because they would sooner reckon with two rigid components than with a single elastic one, although daily experience must teach them that stories awkward in style and illogical in small points are everywhere the rule.

[2] Weiss judges similarly concerning the incompatibility of the two motives given in iv. 16 and iv. 21.

Ἱερουσαλὴμ κατοικοῦντες Ἰουδαῖοι, ἄνδρες εὐλαβεῖς ἀπὸ πάντος ἔθνους τῶν ὑπὸ τὸν οὐρανόν alone appear (*vide supra*), so that we are almost compelled to infer that the story of Pentecost only concerns these Hellenists to the exclusion of the natives of Jerusalem. Or is this only due to the unskilfulness of the writer (see verse 14)?

Chapters i. and ii. and v. 17–42 are the passages of the Acts which are furthest removed from actual history. The account of the Ascension is quite useless to the historian (*vide supra*, pp. 155 *ff.*), the account of the election of an Apostle is at least beyond our control, and the story of Pentecost is so worked up that even St. Luke did not recognise it as a doublet of iv. 31. Neither has he recognised that the story of the imprisonment of the Apostles and their miraculous release (v. 17 *ff.*) is a doublet of iv. 1 *ff.* and xii., because here all the Apostles have taken the place of St. Peter. Finally, our trust in this source is not increased by its profession to know exactly what happened in the Council (v. 34 *ff.*, the speech of Gamaliel). These passages taken together must be accounted the latest and least credible in the book.

IV. In favour of the theory that A (the Jerusalem-Cæsarean source) was a written source, we may advance the following considerations:—

(1) The name of St. John seems to have been interpolated into a text that had already taken form, in which St. Peter alone was mentioned (chaps. iii.–iv.).

(2) The scene of iv. 5 *ff.* seems to have been originally set in the Court of the Temple, and to have been first transferred to the Sanhedrin by St. Luke.

(3) Elsewhere in this passage, so it seems, traces are to be found of the work of an editor.

(4) Such traces are also found in the passage iv. 25–31.

(5) Chap. iv. 32 presents difficulties in both form and subject-matter, and does not agree with iv. 36 *f.*; the same remark applies to iv. 34 *f.*

(6) Chap. v. 14 looks like an interpolation which breaks the thread of the context.

(7) In chapter x. it seems possible to distinguish the work of an editor and a fixed text which he has worked up.

(8) The same seems to be the case in xii. 1–6. Moreover, the brevity of the notice concerning the martyrdom of St. James, and of the sufferings of other Christians at the same time, is best explained on the assumption that the source contained stories about St. Peter, and accordingly only cursorily touched upon other subjects, however important they may have been (*vide supra*, p. 125).

(9) The expression xii. 17: *ἐπορεύθη εἰς ἕτερον τόπον* looks like the concluding sentence of a source, in the reproduction of which the name of the place has been suppressed.

I do not think that I need weary the reader with a detailed investigation of these instances, seeing that I have not yet been able to attain to a quite complete and certain result, and have advanced only a little beyond the position which I formulated in my earlier work ("Luke the Physician," pp. 116 *f.*).

For some passages of this body of tradition it is, in my opinion, very probable that St. Luke depended upon a written document. So, above all, for chaps. iii., iv., and chap. xii. As for the former extensive passage, it is here so obvious that the name of St. John has been interpolated into a story that had already taken a fixed form, that we need only ask whether St. Luke himself inserted it or a later interpolator. Seeing, however, that St. Luke without doubt betrays in his gospel an interest in St. Peter *and St. John* (*vide* especially xx. 8; the other gospels give no names here), it is precarious not to ascribe this interest also to him in the Acts. Then it would follow that the tradition of chaps. iii. and iv. lay before him in a fixed—*i.e.* in a written—form of narrative[1] with which it would also seem necessary to combine chap. v. 1–11. It may, moreover, be maintained that chapter xii. depends upon a written document, both on account of its introduction, the brevity of which would be otherwise incomprehensible, and because of other phenomena it presents. It is not so probable that the passage x. 1–xi. 18 depends upon a written tradition, and such an hypothesis is quite uncertain in the case of chaps. viii. and ix. 32–43. It is not, however, necessary to imagine that because some of these passages with great probability are based upon written tradition, it therefore follows that the same hypothesis must be extended to all the rest. However probable it is that the passages we have included under A form a certain homogeneous whole, it cannot be shown that in matters of form this unity is so complete that it is not possible to suppose that some

[1] Note also that it is only here that our Lord is called ὁ παῖς θεοῦ (*vide supra*)—an important point!

of its elements may have reached St. Luke in writing and others by way of oral tradition, nor to suppose that they *may* depend upon the authority of different persons. The whole of the phenomena seems to be best explained on the supposition that St. Luke received from St. Philip (or from him and his daughters) partly oral information, partly also written tradition, which helped out the oral accounts. This body of tradition referred to St. Philip's own ministry, but above all it was made up of reminiscences concerning St. Peter (and for these St. Mark also comes under consideration). What was written can, however, scarcely have been written in Greek, but must have been composed in the Aramaic tongue; for the Lukan vocabulary and style can be traced into the most intimate details of the narratives, while from the syntax of the sentences, and from many turns of phraseology, we may conclude that the original was *perhaps* Semitic.

As for the historical value of the records in A, we have already considered this question in the preceding chapter. This collection of traditions proceeds from one who thoroughly believed in the miraculous, and was probably himself endowed with supernatural gifts, and it has received some legendary embellishments. But the legendary element can easily be discerned as such; and beneath the whole there lies a nucleus of historical fact. This nucleus appears especially in chapters iii. and iv. (the intelligible development of events leading up to the "outpouring of the Spirit" and the foundation of the Church). In this source the stories of the conversion of the Samaritans and of

Cornelius were not related as stages leading up to the mission to the Gentiles, but simply as stories concerning St. Peter and St. Philip.[1] It was only the way in which St. Luke has used them for his history that first gave them their appearance of stages. Lastly, the facts referred to in chapter xii. may be said to depend upon genuine and trustworthy tradition.

V. It now only remains for us to conclude with the investigation of the extensive Jerusalem-Antiochean source (vi. 1–viii. 4; xi. 19–30; xii. 25 [xiii. 1]–xv. 35). In favour of the written character of this source we may adduce the following weighty considerations:—

(1) The abrupt fashion in which it begins at vi. 1, indeed in which it begins everywhere, when it starts afresh. Note especially the verbal identity of viii. 4 and xi. 19.

(2) Certain terminological and other differences, though not many, which exist between it and the remaining portions of the first half of the Acts.

(3) The consideration that the speech of St. Stephen seems to have been edited (though not to the extent assumed by Weiss), and that its conclusion seems to have been curtailed.

(4) The consideration that ix. 19–30 looks like an extract; while on the other hand xiii. 4–xiv. 28 gives the impression of having been expanded from shorter records.

[1] For this very reason the ordinary objections that are advanced against an historical nucleus in the story of Cornelius fall to the ground.

(5) The consideration that chap. xv. seems to have been based upon a fuller narrative.

(6) The appearance of unity and of gradual development up to a climax which can be traced throughout, and distinguishes all the passages assigned to this source.

(7) The consideration that St. Philip, one of the "seven," plays no part here, though his name is mentioned.

(8) The consideration that the actual circumstances of the story of St. Stephen (a riot in the streets) can still be discerned behind the representation of St. Luke, who has placed the scene in the council-chamber.

(9) The consideration that vii. 57–viii. 3 is best explained as an unskilful shuffling together of two sources, of which *one* at least must have been written.

(10) The consideration that St. Barnabas is here not only treated as of equal authority with St. Paul, but is even set in the foreground.

(11) The consideration that xv. 40 is discrepant with xv. 33.[1]

Not one of these considerations affords a convincing proof of the written character of the source—it is also possible to assume later interpolation and editing[2]—but the impression that part at least of this source,

[1] The discrepancy is indeed so flagrant that one is inclined to conjecture a *later* interference with the text.

[2] It is not probable that the conclusion of the speech of St. Stephen has been curtailed by some later corrector, seeing that a too sharp attack upon the Temple and "the customs delivered by Moses" would also to St. Luke himself have seemed wanting in reverence.

perhaps the whole, was in writing makes itself felt still more strongly than in the case of the source A. If Silas was the authority for this body of tradition —and considering the subject-matter and the relations that existed between himself and St. Paul, what more likely person could we imagine!—it follows that in this case also we may suppose that oral information was helped out by written notes. Such a solution of the problem seems to answer best to the actual situation; but I am far from holding it as certain. St. Luke has—shall we say, unfortunately?—understood how to give his work such a stamp of homogeneity that, with the exception of the vindication of the we-sections for the author himself, of the discovery of the doublets in A and B,[1] and of the separation from the rest of the book of a distinct collection of narratives connected with both Jerusalem and Antioch, there is nothing in the criticism of the sources of

[1] But the following pretty little experience of mine teaches how careful one should be in assuming doublets. On a rainy day beside the Walensee, I was turning over the leaves of the *Jahrbuch des Historischen Vereins des kanton Glarus*, 27. Heft (1892). In an article on "St. Felix and Regula in Spain" I read (pp. 6 *f.*) as follows: "If any one had anywhere read that in the third decade of this century a pupil of the public school of Aarau, the son of one Trümpi, a pastor in Schwanden [Canton Glarus], was drowned near Aarau when bathing in the Aar, and had afterwards read somewhere else that in 1837 one Balthasar Leuzinger, son of M. Leuzinger, the pastor in Schwanden, was drowned when bathing in the Aar close to Aarau, if the reader were at all of a critical turn of mind he would assuredly have drawn the conclusion that one and the same occurrence was evidently referred to in each case. . . . And yet it actually happened that two young natives of Glarus, both of them sons of a pastor of Schwanden, were drowned in the neighbourhood of Aarau [thus a long way from Schwanden]."

the Acts that can be maintained with absolute confidence.

We have already discussed (pp. 195 *ff.* and elsewhere) the high historical worth of this Antiochean source. We owe to it most important information concerning the early history of the Church of Jerusalem and the beginning of the mission to the Gentiles, filling up great gaps in the information we derive from the epistles of St. Paul. Without this source we should have been unable to form any conception concerning certain fundamental historical questions, or we should at least have arrived at a conception which would have been incorrect. But there is *one* account in this source which seems to threaten its trustworthiness—I refer to the Apostolic Decree of the Council of Jerusalem.

Our concern is only with the Decree itself—the rest of the narrative in chapter xv. either presents no difficulties at all, or at least not such as would exclude its composition by St. Luke—*i.e.* by a man who was in a position to make inquiries from the eye-witnesses.[1]

[1] It must not, of course, be forgotten that other points of difference exist between Gal. ii. and Acts xv. The most glaring are these—that, in the Acts, the Apostles seem from the first to have stood upon the side of freedom, and that St. Paul is not represented as standing on an equality with them, indeed they seem rather to form a court of higher instance. But this is partly only appearance. Even according to the Acts the conversion of Cornelius did *not* have the result that the Apostles now became missionaries to the Gentiles, or in plain terms, recognised the Mission (St. Luke makes them refer to the story of Cornelius as an event that had happened long ago), and even from the Acts one can see clearly enough that it was the account which St. Barnabas and St. Paul gave of the success of their mission that led to the final decision. If, however, St. Paul, when compared

But the Apostolic Decree, if it contained a general declaration against eating sacrifices offered to idols, against partaking of blood or things strangled, and against fornication, is inconsistent with the account given by St. Paul in Gal. ii. 1–10,[1] and with the corresponding passages in the First Epistle to the Corinthians. It is, accordingly, unhistorical. But if the Decree is unhistorical, it follows that it is in the highest degree improbable that a companion of Silas and St. Paul either wrote or accepted from others what we read in Acts xv. Both he and his authority must have known the real result of the deliberations of the Council. Neither could St. Luke have been so audacious as to forge the result, nor so simple as to forget it or to exchange it for another tradition, seeing especially that he lays great stress upon the fact that St. Paul and Silas on their missionary journey delivered this very Decree to the churches (xvi. 4), and seeing that he himself refers

with the Apostles, here falls into the background, we must nevertheless allow St. Luke, who was not present on this occasion, the liberty so to picture the scene to himself, seeing especially that we have here a conflict of two representations, and that the religious and apostolic independence which St. Paul claimed for himself by no means excludes that at that time the Church of Jerusalem with its leaders was regarded as the court of ultimate appeal for the whole of Christendom. (Even if the Decree is authentic, I have always regarded the letter as a creation of St. Luke. He perhaps imitated some other letter of the kind.) Besides, we must not forget that even St. Paul has written in Gal. ii. 2: *ἀνεθέμην αὐτοῖς* (the "pillars" of the Church of Jerusalem) *τὸ εὐαγγέλιον ὃ κηρύσσω ἐν τοῖς ἔθνεσιν . . . μή πως εἰς κενὸν τρέχω ἢ ἔδραμον.* This after all is not so very different from the impression which is given by the Acts.

[1] And also with the narrative of Gal. ii. 11 *ff.*

to it again in xxi. 25. It is possible to suppose that a later annalist, who could no longer communicate with eye-witnesses, might have made a mistake about this Decree, or might have mixed up two different decrees—but in the case of a companion of St. Paul who met with the Apostle soon after the promulgation of the Decree, such a supposition is quite inadmissible. The same holds good of the person who formed his authority.

Now it is well known that the Apostolic Decree is handed down to us in a twofold form in the manuscripts and by the Fathers. Following in the steps of other scholars, whose vision, however, had not been keen enough, I have gone most thoroughly into the question in an article published in the *Sitzungsberichte d. K. Preuss. Akad. d. Wiss.*, 2. März 1899. I here arrived at the result—which is now, so far as I know, widely accepted—that the Decree according to one tradition prohibited certain foods (flesh offered to idols, blood, things strangled) and fornication, and that according to the other tradition it was a summary of Jewish ethical catechetics (the abstaining from flesh offered to idols—in the sense of sharing in the idolatrous feasts, and in idolatry generally—from murder and fornication, "and all which ye would not that others should do to you, even so do it not to them"). In this article I attempted to prove a position which up to that time I had agreed with almost every one in accepting, namely, that the first of these two forms of the Decree (we may call it the Eastern form and that of the Uncials) was the original, and that the second form (we may call it that of the

Western Fathers, including Irenæus; it is also that of Codex D) must accordingly be regarded as due to interpolation.

Since that time—and I may say with great reluctance and after long consideration—I have arrived at a different conclusion. I am not fond of correcting myself—and it is not the first time—but *magis amica veritas!* Besides, the main structure of my article still stands firm. The conversion was effected by the excellent and exhaustive treatise of Resch, junior, *Das Aposteldekret nach seiner ausserkanonischen Textgestalt* (*Texte und Unters.*, Bd. 28, Heft 3, 1905).[1] But there were two other contributory influences: (1) A conviction, strengthened by Wellhausen (*Noten z. Apostelgesch.*, s. 19 *ff.*), that the word πνικτόν did not belong to the original text, and (2) the perception that the Decree in its ordinary form did not fit in well with its context in chapter xv.

Πνικτόν is wanting in Dd, Athous, Sahid., Iren., Porphyr., Gigas, Augustine (ep. 82, Specul. and elsewhere), Tertull., Cyprian, Pacian, Hieron, App. ad Eucher. opp., Ambrosiaster, Fulgent. It is combined with αἷμα to form one idea in the Vulgate [*sanguine suffocato*], and by Cyril of Jerusalem [αἵματος πνικτοῦ] and by Gaudentius [*a sanguine id est suffocatis*]; on the other hand, αἷμα is wanting in Orig. lat. in Matth.

[1] In the year 1906 there also appeared a treatise by A. Seeburg entitled, *Die beiden Wege und das Aposteldekret.* In my article in the *Sitzsungsberichten* I had already touched upon the "Two Ways," and used it to illustrate the Apostolic Decree in its Western form. Seeburg in his careful treatise has carried this much further; but I cannot accept his conclusions, seeing that they presuppose the originality of the prohibitions of food in Acts xv.

and in Methodius. Moreover, Wellhausen has decisively proved—*cf.* also Resch's learned notes on πνικτόν—that πνικτόν is included in the prohibition of αἷμα (if αἷμα means "partaking of blood"; it only occurs in those authorities where αἷμα has this meaning), and cannot stand as a separate member of the list.[1] Accordingly, the original decree, as reported by St. Luke, read in its second half as follows: Ἀπέχεσθαι εἰδωλοθύτων καὶ αἵματος καὶ πορνείας ἐξ ὧν διατηροῦντες ἑαυτοὺς εὖ πράξεσθε. *As soon as this is recognised, the question concerning the original meaning of the Decree becomes no longer a question of text but simply of interpretation.* The Western authorities (and D) have made it quite clear, by the interpolation (ὅσα μὴ θέλετε ἑαυτοῖς γίνεσθαι ἑτέρῳ μὴ ποιεῖν), which interpretation they preferred.[2] But is this not really the meaning intended by St. Luke? Resch and—already

[1] It is also in favour of the original absence of πνικτόν that the insertion of the word can be easily explained (*vide infra*), and that as a general rule interpolations into the text [especially in D, but also elsewhere] are far more frequent than omissions [amid the enormous number of additions in D can we point to a single omission which is not due to grammatical considerations or to carelessness?—*vide* Weiss in *Texte u. Unters.*, Bd. 9, s. 37 *ff.*]. If πνικτόν stood originally in the text, and was afterwards omitted, this would have implied gross interference with the text. If it was originally absent, and then inserted with the intention of giving what was thought to be a correct interpretation of αἷμα, this would scarcely have been called interpolation. However, Wellhausen's supposition that in the case that αἷμα means "shedding of blood" πνικτόν may be original (but not if it means "partaking of blood," as he supposes) seems scarcely possible; for it is incredible that any one should have set together in this fashion the abominations of idolatry, murder, fornication, and eating things strangled.

[2] It is here assumed that these words are interpolated. That this was probably so *vide infra.*

before him—Hilgenfeld[1] have answered in the affirmative, in opposition to all other scholars. What support, then, can be found for the usual interpretation (prohibition of meats and of fornication), if πνικτόν does not belong to the original text? *Nothing certainly in the context of the Acts*—whether one considers only chapter xv. or the whole book—*nor in the epistles of St. Paul.* Moreover, the united testimony of the exegesis of the ancient Western Fathers is opposed to this interpretation. So far as I can see, the conception that the Decree originally included prohibition of meats can be based only on the following considerations:—

(1) Upon the exegesis of the Eastern Fathers, but not until St. Clement and Origen;

(2) On passages in very ancient documents (*e.g.* The Revelation), in which the eating of flesh offered to idols appears as something that is altogether abominable;

(3) On the consideration that as eating is referred to in the word εἰδωλόθυτον, it may also be understood in the case of αἷμα;

(4) Upon the consideration that it would seem superfluous to insist upon plain and obvious moral commandments, and that the Decree must therefore have dealt with more special precepts;

(5) Upon the consideration that it is more probable that ceremonial ordinances should have been transformed in course of tradition into general ethical commandments than the opposite case.

[1] *Ztschr. f. wiss. Theol.*, 1896, s. 625 *ff.*; 1899, s. 138 *ff.*; *Acta App. Græce et Latine*, 1899.

Of these five arguments the first has no weight, because the exegesis of the Eastern Fathers begins after the time that *πνικτόν* had found its way into the text. Neither is the second to the point; for the Decree *in either form* forbids *πορνεῦσαι καὶ φαγεῖν εἰδωλόθυτα* (Revelation). The question is only what range of meaning "*ἀπέχεσθαι εἰδωλοθύτων*" is intended to have in the Decree (taking part in sacrificial feasts may be meant; but partaking of any flesh that was used in sacrifice may also be understood); and this cannot be decided from the wording alone, but only from the context. The third argument is likewise without force; for *πορνεία* has nothing to do with eating, neither therefore need *αἷμα* be so interpreted. It cannot be allowed that it is more natural to translate *ἀπέχεσθαι τοῦ αἵματος* by the words "to abstain from partaking of blood," than by the words "to abstain from murder."[1] When *αἷμα* stands by itself, or side by side with Idolatry or Fornication, it is rather to be understood as "murder," unless there are strong reasons to the contrary, *vide*—Lev. xvii. 4: *λογισθήσεται τῷ ανθρώπῳ αἷμα*, Deut. xvii. 8: *ἐὰν ἀδυνατήσῃ ἀπὸ σοῦ ῥῆμα ἐν κρίσει ἀνὰ μέσον αἷμα αἵματος καὶ ἀνά μέσον κρίσις κρίσεως*, Sirach xxxiv. 25: *ἄρτος ἐπιδεομένων ζωὴ πτωχῶν, ὁ ἀποστερῶν αὐτὴν ἄνθρωπος αἱμάτων*, St. Matt. xxiii.

[1] 1 Thess. iv. 3: *ἀπέχεσθαι ἀπὸ τῆς πορνείας*, 1 Thess. v. 22: *ἀπὸ παντὸς εἴδους πονηροῦ ἀπέχεσθαι*, 1 Pet. ii. 11: *ἀπέχεσθαι ἀπὸ τῶν σαρκικῶν ἐπιθυμιῶν*, 1 Tim. iv. 3: *ἀπέχεσθαι βρωμάτων*. At the third place in which the Decree appears in the Acts (xxi. 25) *ἀπέχεσθαι* is replaced by *φυλάσσεσθαι*. In the N.T. *φυλάσσεσθαι* is never found in combination with prohibitions concerning meats (though it does occur in combination with *πλεονεξία* in St. Luke xii. 15).

30: κοινωνοὶ ἐν τῷ αἵματι τῶν προφητῶν.[1] There thus remain only the two last arguments—general considerations whose validity shall be straightway tested.

On the other hand, in favour of the interpretation of the Apostolic Decree as giving moral precepts, we have the following arguments:[2]—

(1) In the whole of St. Luke's book, where it deals with the Gentile Christian controversy, there is no other reference to the question of prohibited meats, but only to questions of capital importance—namely, to *Circumcision and the Mosaic Law as a whole.* It is most strange that in a single passage, and that a passage so important, St. Luke should suddenly introduce rules concerning meats without making any further remark, or giving any reason for their appearance. Fundamental ethical directions, on the other hand, do not suffer from this difficulty.[3]

[1] This use of the word is also found in the profane writers (*vide* Resch, p. 42). We need no examples to prove that αἷμα, when placed side by side with Idolatry and Fornication, as a rule means "shedding of blood."

[2] I omit the arguments in favour of this interpretation which may be derived from the Pauline epistles, although, after all, there is no reason for this forbearance.

[3] St. Peter's vision in chapter x. (the sheet with the unclean animals) ought not to be adduced here. But even if it is thought necessary to take notice of this instance, it will be found that it does not favour the view that chapter xv. deals with regulations concerning meats. The import of chapter x. is that these regulations were an especially characteristic element of the Law of the Old Testament from which St. Peter was to shake himself free. How, then, could St. Luke have related, without turning a hair, that regulations concerning meats were nevertheless imposed upon Gentile Christians?

(2) The combination of prohibition of meats and fornication—why this selection?—is a detail that no one has yet been able to explain satisfactorily.[1] On the other hand, the combination of Idolatry, Murder, and Fornification is quite intelligible, and can be instanced from the ethical catechisms of contemporary Judaism.

(3) If the commandments of the Decree prohibited meats they undoubtedly formed part of the Jewish Law; but we read just beforehand (xv. 19 *f.*) that nothing of the Jewish Law was to be imposed upon the Gentile Christians, seeing that this Law still continued in force and in practice among the Jews; accordingly (if the commands of the Decree are interpreted as forbidding certain meats) a discrepancy, not easy to be removed, arises between "μὴ παρενοχλεῖν τοῖς ἀπὸ τῶν ἐθνῶν ἐπιστρέφουσιν ἐπὶ τὸν θεόν" (and μηδὲν πλέον ἐπιτίθεσθαι ὑμῖν βάρος) and this "ἀπέχεσθαι." On the other hand, though the moral injunctions were also Mosaic commandments, still they would have been generally regarded as commandments of the universal Moral Law; for the conscience of Judaism had at that time already advanced as far as this.

(4) It is difficult to understand why it is that just

[1] I have emphasised this point also in my earlier article (p. 19): "It only remains for us to admit that we cannot explain the object and the selection here. We do not know whether we ought to give 'πορνεία' a quite general meaning, or whether we must understand it in its more special significance; we cannot tell why just these four commands have been selected out of the abundance of legal ordinances; more particularly our attitude towards the combination of prohibition of meats with πορνεία is one of total ignorance."

these points (prohibition of meats!) are described as absolutely essential (ταῦτα τὰ ἐπάναγκες), and how it could be regarded as a necessary condition of the εὖ πράσσειν of Christians that they should observe them (ἐξ ὧν διατηροῦντες ἑαυτοὺς εὖ πράξετε).[1] On the contrary, there is here no difficulty if the Decree deals with moral precepts; these are, in fact, the necessary presupposition of εὖ πράσσειν.

(5) The meaning of the word "εἰδωλόθυτον" is to be derived from the first passage in which the Decree appears (xv. 20). Here, however, we read "ἀπέχεσθαι τῶν ἀλισγημάτων τῶν εἰδώλων." Accordingly, εἰδωλόθυτον does not specially refer to the sacrificial flesh that was on sale in the markets, nor indeed even exclusively to the flesh of the sacrificial feasts, but simply to Idolatry in general. Participation in the idolatrous feasts is especially emphasised, simply because this was the crassest form of idolatry.[2]

(6) The objection that the prohibition of murder is in such a document strange and superfluous has no force;[3] for, in the first place, the combination of the three elements of the Decree is formal, depending upon the Decalogue and the "Two Ways";

[1] It would be otherwise if we read—"on these conditions we will enter into fellowship with you"; but we do not read this, nor is this idea introduced. Nothing at all is said about fellowship and intercommunion.

[2] In the first passage where the Decree occurs in the Acts we may assume with some probability that there is absolutely no intention to prohibit meats. But the other passages must be interpreted by the first, *i.e.* εἰδωλόθυτον is accordingly to be understood as *pars pro toto*.

[3] Wellhausen writes: "This for Christian Gentiles seems surely too self-evident."

secondly, more refined as well as gross forms of αἷμα were very prevalent in Heathendom, and these needed to be earnestly combated (exposure and slaying of children, abortion, murder of slaves, &c.); thirdly, it was already a part of Jewish teaching that "murder" included every injury to the life of one's neighbour. Lastly, let us recollect that St. Peter writes (1 Pet. iv. 15): μή τις ὑμῶν πασχέτω ὡς φονεύς, that we read in the First Epistle of St. John (iii. 15): πᾶς ὁ μισῶν τὸν ἀδελφὸν αὐτοῦ ἀνθρωποκτόνος ἐστίν, that the Revelation—as if in dependence upon the Apostolic Decree—proclaims (xxii. 15): ἔξω . . . οἱ πόρνοι καὶ οἱ φονεῖς καὶ οἱ εἰδωλολάτραι, and that St. James writes, even in reference to Christians (iv. 2): φονεύετε καὶ ζηλοῦτε. Moreover, Irenæus expressly says that when heathens were converted it was necessary to teach them the most elementary moral precepts. Indeed, seeing that at the Apostolic epoch conversions were often—perhaps as a rule—ecstatic in character, *i.e.* wrought "by the Spirit," it was doubly necessary to insist most strongly upon the great general principles of morality, especially in cases where the authority of the Mosaic Law was not felt. It is therefore far from being strange that these ethical commandments should occur in the context of the Apostolic Decree; they are rather proved to be necessary and very much to the point. These three ordinances against Idolatry, Murder, and Fornication are intended to exclude the whole sphere of non-moral conduct.

(7) Resch quite rightly points out that the existence of an authoritative law against partaking of

blood is not to be found in the most ancient Christian documents earlier than the Epistle from Lyons and Vienne, and that there is absolutely no evidence in primitive times for the prohibition of sacrificial flesh sold in the markets. The prohibition in the Epistle from Lyons is not based upon the Apostolic Decree—indeed we know from Irenæus that in that part of the world the Apostolic Decree was at that time regarded as a code of ethical precepts. But the polemic against εἰδωλόθυτον was, as a rule, a polemic against participation in idolatrous sacrificial feasts. The Apostolic Fathers and the Apologists know nothing of regulations concerning meats binding upon Christians. If it is otherwise with the φαγεῖν εἰδωλόθυτα of the Revelation, and with the εἰδωλόθυτον of the Didache (vi. 3)—and this cannot be proved—no reference is at any rate made to the Apostolic Decree.

(8) The whole Western Church understood the Apostolic Decree as an *ethical rule, and even Fathers (like Tertullian*[1]*) who already recognised the prohibition of blood and of things strangled as binding upon Christians, so understood it.*

From these considerations, as it seems to me, it follows that St. Luke (who did not write πνικτόν at all) understood the three clauses ἀπέχεσθαι τῶν ἀλισγημάτων τῶν εἰδώλων (εἰδωλοθύτων) καὶ τῆς πορνείας καὶ τοῦ αἵματος as an abstract of an ethical catechism, and that he intended his readers so to understand

[1] Tertullian when mentioning the prohibition of blood does not appeal to the Decree (Apol. 9; De Monog. 5; De Jejun. 4); neither does he appeal to the Decree in support of abstaining from flesh offered to idols, but to Revelation and 1 Corinthians (De Spect. 13; De Corona 10; De Præsc. 33; De Jejun. 15).

them. If this is accepted, then everything in the Decree and in the narrative at once becomes consistent and clear. We also see clearly that it was not necessary for St. Paul to mention these stipulations in the Epistle to the Galatians, and that in spite of the silence of this epistle they may very well be historical.

Moreover, we now see clearly how the false interpretation arose.[1] In the course of the second century, but quite independently of the Apostolic Decree or any other decree, the Jewish prejudice against partaking of blood (like much else from the Old Testament in spite of freedom from the Law) crept into the Church. Then it was that early—indeed, very early—πνικτόν was added to αἷμα in the margin of the Decree,[2] in order to give the prejudice against the partaking of blood the sanction of a commandment. This πνικτόν transformed the whole Decree! (The transformation could scarcely have been carried out if the words καὶ ὅσα μὴ θέλετε ἑαυτοῖς γίνεσθαι ἑτέρῳ μὴ ποιεῖν had been original; it is therefore probable [not certain] that they are an ancient interpolation which was intended to fix the character of the Decree as a summary of moral precepts.) This could the more easily happen since the brevity of the Decree made its meaning not quite clear, and since a simple ethical catechism in a document like this *may* have seemed superfluous to a later generation. But it was at first only in the East —and very slowly—that πνικτόν and the new inter-

[1] Further details will be found in Resch, s. 151–170, to whose discussion of this point I expressly refer.

[2] The earliest direct testimony to this word is found in Clement of Alexandria and Origen, but the consensus of almost all the Uncials throws it back much further.

pretation of the Decree spread from Alexandria and gained general recognition.[1] In the West it was not until the time of Augustine that, under Greek influence, the false interpretation replaced the true.

If this conception of Acts xv. is correct, then we can close whole libraries of commentaries and investigations as documents of the history of a gigantic error! What has not been written concerning the Apostolic Decree as prohibiting meats—concerning the relation of Gal. ii. and Acts xv. on the assumption that Acts xv. deals with the question of prohibited meats—concerning Jewish and Gentile Christianity—concerning the "commandments of the Covenant with Noah"—and concerning the historical worthlessness of the Acts of the Apostles! The scribe who first wrote the little word *πνικτόν* opposite *αἷμα*, on the margin of his exemplar, created a Flood which has for almost two thousand years swamped the correct interpretation of the whole passage! The joy that the truth has been at last discerned is mingled with sorrow and vexation over labour that has been unspeakably great and utterly useless!

If the interpretation which we have here demonstrated is correct, then according to Acts xv. the only question in debate was this—whether Gentiles who wished to become brother Christians were to be circumcised and subjected to the yoke of the Mosaic

[1] The consensus of all the Uncials (except D) in support of an interpolation is a new and strong proof that this consensus offers no guarantee that the text is genuine, and that it points to an *Alexandrian* recension. The importance of Codex D—supported, to be sure, by all the Western authorities—is here brought into great prominence!

Law. This question was answered in the negative; indeed, even St. James declared that the burden of the Law was not to be placed upon their shoulders, but that they must simply observe the great moral precepts. They were therewith recognised as Christians; but nothing is said in the Decree regarding the *practical* attitude which the Jewish Christians intended to adopt towards them in the future. Nothing, however, is said about this in Galatians. Though the words of that epistle: "ἐμοὶ οἱ δοκοῦντες οὐδὲν προσανέθεντο," and "δεξιὰς ἔδωκαν ἐμοὶ καὶ Βαρνάβᾳ κοινωνίας, ἵνα ἡμεῖς εἰς τὰ ἔθνη, αὐτοὶ δὲ εἰς τὴν περιτομήν," as well as "ἀλλ' οὐδὲ Τίτος . . . ἠναγκάσθη περιτμηθῆναι," do not contain verbal confirmation of the record of the Acts; yet no one can any longer maintain that the Acts gives at this point a representation which conflicts with the account given by St. Paul—an account that has evidently a distinct personal colouring and reference. We have here two entirely independent reports (one by St. Paul, the other by a man who was equally interested in Jerusalem and Antioch), accounts which can quite well be reconciled with each other, and which both of them show that the result arrived at by the Council was simply a theoretical recognition of the Gentiles, together with only an unsatisfying and an unsatisfactory determination to keep the peace.[1] Nevertheless, the advance was

[1] The scene in Antioch between St. Peter and St. Paul is now, even after what the Acts tells us, not unintelligible. If we are obliged to regard the Decree as prohibiting meats, the scene would be difficult to explain; for such regulations could only have been enjoined in order to make it possible for Jewish and Gentile Christians to have fellowship with one another and to eat together.

of course tremendous: strict Jewish Christians now recognised that Gentiles by birth could be Christians without circumcision and the observance of the Law.

The Antiochean source is accordingly free from objection also in this point, and St. Luke in following this source has trusted to a good authority, nor has he told us anything that he could not have told us as a companion of St. Paul. But critics have always accounted Acts xv. as their chief support for the hypothesis that the Acts could not have been composed by St. Luke. This support is now, I think I may assume, withdrawn. Perhaps I am not too bold in hoping that they will draw therefrom the logical conclusions.

EXCURSUS I

SURVEY OF THE NARRATIVES OF ST. LUKE (CONCERNING THE PRIMITIVE COMMUNITY AND THE EARLIER HISTORY OF ST. PAUL, ACTS I.–XIV.) WHICH ARE CONFIRMED BY THE PAULINE EPISTLES.[1]

(1) Jerusalem, not some town in Galilee, is the seat of the Primitive Community, the centre and, so to speak, the Forum of the Christian Movement (Acts *passim* Gal. ii. &c.).

(2) Christian communities were also in existence outside Jerusalem, and especially in Judæa, at a very early date; there was a time when Christendom was described as "the Churches of Judæa" either *a parte fortiori* or in the literal sense (Acts ix. 31: ἡ ἐκκλησία καθ' ὅλης τῆς Ἰουδαίας, Acts xi. 1: οἱ ἀπόστολοι καὶ οἱ ἀδελφοὶ οἱ ὄντες κατὰ τὴν Ἰουδαίαν, xi. 29: οἱ κατοικοῦντες ἐν τῇ Ἰουδαίᾳ ἀδελφοί, 1 Thess. ii. 14; Gal. i. 22).

(3) The Christian communities are called both *αἱ ἐκκλησίαι* (Acts and Pauline epistles, vv. ll.) and ἡ

[1] The comparison of the second half of the history of St. Paul (including Acts xv.), according to the record of the Acts and of St. Paul himself, though it is still by no means superfluous labour, may here be left out of consideration. We are here practically concerned only with Acts i.–xiv., and our purpose is to show to what extent these chapters also receive confirmation from the epistles of St. Paul.

264

ἐκκλησία (Acts ix. 31; xii. 1; Gal. i. 13); they therefore form in some fashion a united body.

(4) The Christians are called both οἱ ἅγιοι and οἱ ἀδελφοί (Acts and Pauline epistles *passim*).[1]

(5) The Churches of Jerusalem and Judæa had to endure persecutions at the hands of their compatriots, indeed these persecutions were a characteristic circumstance of their existence (Acts *passim*, 1 Thess. ii. 14).

(6) These Churches held fast to the observance of the Law (Acts xv. 1 *ff.*; xxi. 20; Gal. ii. 12), and for this very reason St. Paul, even towards the end of his career, was not quite sure of the attitude of the Church of Jerusalem towards himself (Rom. xv. 31).

(7) At the head of the Church of Jerusalem, and therefore at the head of these Churches, stood "the Twelve," who are also called "the Apostles" (Acts i. 13; vi. 2, &c.; Gal. i. 17; 1 Cor. xv. 5); the character of their primacy is defined neither in the Acts nor by St. Paul.

(8) Beside the twelve Apostles there were also other

[1] St. Paul never uses the name "Christian"; but the Acts also avoids it, and only informs us that it was used (xi. 26: χρηματίσαι =vocari) by outsiders (first in Antioch), therefore also by King Agrippa (xxvi. 28). Thus here also there is complete agreement. It is otherwise in 1 Pet. iv. 16 and in Ignatius (*cf.* Tacitus and Pliny). The fact that οἱ μαθηταί is so frequent in the Acts, while this designation is entirely absent from the Pauline epistles, is by no means a proof of a later date for the Acts; on the contrary, it is surprising that the designation should be wanting in the epistles. The reason can only be that St. Paul purposely avoided the term as liable to misconstruction, just as he never speaks of our Lord as "The Master." "St. John" did not share in this feeling.

apostles; St. Barnabas in particular was an apostle (Acts xiv. 4, 14; 1 Cor. xv. 7; 1 Cor. ix. 5, 6).[1]

(9) St. Peter and St. John stand out from the number of the Twelve Apostles (Acts iii. 1 *ff.*; viii. 14 *ff.*; Gal. ii. 9).

(10) The real head, however, is St. Peter (Acts ii. 37, &c.; Gal. i. 18; 1 Cor. xv. 5).

(11) He is also commissioned to be the head of the Mission (among the Jews), and as such makes journeys (Acts vv. ll.; Gal. ii. 7,8; Gal. ii. 11).

[1] We can discern both in the Acts and in the writings of St. Paul the twofold character of the twelve Apostles—as "the Twelve" they were the leaders, but they also possessed the apostolic character which of itself had nothing to do with the number twelve (the term apostle is applied in the Acts to an individual or to individuals in pairs); but the process of limitation of the conception of apostleship to "the Twelve" is much further advanced with St. Luke than with St. Paul. St. Paul and St. Barnabas alone appear as apostles side by side with the Twelve (xiv. 4, 14). In the second half of the book the word apostle is entirely wanting—probably accidentally, or because there was no occasion to use it. In the first half the use is in general quite unambiguous, *i.e.* the Twelve Apostles are the ruling body. Yet it must be pointed out that the wider use of the word, as well as the term "*οἱ δώδεκα*" (without *ἀπόστολοι*), is found only in the Antiochean source, while on the other hand it is only in the source B that the phrases "Peter and the rest of the Apostles" (ii. 37), or "Peter and the Apostles," are to be found.

Moreover, it is only in the Antiochean source that *οἱ πρεσβύτεροι* are found side by side with *οἱ ἀπόστολοι* in Jerusalem (xv. 2, 4, 6, 22, 23; xvi. 4), while previously in xi. 30 (thus in the same source) they are introduced without the Apostles. It is probable that we have here a very accurate representation of events. When St. Paul and St. Barnabas came to Jerusalem from Antioch the Herodian persecution had begun and the Apostles had taken flight. In their place St. James, at the head of a college of presbyters, had taken over the leadership of the Church of Jerusalem (xii. 17), and this arrangement established itself (xx. 18): the rule of "the Twelve"

(12) The Brethren of the Lord form a group side by side with the Apostles (Acts i. 14; 1 Cor. ix. 5).

(13) St. James stands at their head, and is, like St. Peter and St. John, a "pillar"—indeed, from a definite point of time he occupies in Jerusalem a position of monarchical authority (Acts xii 17; xxi. 18; xv. 13 *ff.*; 1 Cor. xv. 7; Gal. ii. 9; Gal. ii. 12).

(14) St. Barnabas appears as the most important of the missionaries to the Gentiles together with St. Paul (*and* set upon an equality with him), and he is governed by the same principles of missionary work as St. Paul (Acts ix. 27; xi. 22 *ff.*; xiii.–xv.; Gal. ii. 1 *ff.*; 1 Cor. ix. 6).

was thus never restored. It is, however, probable that individual members of the Twelve, who were now only apostles, returned afterwards to Jerusalem on temporary visits. On such occasions they would naturally take a part, and a very prominent part, in the government of the Church in that city. So it was when St. Paul came to Jerusalem for the so-called Apostolic Council. St. Peter and St. John were present in Jerusalem, and strengthened by their authority the rule of St. James and the presbyters. We do not know whether any other members of the Twelve, and if so how many, were then in Jerusalem. If these plain and obvious deductions from the record of the Acts answer to facts, then Wellhausen's hypothesis (s. 5 *f.*) that the presbytery of the Church of Jerusalem was coincident with "the Twelve," and that the phrase *οἱ ἀπόστολοι καὶ οἱ πρεσβύτεροι* is therefore a hybrid, is not only very daring but also quite inadmissible. Again, Wellhausen makes a mistake when he adds: "The sharp-sighted revisor, to whom we owe the recension of D, took offence at the hybrid and corrected it in Acts xv." In none of the six places where the phrase occurs has the revisor corrected it. The mistake has probably arisen because in D the article "*οἱ*" is wanting before "*πρεσβύτεροι*" in xv. 6. Wellhausen evidently regarded the note "om. *οἱ*" as referring also to "*πρεσβύτεροι*." Besides, even if *οἱ πρεσβύτεροι* had been omitted in only one place out of six, this would have had no significance, and must have been simply accidental.

(15) According to the Acts (iv. 36 *ff.*) this Barnabas was a member of the Primitive Community; according to Gal. ii. 11 *ff.* he feels more strongly than St. Paul his dependence upon the authority of the Primitive Community, especially of St. Peter and St. James; from this it is allowable to conclude that he belonged to the Primitive Community.

(16) In the Acts St. Mark appears in especially close connection with St. Barnabas (xv. 37 *ff.*); from Col. iv. 10 we learn that he was his "ἀνέψιος."

(17) According to Acts xv. 40 *ff.* Silas, a member of the Primitive Community, was a companion of St. Paul, who as a missionary was in a position of almost equal authority with that Apostle; while the position of Timothy (xvi. 1 *ff.*) was more subordinate; according to 1 Thess. i. 1; 2 Thess. i. 1; 2 Cor. i. 19, Silas stands before Timothy.

(18) In the Acts, even in the earliest period of the history of the Church of Jerusalem, the number of members is very considerable (ii. 41; iv. 4); according to 1 Cor. xv. 6, before the appearances of our Lord to St. James and to "the Apostles" (in a body) there were already more than five hundred brethren in one place (thus in Jerusalem).

(19) According to the Acts and St. Paul, reception into the community was consummated by an act of baptism; but according to the Acts, Baptism does not appear as one of the specific functions of the apostolic office; these were rather preaching and the imparting of the Spirit (viii. 14 *ff.*); here 1 Cor. i. 14, 17, forms a striking parallel.

(20) Baptism was in the name of Jesus (Acts ii. 38,

&c.; Rom. vi. 3; Gal. iii. 27; 1 Cor. i. 13 *f.*, 17, &c.).

(21) Baptism had for its object the *ἄφεσις τῶν ἁμαρτιῶν* (Acts ii. 38; Rom. vi. 1 *ff.*; Col. ii. 12 *f.*).

(22) The *κλάσις ἄρτου* is the social and religious bond within the community (Acts ii. 42, 46; xx. 7, 11; 1 Cor. x. 16; xi. 17 *ff.* 24).

(23) *Εὐχαριστία* and *κλάσις ἄρτου* belong together (Acts xxvii. 35: *λαβὼν ἄρτον εὐχαρίστησεν . . . καὶ κλάσας ἤρξατο ἐσθίειν*, 1 Cor. xi 23 *f.*: *ἔλαβεν ἄρτον καὶ εὐχαριστήσας ἔκλασεν . . . ὁσάκις ἐὰν ἐσθίετε*).

(24) The "Doctrine of the Apostles" is the fundamental principle of the community and its bond of unity (Acts ii. 42); we may here compare 1 Cor. xv. 1–3.

(25) In Acts ii. 42, next to the Doctrine of the Apostles and before the *κλάσις ἄρτου*, stands the "*κοινωνία*"; for this conception, which was also of great importance in St. Paul's teaching, compare Gal. ii. 9; 1 Cor. i. 9; x. 16, 18, 20; 2 Cor. 1, 7; vi. 14; viii. 4, 23; xiii. 13; Phil. i. 5; ii. 1; iii. 10; Philem. 17.

(26) In Acts ii. 42 "the prayers" are introduced as the fourth chief article of the summary there given; also in the Pauline epistles the basis and the sphere of the Christian life are summed up in these four articles (together with Baptism).

(27) From the speeches of St. Peter we see that the most important subjects of the Apostolic teaching were the Crucifixion and Death of our Lord: further, the fact that He did not abide in the grave but rose again and manifested Himself *οὐ παντὶ τῷ λαῷ ἀλλὰ*

μάρτυσιν προκεχειροτονημένοις (Acts x. 41; *cf.* xiii. 31)—all these things happened as had been foretold in Holy Scripture; just the subjects which St. Paul specifies as fulfilments of prophecy, and to which he himself bears witness that they formed the content of the Apostolic teaching (1 Cor. xv. 1–11: *παρέδωκα ὃ καὶ παρέλαβον . . . κατὰ τὰς γραφάς . . . εἴτε οὖν ἐγὼ εἴτε ἐκεῖνοι, οὕτως κηρύσσομεν καὶ οὕτως ἐπιστεύσατε*). In the Acts (including the speeches of St. Paul) the theoretical and practical content of Christian doctrine is not unfrequently summed up in the term "*ἡ ὁδός*"; in 1 Cor. iv. 17 St. Paul speaks of *τὰς ὁδούς μου τὰς ἐν Χριστῷ, καθὼς πανταχοῦ ἐν πάσῃ ἐκκλησίᾳ διδάσκω.*

(28) In the Acts the power to work miracles and signs appears as part of the equipment of an apostle and missionary (Acts ii. 43; iii. 12 *ff.*; viii. 6 *ff.*; xiv. 3, &c.); but also in 2 Cor. xii. 11 *f.* we read: *οὐδὲν ὑστέρησα τῶν ὑπερλίαν ἀποστόλων, εἰ καὶ οὐδέν εἰμι. τὰ μὲν σημεῖα τοῦ ἀποστόλου κατειργάσθη ἐν ὑμῖν . . . σημείοις τε καὶ τέρασι καὶ δυνάμεσιν*, *cf.* Rom. xv. 18 *f.*: *οὐ γὰρ τολμήσω τι λαλεῖν ὧν οὐ κατειγάσατο Χριστὸς δι' ἐμοῦ εἰς ὑπακοὴν ἐθνῶν, λόγῳ καὶ ἔργῳ, ἐν δυνάμει σημείων καὶ τεράτων, ἐν δυνάμει πνεύματος ἁγίου.* With the special instance of the display of Apostolic power in Acts v. 1 *ff.* compare 1 Cor. v. 1 *ff.*

(29) In Acts xx. 3 (&c.) St. Paul says: *ἐγώ εἰμι Ἰουδαῖος*, *cf.* Phil. iii. 5: *ἐκ γένους Ἰσραὴλ . . . Ἑβραῖος ἐξ Ἑβραίων*, and 2 Cor. xi. 22.

(30) In Acts xxvi. 5 St. Paul says: *κατὰ τὴν ἀκριβεστάτην αἵρεσιν τῆς ἡμετέρας θρησκείας ἔζησα*

Φαρισαῖος, *cf.* Phil. iii. 5 *f.*: κατὰ νόμον Φαρισαῖος . . . κατὰ δικαιοσύνην τὴν ἐν νόμῳ γενόμενος ἄμεμπτος. Also the words προέκοπτον ἐν Ἰουδαϊσμῷ ὑπὲρ πολλοὺς συνηλικώτας κτλ. (Gal. i. 14) are illustrated by Acts vii. 58 and ix. 2.

(31) In Acts ix. 1 *f.*, &c., we are informed that St. Paul originally persecuted the Christians; compare with this Gal. i. 13 *f.*; 1 Cor. xv. 9; Phil. iii. 6.

(32) In the Acts St. Paul appears as an apostle on a level with St. Peter (and the rest), *cf.* Gal. ii. 7 *ff.*; 2 Cor. xi. 23.

(33) According to the Acts St. Paul's conversion was brought about near Damascus by a revelation of our Lord, *cf.* Gal. i. 12, 17, and 1 Cor. xv. 8.

(34) According to the Acts St. Paul fled secretly from Damascus (he was let down from the city wall ἐν σπυρίδι); *cf.* 2 Cor. xi. 32 *f.*

(35) According to the Acts St. Paul then went to Jerusalem—but no time is given (ix. 26), St. Luke seems to mean that he went at once—and saw the Apostles there; *cf.* Gal. i. 18 *f.* (after three years; he saw St. Peter and St. James). With Acts xxiii. 11 (ὡς διεμαρτύρω τὰ περὶ ἐμοῦ εἰς Ἱερουσαλήμ) we may compare Rom. xv. 19 (ὥστε με ἀπὸ Ἱερουσαλὴμ καὶ κύκλῳ . . . πεπληρωκέναι τὸ εὐαγγέλιον).

(36) In the Acts St. Paul appears as the missionary who laboured most in the Mission; *cf.* 1 Cor. xv. 10; 2 Cor. xi. 23.

(37) In Acts xiii.–xiv. we have a homogeneous narrative of the ministry and of the sufferings of St. Paul in Pisidian Antioch, Iconium, and Lystra;

cf. 2 Tim. iii. 11: *τοῖς διωγμοῖς, τοῖς παθήμασιν, οἷά μοι ἐγένετο ἐν Ἀντιοχείᾳ, ἐν Ἰκονίῳ, ἐν Λύστροις.*

(38) According to Acts xiv. 23, St. Paul established presbyters in the churches of Lycaonia; compare with these the *προιστάμενοι* of 1 Thess. v. 12 *f.* (the name *οἱ πρεσβύτεροι* is probably only accidentally absent from the genuine Pauline epistles).

(39) In Acts xiii. 38 *f.*, St. Paul says: *διὰ τούτου* [through the Risen Christ] *ὑμῖν ἄφεσις ἁμαρτιῶν καταγγέλλεται* [*καὶ*] *ἀπὸ πάντων ὧν οὐκ ἠδυνήθητε ἐν νόμῳ Μωϋσέως δικαιωθῆναι, ἐν τούτῳ πᾶς ὁ πιστεύων δικαιοῦται.* This is a summary of the great principle of St. Paul's doctrine as it is taught in his own epistles —but from the standpoint of St. Luke.

The agreement which in these numerous instances exists between the Acts (chaps. i.–xiv.) and the Pauline epistles, although the latter are only incidental writings belonging to the later years of the Apostle, is so extensive and so detailed as to exclude all wild hypotheses concerning those passages of the Acts that are without attestation in those epistles. The Acts is *an historical work* that has nothing in common with the later "Acts of the Apostles," and is not to be judged by the standard nor criticised by the method which suits these. If we divide the remainder of Acts i.–xiv. into two parts, the first containing the passages, the statements, and notices which have no Pauline attestation, the second containing those which are distinctly contradicted by St. Paul, we shall find that the latter is almost a vanishing quantity. Only in making our division we must dispense with that self-complacent method whereby from our own really great and at present insuperable ignorance of events, institutions, and other details of that period, a rope is made to hang the author of the Acts. The axiom: "What we do not know or cannot prove cannot be right" still exercises a tyrannical sway in the sphere of history, though we have learned by experience that better understanding of known authorities, and the discovery of new ones, have again and again proved how mistaken it is to form hasty judgments concerning primitive Christian tradition. Hence in the case of an historical work like the Acts, our attitude towards passages containing elements that are strange and extraordinary should be one of critical caution. This does not mean that we are to forget that some passages have been worked up, and that the author is superstitious—but who was not superstitious in those days!

Finally, the character of the vocabulary of the Acts is also just what we should have expected in one who was a companion and friend, but not a dependent disciple of St. Paul. I have already dealt with this question in "Luke the Physician" (pp. 19 *ff.*). The gospel of St. Luke and the genuine Pauline epistles have in common 83 words which are not found elsewhere in the gospels; of these 32 also occur in the Acts; but in addition to these there are about 65 words which only occur in the Acts and the genuine Pauline epistles. These words common to St. Paul and St. Luke, about 148 in number, well deserve a more detailed investigation (*vide* the careful collection in Plummer's "Commentary on St. Luke," 1896, pp. liv. *ss.*).

From yet another point of view it is possible to establish the affinity between the Lukan writings and the Pauline epistles. Hawkins (*Horæ Synopticæ*, 1899, pp. 1 *ff.*) has drawn up lists of words and phrases characteristic of the three synoptists—86 for St. Matthew, 37 for St. Mark, 140 for St. Luke. Of the 86 characteristic of St. Matthew 46 are also used by St. Paul (*loc. cit.* p. 155), of the 37 Markan words St. Paul has 19, but of the 140 Lukan words St. Paul has 94. We may then speak of a certain kinship in style and vocabulary between St. Luke and St. Paul—it is not, however, very significant; the epistles which stand nearest to the Lukan writings are those to the Colossians and Ephesians. Only the most general and most important characteristics of the teaching of St. Paul and the success of his preaching had really made deep impression upon St. Luke. For the rest he was not spiritually nor intellectually dependent, still less slavishly dependent, upon the Apostle. He remained himself! The work of St. Paul decided and influenced him far more strongly than the personality of the Jew, whose character in all its intensive grandeur had not fully disclosed itself to him. And yet it was St. Luke that continued with St. Paul, indeed was the only one to continue with him! And how can we find fault with him, a genuine Hellene, for not fully comprehending the genius of the Apostle.

EXCURSUS II

ON THE PLAN OF THE GOSPEL OF ST. LUKE AND THE ACTS OF THE APOSTLES

In the Introduction we have already stated that St. Luke could not form his type of narrative for the Acts upon the type of his gospel as it was created by St. Mark and developed by himself. The subject-matter was too different; so that St. Luke was obliged to form for himself a new type. Yet in *one* point a certain likeness prevails between the plans of the two works. In his gospel St. Luke has arranged his material under the headings: Jesus in Galilee; Jesus on His way from Galilee through Samaria, &c., to Jerusalem; Jesus in Jerusalem. In the Acts the plan is analogous: the Gospel in Jerusalem; the Gospel on its way from Jerusalem through Samaria, &c., into the Gentile World and to Rome; the Gospel in Rome. In both cases the *progression* within the "καθεξῆς" is the chief consideration, and forms the thread of the narrative.

Whilst the reader of the prologue to the gospel receives exact information as to what he may expect in the book (διήγησιν περὶ τῶν πεπληροφορημένων ἐν ἡμῖν πραγμάτων according to the tradition of the eye-witnesses of our Lord), no such summary of the contents of the work is given in the Acts of the Apostles (on the other hand, the contents of the Gospel are yet again summarised in Acts i. 1 *f.*).

We must read as far as verse 8, where we already find ourselves in the narrative itself, in order to learn St. Luke's aim in his second book. But that this verse gives the programme of the book is only to be discovered from the book itself, and not from the form of the verse. It is the same with the conclusion: the gospel comes to a solemn close, after which one expects nothing more. But it is not at once clear that the conclusion of the Acts is really a conclusion—indeed, judging from i. 8 (ἕως ἐσχάτου τῆς γῆς), one might expect a further continuation. From this difference between the two books we are scarcely justified in concluding that St. Luke did not give the finishing touches to the Acts—this is indeed probable on other grounds—, but we must rather recognise that the theme which St. Luke set himself in the Acts was of a kind that it was difficult to summarise in a short argument. In the Introduction we have already defined this theme as follows: "The power of the Spirit of Jesus in the Apostles, manifested in expansion of the mission even to Rome, in the Conversion of the Gentile world, and in the hardening of the heart of the Jewish nation." We at once see that this theme was too unwieldly to be framed within a short argument. It was probably for this reason that St. Luke abstained from giving such an argument, though the theme of the book was quite distinctly formed in his mind and kept well in view throughout the work.

EXCURSUS III

ST. LUKE AND CHRISTIAN JOY

The high note of Christian Joy was, so far as we know, first struck by St. Paul. He experienced, and could proclaim as an experience, both "the joy in the Lord" and "the joy in the Holy Spirit." How much he regarded joy as the necessary and constant condition of the Christian is shown in many passages of his writings, but above all in 2 Cor. i. 24: *συνεργοί ἐσμεν τῆς χαρᾶς ὑμῶν*. We cannot here go into the question of the importance and the peculiar significance which this conception of joy has reached in the Johannine literature.

In the ancient evangelic tradition, and in St. Mark and St. Matthew, not very much of this joy is to be traced. Apart from the references to the stern joy because of persecutions (St. Matt. v. 12; St. Luke vi. 23), to the joy over the penitent (St. Matt. xviii. 13; St. Luke xv. 5, 7, 10), and to the joy at the reception of the Word (St. Mark iv. 16; St. Matt. xiii. 20, 44; St. Luke viii. 13)—yet the latter is certainly very important—we can scarcely find another passage of the kind.

It is otherwise with St. Luke. In his expression of joy he speaks in unison with St. Paul and St. John. Indeed in the New Testament it is in his writings alone that we find the word *εὐφροσύνη* as well as the more usual words *χαρά* and *χαίρειν*—*εὐφραίνεσθαι* is more frequent with him than in all the other writings of the New Testament taken together, and various expressions for "joy" run through both his works.

The gospel begins with "joy" (joy of many over the birth of St. John the Baptist, i. 14; "Behold, I bring you tidings of great joy; for to you is born this day the Saviour," ii. 10), and with "joy" it closes (the disciples are *ἀπιστοῦντες ἀπὸ τῆς χαρᾶς*, xxiv. 41; and they return to Jerusalem with great joy, xxiv. 52). St. John leaps for joy in his mother's womb (i. 44), Elizabeth rejoices *ἐπὶ τῷ θεῷ τῷ σωτῆρί μου* (i. 47), and our Lord rejoices in the Spirit in His Thanksgiving to the Father (x. 21). The seventy disciples return from their mission with joy (x. 17), and are taught in what they should rejoice and in what not (x. 20). The people rejoice over all the glorious actions of our Lord (xiii. 17), and the multitude of the disciples rejoice with cries of praise at His entry into Jerusalem (xix. 37). Zacchæus rejoices because he is allowed to entertain our Lord in his house (xix. 6), and the whole second half of the parable of the Prodigal Son is filled with joy (xv. 23, 24, 29, 32).[1]

It is the same in the Acts. In his first great speech St. Peter quotes the joyous words (ii. 26, 28):

[1] From these passages, and from xii. 19 and xvi. 19, one sees that St. Luke likes to connect, indeed almost exclusively connects, *εὐφραίνεσθαι* with the partaking of food. Just in the same way we read in Acts xiv. 17 that God fills men's hearts with *τροφὴ καὶ εὐφροσύνη* (see also Acts vii. 41), and in Acts ii. 46: *μετελάμβανον τροφῆς ἐν ἀγαλλιάσει*.—St. Luke evidently had a feeling for the joy that springs from the common festal meal, and regarded it also in a religious light. These social meals *ἐν ἀγαλλιάσει καὶ ἀφελότητι καρδίας* replace the ancient sacrificial feasts.

διὰ τοῦτο ηὐφράνθη μου ἡ καρδία καὶ ἠγαλλιάσατο ἡ γλῶσσά μου . . . πληρώσεις με εὐφροσύνης μετὰ τοῦ προσώπου σου—here we have an obvious parallel to the Magnificat of Elizabeth, which also stands near the beginning of the gospel. St. Peter's Sermon results in the foundation of the Church, which henceforth eats its bread ἐν ἀγαλλιάσει (ii. 46). The disciples come with joy from the Jewish tribunal (v. 41); great joy prevails among the converts of Samaria (viii. 8); the baptized eunuch goes on his way rejoicing (viii. 39); St. Barnabas sees with joy the work of the mission to the Gentiles in Antioch (xi. 29); the Gentiles of Pisidian Antioch are glad because St. Paul teaches that the word of Salvation was intended for them (xiii. 48), and they are filled with great joy *and with the Holy Spirit* (xiii. 52). St. Paul holds up as the most striking instance of God's gracious Providence the fact that He fills our hearts with food and gladness (xiv. 17). The reports given by St. Paul and St. Barnabas of their success in Asia Minor fill the brethren in Phœnicia and Samaria with great joy (xv. 3), and the converted jailor in Philippi ἠγαλλιάσατο πανοικεὶ πεπιστευκὼς τῷ Θεῷ (xvi. 34).

This joyous characteristic of the book, though there is in it no want also of tears, is not only important for our knowledge of St. Luke, but also—in conjunction with the testimony of St. Paul and St. John (also of the First Epistle of St. Peter)—for the accurate knowledge of the temperament of the Greek Christians of his times. Their sacred feasts were feasts of joy, and those who were leaders in the churches bestirred themselves to create and to preserve among Christians the atmosphere of joy. Even if this implied some forcing of the note, and even if the purpose was stronger than the result—though this cannot be proved—still the purpose must be specially noted.

To Joy belongs *Peace*. In St. Paul (also in St. John) they stand close together (*vide* Gal. v. 22; Rom. xv. 13); God is the God of Peace (Rom. xv. 33; xvi. 20; 1 Cor. xiv. 33; 2 Cor. xiii. 11; Phil. iv. 9; 1 Thess. v. 23; and the formularies of greeting); there is not only a peace of Christ (Col. iii. 15), but Christ is our peace (Ephes. ii. 14), &c. In St. Mark and St. Matthew nothing of the kind is to be found—on the contrary, we read in St. Matthew (x. 34): *οὐκ ἦλθον βαλεῖν εἰρήνην*. It is otherwise with St. Luke. The word occurs no less than twenty-one times in his works. His gospel begins with the proclamation of "peace" as well as of joy (i. 79; ii. 14, 29), and the greeting of peace (xxiv. 36) stands near its close. Though St. Luke has also taken up into his work the harsh-sounding saying against peace (xii. 51), because he could not conscientiously pass it by, still Christ is for him the bringer of peace (*vide* xix. 38), and so we read in the Acts (x. 36): *τὸν λόγον ἀπέστειλεν τοῖς υἱοῖς Ἰσραὴλ εὐαγγελιζόμενος εἰρήνην διὰ Ἰησοῦ Χριστοῦ*. In this respect also St. Luke has imprinted upon his work an homogeneous character.

Finally, there is yet another word belonging to this sphere of feeling and forming a bond between St. Paul, St. John, and St. Luke—I mean *παρρησία*. Though it is wanting in St. Luke's gospel, yet in the Acts it occurs both at the beginning and at the close in most important passages; in St. Paul it is found seven times, in St. John thirteen times. The Acts uses the word in ii. 29; iv. 13, 29, 31 (the two last instances are important), and the book closes with the record that in Rome St. Paul preached and taught concerning the Lord Christ *μετὰ πάσης παρρησίας ἀκωλύτως* (with *πάσης* here compare iv. 29 and Phil. i. 20). *Χαρά, εἰρήνη, παρρησία*, and in addition *σωτήρ* and *σωτηρία*—the spiritual sphere characterised by these words is common to the Pauline, Johannine, and Lukan writings. With the ultimate origin of these terms as denoting religious conceptions we are not sufficiently acquainted; but the question of the origin of the terminology is of secondary importance. The terminology could only be accepted when men had the thing itself, and the thing itself was not imported but was a fact of Christian experience.

EXCURSUS IV

ST. LUKE AND THE DEVELOPMENT OF CHRISTIANITY FROM THE RELIGION OF A JEWISH SECT TO A UNIVERSAL RELIGION

When one speaks of the development of Christianity from the religion of a Jewish sect to a universal religion, one at once thinks of St. Paul, and rightly so. He not only laboured more than the rest, but he also realised the opposition between the religion of the Old Testament and the Gospel in its profundity.

But one must also recollect the limitations which must be drawn here. St. Paul was not the first to begin the mission to the Gentiles—the real originators were anonymous men of Cyprus and Cyrene—; he allowed that the Law remained in force for the Jewish Christians, provided only that they did not believe that righteousness was gained by keeping it; and, what is more, he taught that a special rôle was reserved for the nation of Israel, that the promises given to it would still be fulfilled, and that the time would come when "all Israel will be saved." In this sense he remained a Jewish Christian. Lastly, though his demonstration of universalism and of the abrogation of the Law is most profound, it is also most difficult to comprehend. Scarcely any one understood it, and it did not make its way into the thought of the Churches. St. Paul always regarded the question as a problem—a problem capable indeed of solution yet still to be solved; and so long as a man regards important principles as being still problems, he will not be able to commend his thought to others. Only trivial truths are successful. A thought in which there is still something to be thought out has no prospect of being widely accepted.

Thus the teaching and the procedure of St. Paul left much to be desired. Ought a Jewish Christendom to be left in continuous existence side by side with Universal Christendom? Must not its simple existence exert a perplexing and disturbing influence? Could a special Hope for Israel *κατὰ σάρκα* be recognised side by side with the general Hope of all Christians? Must it not appear a gigantic paradox that for this nation, in spite of the Divine sentence of hardening of heart, there should yet be reserved a special promise in the Kingdom of God? Finally—was it possible that the appalling contradiction which lies in the Pauline criticism of the Law could have been allowed to stand? Could one believe at one and the same time that the Law in its verbal meaning was Divine and holy, but that the Gentile Christian who kept it denied Christ?!

Three points were here in question—the *Law*, the judgment to be passed upon the *Jewish nation*, and the property in the *Old Testament* as a whole. On all these points the attitude which St. Paul had adopted seemed unsatisfactory. Things must be carried further. The only satisfactory element was the *fait accompli*—universalism, and freedom from the yoke of the Law. But the necessary consequences did not seem to have been yet drawn by St. Paul.

In regard to the Law—the Gentile Christians could not arrive at complete peace of mind until the allegorical method of interpretation became decisive. Men could not believe that they were really freed from the Law until it was recognised that the import of the Law was the same as that of the Gospel, and that the ceremonial ordinances could all be spiritually interpreted.

In respect to the *Jewish people*, there could be no settlement of mind until it was recognised that the nation was not only now subject to the sentence of hardening, but that it had never possessed any promises—for all the promises of the Old Testament referred to the new nation—and that it therefore had absolutely nothing more to expect from God in the future.

Lastly, in regard to the *Old Testament*, there could be no satisfaction until absolutely every kind of claim that the Jews might advance to its possession was disproved, and it was clearly shown that the book belonged *exclusively* to the Christians.

In the writings of the Apologists, and in the Epistle of Barnabas, these points of view have been already reached. Between them and the Doctrine of St. Paul as the starting-point, we can distinguish stages of development. In regard to the question of the nation of Israel, these stages have been briefly sketched above on pp. xxv. *s.* What station in this process of development may now be assigned to the writings of St. Luke?

Let us at once say—*one that is still very ancient*, one that by no means coincides with that of St. Paul, yet is of equal standing with it in point of age, and is more archaistic than that of "St. John," to say nothing of "Barnabas" and the Apologists.

As for the *Law*, he has an extraordinarily high opinion of its importance for the Jew by birth. From the first leaf of his gospel he shows this. The Jew's pious observance of the Law is with him a thing worthy of the highest honour (*cf.* Elizabeth and Zacharias, &c.). People who were to be found daily in the Temple are to him worthy of reverence, and it appears to him most praiseworthy that the members of the early Church were so conscientious in their visits thither. It has also his full approval that St. Paul behaved himself as a pious Jew, both in Jerusalem and elsewhere. The Law according to St.

Luke maintains its authority among Jews, whether Christian or non-Christian. This he makes St. James say expressly. No one ought to offend against the Temple and the Law; St. Paul also had never done this (Acts xxv. 8). It appears to have been otherwise in the case of St. Stephen, but St. Luke evidently takes the speech—which he had not drafted himself—in such a way that its point lies in the announcement of the future downfall of the Temple. This was a thing that St. Luke could not pass over, because it had been prophesied by our Lord Himself. As for St. Stephen's reference to a change in the customs delivered by Moses, St. Luke understood this to mean that now, seeing that the Jews had hardened their hearts, Salvation would pass over to those who were not bound to observe the Law; for with those who were Gentiles by birth the Law and Circumcision were not in force—as St. Luke had learned from St. Paul. Yet it was still clearly recognised by St. Luke that this view and the ultimate recognition of Gentile freedom from the Law were arrived at by a process of historical development which he seeks to investigate and to describe to his readers (*vide supra*, pp. xxvi. *ff.*). But though St. Luke acknowledges that the Law was not in force for Gentiles by birth, he does not by any means therefore imply that the Law possessed no saving power. It is true that he not only appropriated the Pauline doctrine of Universalism, but also the Pauline doctrine of Justification. Yet in sharp contrast with St. Paul he regarded the latter doctrine as only *complementary*, at least for Jews by birth. The Gentiles must trust in Justification by Faith alone,[1] but for the Jews this doctrine was only necessary in so far as they fell short of the fulfilment of the Law, and therefore, beside and apart from the Law, still required the forgiveness of sins in order to be quite righteous (xiii. 38, 39). On the whole St. Luke, though himself a Gentile, stands nearer than St. Paul to the Law—we may therefore also call his attitude more primitive; for it is certainly not to be regarded as reactionary, but as the reflexion of the historical conditions of a time when the Jewish Christians still played a very important part, and when the Gentile Christians had not yet lost their reverence for the *religio antiqua*, and had not yet arrived at a distinct self-consciousness of their own in the face of Judaism. *Though St. Luke may even give an allegorical interpretation of a passage in the Law, he still regards Law, Temple, and Vow as what they really were, and he values them as such very highly.*

This position of his becomes still more clear as we consider his attitude towards the *Jewish nation.* He took over from St. Paul the theory of the predetermined hardening of the heart of the Jewish nation, and he seems here to have gone further than St. Paul, since he does not repeat the Pauline thought that still at last πᾶς Ἰσραὴλ σωθήσεται. But upon closer consideration it will be seen that his judgment of the Jewish people is not sterner than that of St. Paul. In the first place, the disparaging "οἱ Ἰουδαῖοι" of "St. John" is found very rarely in his writings, though it is already coming into use with

[1] Yet also this may be disputed with reference to x. 35 (ἐν παντὶ ἔθνει ὁ φοβούμενος αὐτὸν καὶ ἐργαζόμενος δικαιοσύνην δεκτὸς αὐτῷ ἐστιν).

St. Paul. In spite of the theory of "final hardening," St. Luke does not regard the Jews as a *massa proditionis et perditionis*, but differentiates between them according to their natural and spiritual qualities (*vide supra*, pp. xxiii. *ff.*). Again, passages like St. Luke i. 72–79; ii. 31, 32, &c., show that he conceived of the Gospel as the "consolation of Israel," and that he recognised in it a twofold function: *it both fulfilled the promises given to the people of Abraham* κατὰ σάρκα, and it was a light to the Gentiles.[1] If St. Luke held this view of the Gospel it necessarily follows that a thought like that of Rom. xi. 25 *ff.* could not have been so very far from him, or that he at least cherished similar thoughts. According to him, St. Paul contended for the Resurrection as for a hope that was common to both Jews and Christians. Above all, we must once again (*vide supra*, pp. 50 *f.*) point out that "ὁ λαός" (ὁ λαὸς τοῦ θεοῦ) is for St. Luke the Jewish nation. *Before his eyes Christendom stands in two camps*—still, indeed, separate from one another—*first the Jewish people, that is, the pious Israelites who had accepted Jesus as the Lord; secondly, the* ἔθνη, *who had been afterwards called to the standard.*[2] This Gentile Christian author is still very retiring, and his self-consciousness as a Gentile Christian is still undeveloped. He is certain that he and his fellow

[1] The canticles in St. Luke i. ii. are, in vocabulary, style, and thought, the property of St. Luke. If, however, it is thought that he received them from elsewhere, we can prove from other passages in the Lukan writings that these conceptions are Lukan.

[2] St. Luke nowhere regards Jewish and Gentile Christians as bound together in such unity as is pictured in the Epistle to the Ephesians. Their separation from one another does not disturb him.

Gentiles have been freed from the observance of the Law; he knows that the great majority of the Jewish nation have fallen under the sentence of "final hardening"; but he feels that only the more respect is due to those Jews who, while observing the Law, believed in Christ. They are "the nation" for whom, in the first place, all the promises have been and are being fulfilled, and their *observatio legis* is for him an object of admiration.

This attitude of St. Luke towards the Law and the Jewish nation [1] reflects very early conceptions, and expresses historical relations which existed at the time of St. Paul, but can scarcely have continued much later. Hitherto this has not been clearly recognised, rather the standpoint of St. Luke has been obscured by all kinds of distorting theories. These theories all proceed *a priori* from the assumption that St. Luke's point of view can only be regarded as a stage in the development of post-Pauline doctrine. Hence we hear of compromises between Jewish and Gentile Christianity which may be discerned in these writings, or of a Gentile Christianity which had "already" absorbed Jewish Christianity and so modified itself, &c. But the real situation is much simpler. In these writings we must recognise a position parallel with that of St. Paul, just such a position as must have been taken up by a Christian Greek of the earliest period; one who was more humane but also

[1] After what has been already said there is no need of a special discussion of St. Luke's attitude towards the Old Testament. It is now self-evident that he never doubted that this book had been given to and belonged to the Jewish nation. In that the Gentiles are called, they take a share in the inheritance of the nation.

more superficial than St. Paul—one who, with all his universalism, could yet feel a respect for the Jewish Law as well as for the Jewish religion, and more especially could regard devout Jewish Christians with an esteem and reverence such as the Apostle, who had recognised that Christ was the end of the Law, could no longer bring himself to feel. All that remained to St. Paul for his own nation he casts into the future (ἄχρις οὗ τὸ πλήρωμα τῶν ἐθνῶν εἰσέλθῃ), while St. Luke, who had never experienced the terror of the Law, stands full of reverence before the *antiqua religio.*

Gentile Christendom advanced in self-consciousness far beyond the standpoint of St. Luke, indeed even of "St. John."[1] In the interests of its own self-preservation it allegorised the Law, declaring that the verbal sense was a deception of the devil, or was a penal and disciplinary ordinance devoid of blessing and promise; it delivered the Jewish nation to Satan and the dæmons, and claimed the Old Testament with all the promises and with all the patriarchs, men of God, and prophets *exclusively* for itself.[2] But this attitude did not remain final in the Church; rather since the end of the second century it experienced forcible modification. The great conflict with Gnosticism and Marcionitism compelled the Church to attend to the verbal sense of the Old Testament,

[1] For "St. John" the statement: ἡ σωτηρία ἐκ τῶν Ἰουδαίων ἐστὶν still held good.

[2] This development was assisted by the enduring and increasing enmity of the Jews, by the numerical weakness of the Jewish Christians, and by the destruction of the Temple, the capital city, and the Jewish people as a nation.

and to restore to it its rightful position. If the verbal sense were to be finally given up by the Church, the consequence that would be drawn by her dangerous opponents—namely, the rejection of the whole book—was too obvious. But when the Church again required of its members that they should attend to the verbal sense, indeed even regard it as divine, and seeing that they could not appropriate to themselves the difficult teaching of St. Paul, *St. Luke's way of thinking came again to their aid.* In fact, we see that the great early Fathers of the Church—above all, Irenæus in the long chapters of Book iii., where he follows the Acts—walk in the very footsteps of St. Luke; with them the religion of the Old Testament is holy and good, the Law even in its verbal sense, and although it was a *legislatio in servitutem*, is right and good; the saints of the Old Testament are worthy of reverence, &c. Of course the high esteem in which St. Luke held the Jewish Christians as the ancient people of God never returned—the time for this had passed away; but in all other directions it was St. Luke, the Hellene of the first ages, who marked out the paths by which the theologians and historians of the Church approached the problem of the relation between Universalism and the Old Testament.

EXCURSUS V

THE DATE OF THE ACTS

The following remarks are not intended actually to commend the earliest date for the composition of the

Acts, but to warn critics against a too hasty closing of the chronological question. It is well known how quickly hypotheses that are questionable and burdened with the greatest difficulties—such, for example, as the hypothesis that Rom. xvi. is an epistle, or part of an epistle, to Ephesus—have arrived at even unquestioned recognition.

In my *Chronologie der altchristl. Litt.*, I. (1897), s. 246–250, 718, I have produced the reasons in favour of the hypothesis that the Acts was not composed before the year A.D. 78. They reduce themselves to *three* in number—all the rest are not of great weight, to say nothing of being convincing: (1) The prologue of St. Luke's gospel seems to demand that at least half a century should have elapsed since the death of Jesus; (2) the gospel with its detailed prophecies concerning the destruction of Jerusalem and the Temple seems to presuppose that the catastrophe of the year A.D. 70 had already occurred—moreover, the omission by St. Luke of the warning: ὁ ἀναγιγνώσκων νοείτω (St. Mark xiii. 14; St. Matt. xxiv. 15) suggests that the fulfilment itself already lay before men's eyes; (3) the legends concerning the appearances of the Risen Christ and the Ascension are difficult to explain, on the assumption that they arose before the destruction of Jerusalem.

Of these three arguments the second and third are weighty, while the first upon closer consideration is only of quite slight importance. Unfortunately we know absolutely nothing, nor can we form a conjecture as to how many, even at the earliest period, wrote concerning the "πεπληροφορημένα ἐν ἡμῖν πράγματα," nor when this literary activity began. Why must we suppose that the wording of the prologue necessitates the lapse of a period of fifty years? Would not about thirty-three years be sufficient? Just as to-day in reference to the restoration of the German Empire one could write: "Since many have undertaken to describe this restoration καθὼς παρέδοσαν ἡμῖν οἱ ἀπ' ἀρχῆς αὐτόπται γενόμενοι, &c.," so also an author even at the beginning of the seventh decade of the first century could have written concerning the history of Jesus. And even if γενόμενοι is pressed, no difficulty arises; for even after the lapse of only thirty years the great majority of the eye-witnesses of events are no longer alive. We must therefore dispense with the argument derived from the prologue. There remain only the destruction of Jerusalem and the above-mentioned legends; for the arguments that are derived from the conception one forms of the inward development of things are quite unsafe, and therefore inadmissible, so long as the chronological question remains unsolved. But if it is pointed out that the idea that St. Luke wrote, so to say, under the eyes of St. Paul is hampered with psychological difficulties, it must be of course admitted that this is undeniable; but seeing that we can form no accurate conception of the relations between these two great men, it is a precarious proceeding to appeal to such difficulties.[1]

[1] If stress is laid upon the difficulties involved in the hypothesis that St. Luke wrote as a personal acquaintance of St. Paul, and even during the lifetime of the Apostle—but not under his eyes—it is only necessary to point, in the first place, to the *memorabilia* concerning great men of antiquity, which were confessedly written

What, then, is to be said in favour of the Acts (and therefore also of the gospel) having been already written at the beginning of the seventh decade of the first century. There are, in my opinion, the following very weighty considerations:—

(1) The great difficulty presented by the conclusion of the Acts is undoubtedly removed in the simplest way if St. Luke wrote his work soon after the two years which St. Paul spent in Rome, and thus while the Apostle was still alive.[1] We can also explain away this difficulty on other hypotheses (*vide supra*, pp. 38 *ff.*)—for it *must* be explained!—but none of them are quite satisfactory or very illuminating.

(2) The discrepancy of the passage, Acts xx. 25: "Ye will see my face no more" (*cf.* xx. 38), with the genuine information given in 2 Timothy is thus

by their disciples or acquaintances. Does any one deny that Xenophon was personally acquainted with Socrates because his *Memorabilia* is such a defective work and betrays so little of the spirit of the great thinker? Or does any one deny such acquaintance to Plato because he has so drawn the portrait of Socrates with such freedom in his dialogues? Or must we refuse to ascribe the Life of Constantine to Eusebius because it contains much that is of questionable authority concerning the emperor? Need I even mention the case of Sulpicius Severus and Martin of Tours, or of Athanasius and Anthony?

[1] I do see see that in any passage of the book St. Peter and St. Paul are so treated that we may presume that they were already dead; rather the contrary. In xi. 24 we read of St. Barnabas: *ὅτι ἦν ἀνὴρ ἀγαθὸς καὶ πλήρης πνεύματος ἁγίου.* It seems, therefore, to be presupposed that he was already dead. But even this inference is unsafe; compare xxi. 9: *Φιλίππῳ ἦσαν θυγατέρες τέσσαρες.*—It has been remarked above on p. 41 that the Acts could not have been written at the close of the *διετία* spoken of in the last verse; but the book could very well have been composed after these two years had elapsed, and before the death of the Apostle in Rome.

explained. St. Luke allows St. Paul to say, or St. Paul said, something about his future which afterwards proved to be incorrect. St. Luke, when he wrote, could not as yet have known that it was an incorrect prophecy.

(3) In the Acts the Jews never appear as oppressed and persecuted, but rather as the persecutors. This seems to me a very weighty argument! How comes it that the terrible events which befell this nation since the second half of the seventh decade, and which also affected the Diaspora, have left absolutely no trace of themselves in this historical work? The Jews both in Jerusalem and in the Diaspora are the *beati possidentes!* How remarkable it is that a vivacious story-teller like St. Luke should remain so "objective" that, simply because he is dealing with the times before A.D. 66, he gives no hint of the tremendous change that came with the year A.D. 70! Though in xi. 28 he expressly notices that the prophecy of the famine was actually fulfilled in the reign of Claudius; *yet this historian nowhere says that the prophecy of the destruction of Jerusalem was fulfilled*, and though at the close of his work he casts in the teeth of the Jews the prophecy of Isaiah concerning "the hardening of their hearts," yet he does not think of referring to the terrible judgment that had actually come upon the nation.

(4) But even in the case of the gospel, under the assumption that the destruction of Jerusalem had already taken place, by no means everything is quite clear. With the prophecy of this destruction St. Luke, like the other synoptists, still combines the

proclamation of the great *Final Catastrophe* (xxi. 25 *ff.*), of convulsions of the heavenly bodies, and of *the Coming of the Son of Man* (xxi. 27, 28), and brings all this to a conclusion with the words (xxi. 32): ἀμὴν λέγω ὑμῖν ὅτι οὐ μὴ παρέλθῃ ἡ γενεὰ αὕτη ἕως ἂν πάντα γένηται! Are we then to suppose that the destruction of Jerusalem, which had been followed by none of these events, was for the author a thing of the past? The supposition is exceedingly difficult! Again he repeats the direction (xxi. 21): τότε οἱ ἐν τῇ Ἰουδαίᾳ φευγέτωσαν εἰς τὰ ὄρη—yet the Christians, as is well known, did not flee to the mountains, but to Pella, and so in later days a special command from Heaven was invented in order to explain the discrepancy of this conduct with the original command. There is also much else in the great eschatological discourse that is more easily intelligible if it were written before the destruction of Jerusalem than on the contrary assumption; and the omission of ὁ ἀναγιγνώσκων νοείτω may be due to the circumstance that St. Luke did not intend his work for public reading.

(5) The fact that no use is made of the Pauline epistles in the Acts is easily intelligible about the beginning of the seventh decade, it is not so about A.D. 80, and the later the date the more unintelligible it becomes.

(6) In his use of the word "Christ," St. Luke is even more primitive than St. Paul; in the Lukan writings it has not yet become a proper name, but everywhere means "the Messiah"; the name "Christians" (otherwise than in the First Epistle of St. Peter, *vide supra*) is not yet applied by Christians to themselves, and

the "*nomen Christianum*" as such is not yet proscribed (as it must already have been in the Flavian period). There are, besides, certain delicate terminological traits which seem to point to a high antiquity,[1] as well as the primitive standpoint adopted in the treatment of Judaism and Jewish Christianity (*vide* pp. 281 *ff.*).

These are, so far as I see, the most important arguments for the composition of the Acts at the beginning of the seventh decade. On the other side —unless prejudice or "critical intuition," things that we, of course, cannot search into, are brought into play—we have simply the considerations that the prophecy concerning the destruction of Jerusalem coincides in some remarkable points with what really happened, and that the accounts of the appearances of the Risen Christ and the legend of the Ascension are scarcely intelligible on the assumption that they arose before the destruction of Jerusalem.[2] A deci-

[1] Among these traits I reckon the absence of the title "ὁ βασιλεύς" for the emperor (*vide supra*, p. 36); the use of the name "οἱ μαθηταί" for the Christians (not used even by St. Paul) as the more solemn and ceremonious term (*vide supra*, p. 265); the application of the designation ὁ λαὸς [τοῦ θεοῦ] exclusively to the Jewish nation, not to the Christians (*vide supra*, pp. 50 *f.*); the fact that παροικία and πάροικος have not acquired a technical significance, the as yet undeveloped conception of the Church (*vide* "Luke the Physician," pp. 34 *ff.*), and much else.

[2] Here, however, we are ought to forget that in reference to the origin of these legends we are destitute of the help of any accompanying tradition, and are left simply to considerations of probability, which at all events are not in favour of an early date.—A further great difficulty lies outside the Lukan writings, but at once announces itself. Is it possible that the Gospel of St. Mark, the source of St. Luke, could have been already written about the year A.D. 60—this would be the latest date on the assumption of the earlier date for St. Luke? I cannot here enter into this question.

sion here is difficult. These remarks, which contain scarcely anything that is new, though much that has not been sufficiently considered, are only intended to help *a doubt* to its just dues. It is not difficult to judge on which side lies the greater weight of argument; but we must remember that in such cases of doubt the more far-reaching are the effects of definite decision the greater is the demand for caution. Therefore, for the present, we must be content to say: *St. Luke wrote at the time of Titus or in the earlier years of Domitian, but perhaps even so early as the beginning of the seventh decade of the first century.* The political rule: "*Quieta non movere*" does not hold good for science. She must therefore determine also to submit this question to fresh investigation or—if convincing arguments are wanting—to leave it open.

CONCLUSION

The truth of the description of the characteristics of the Acts of the Apostles which I have given in the first pages of these investigations is, I hope, proved. The book has now been restored to the position of credit which is its rightful due. It is not only taken as a whole a genuinely historical work,[1] but even in the majority of its details it is trustworthy. Except for a few panegyric aberrations in the direction of the Primitive Community, it follows no bias that distorts its representation of the actual course of

[1] According to von Wilamowitz-Moellendorff, *Die griech. Literatur des Altertums*, s. 188 *f.*, "The Acts of the Apostles has as little intention of being history as the *Res gestæ divi Augusti*. A record is given of "Acts" in which the supernatural mission of a hero was revealed; with a god they would have been ἀρεταί. We possess the 'Acts of Heracles' graven in stone; we may compare the legends of St. Francis." It seems to me that this piece of criticism may serve as a warning against the too hasty subsuming of ancient Christian literature under the same category as the general Greek literature of the same period. While attending exclusively to the points in which the two appear to be similar, the critic shuts his eyes to the points in which they differ, and by his demonstration of real or supposed analogies obliterates the peculiar characteristics of ancient Christian literature. This is not what von Wilamowitz has done elsewhere; *cf.* his excellent review of the characteristics of St. Paul and St. John. Certainly St. Luke, in higher measure than these, invites illustration of his work by comparison with the contemporary literature; but by this means we are only brought into little closer touch with the objects, the character, and the essential value of his work.

events, and its author had sufficient knowledge to justify him in coming forward as an historian. Judged from almost every possible standpoint of historical criticism it is a solid, respectable, and in many respects an extraordinary work; and its author's courage is also extraordinary—the courage with which he approaches the task of describing the complicated history of a religious movement still in process of most active development. The talent of personal characterisation was certainly wanting to the author; miracles and supernatural cures so fascinated him that he practically dispensed himself from all profounder consideration of the inner life of his characters. Neither is this to be wondered at. In these workers of miracles nothing seemed so great as the very fact that they worked miracles, that they possessed this gift, that the Divine power had become their own. What value in comparison could be assigned to the personal qualities of these men, however rich their characters might have been? All these things necessarily paled in the light of that tremendous gift!

If the results that we have arrived at are correct, it will be necessary to revise no small portion of the history of the Apostolic Age as it is related by critics of to-day. A work like Weizsäcker's "Apostolic Age," with its thorough-going depreciation of, indeed contempt for, the Acts of the Apostles, will need correction in many chapters. Moreover, we now learn that St. Paul ought no longer to be judged so exclusively by his own works. This has been done by critics since Baur with a self-confident exclusiveness such as they are not accustomed to show when dealing with the autobiographical notices of other heroes—especially in letters. For their mistrust of the Acts they had, of course, the very best excuse that could be given: they possessed no other sources! But even because of this—indeed still more because of this—in dealing with the epistles of the Apostle as the sole authorities for his history, they ought to have treated these with more caution and with more elasticity of judgment, and above all, with a greater sense of proportion and with more impartiality in regard to *all* the traits which appear therein. Here the work of Weinel on St. Paul forms an honourable exception; it would be difficult to name a work in which these necessary critical qualities are more brilliantly displayed. But even his representation would have gained if he had placed more dependence upon the Acts. St. Paul was not so "Pauline"—if I may venture the word—as his biographers would have us think. This has been already shown by Weinel, but we may and must go a step further. The Apostle will lose nothing thereby: the man who did the most to deliver the faith in God and in Christ from the fetters of Judaism, who recognised the Gospel as a new stage in the development of religion, superior to the earlier Revelation, and who conceived it both in his thought and his life as a religion of the Spirit and of Freedom—he has nothing to fear from any correction of the impression men have formed of him. And even if he had, criticism would have no right to trouble itself about such consequences.

The process of crystallisation of the primitive Christian tradition in the Acts, where it deals with the appearances of the Crucified and the events which immediately followed, lies entirely within the charmed circle of a legend whose development was almost incomprehensibly speedy. Yet the sacred historian extraordinarily quickly extricates himself from the bonds of enchantment. He at first walks upon quaking ground, but soon finds firm footing and, thanks to his sources and his own personal experience, up to the end of his course he never again, or only seldom, loses it. Thus in the Acts he has created an historical work which upon the whole gives a correct representation of the actual development of events. But he has done much more than this! In that he has set this historical work side by side with his gospel as a second and equally important part of one and the same work, he laid the foundation both of the New Testament and of that reverence for the Apostolic side by side with the Evangelic, from which arose the conception of Apostolic tradition. It is true that St. Peter, and above all St. Paul himself, laid the deepest foundation for this reverence. But if these heroes had found no historian, it is highly probable that in spite of Marcion we should have had no New Testament; for in the Catholic Church the combination of the isolated Pauline epistles with the Gospel would have been an impossibility. Accordingly St. Luke is really the creator of the New Testament, and in the same sense the creator of the Apostolic, side by side with the Evangelic tradition.

In conclusion, I owe an explanation to Professor Blass (lately deceased), and to Professors Ramsay,

Weiss, and Zahn. The results at which I have arrived not only approach very nearly to, but are often coincident with, the results of their research. The conclusion will be at once drawn that in my case as in theirs there is little prospect of claiming the attention of critics, and compelling them to reconsider their position. So it may actually happen to be. But the cases present points of difference. These scholars are influenced partly by prepossessions in reference to the Canon of the New Testament, partly by the conviction that miracles really happened, partly by both these prejudices. This attitude of theirs has most unfortunately rendered their research and their demonstrations subject to suspicion, even in those points that have nothing to do with the aforesaid prepossessions. In the history of the criticism of the New Testament an Apologetic with a dogmatic bias has always promoted radicalism, or has at least made critics deaf to proofs. This is just the effect that it has had upon its opponents in the case of the Acts. They were led to imagine that everything must be cleared away, and thus together with what is worthless they cast from them traditions that are certainly historical and information that is most valuable. To make matters worse, Blass went on to insult the work that had been hitherto done by the critical school, though at the same time he betrayed a very slight conception of deeper historical questions; again Ramsay set his clear eye, his powers of picturesque description, and his great learning, at the service of a method which seeks to extract from the sources more than is really in them; while

Zahn cannot efface the impression that he conducts historical investigations like a counsel for the defence *à tout prix*. Moreover, all these scholars, and those allied with them, showed little sense of the debt we owe to Baur and his followers, of the deepening of our insight into historical questions, and the broadening of our outlook that have been brought about by their labours. Thus it is that the criticism of the Acts of the Apostles has arrived at the position in which it now stands. This book may perhaps succeed in effecting some alteration, and in bringing the opposing camps nearer to one another. Perhaps it will at last be seen that criticism, after its long and painful exertions, must return to the occupation of positions that it has deserted. These exertions were certainly not fruitless, but they sought to facilitate the solution of difficult historical problems by extending the periods of time traditionally assigned to the processes of historical development, by the rejection of some traditional authorities, and by the analysis of others into various sources—a method well known, very popular, and quite justifiable in every branch of historical criticism whenever there is absolutely no other way out of a difficulty! In this case, however, the witness of the source in most points, and those essential points, stands the test of reliability, and on this assumption the historical problems admit of a solution which does no violence to probability.